D1547041

GIBBON'S SOLITUDE

GIBBON'S SOLITUDE

THE INWARD WORLD OF
THE HISTORIAN

W. B. CARNOCHAN

1987
STANFORD UNIVERSITY PRESS
Stanford, California

Published with the assistance of the
National Endowment for the Humanities

Stanford University Press
Stanford, California
© 1987 by the Board of Trustees of the
Leland Stanford Junior University
Printed in the United States of America

CIP data appear at the end of the book

FOR BRIGITTE

ACKNOWLEDGMENTS

M y obligations are many. I have a long-standing debt to Walter Jackson Bate, who may not accept my view of Gibbon but without whose example, years ago, this book would not have been written. Ian Watt read the manuscript and was encouraging at a discouraging time. Many other colleagues helped along the way, including Nicolas Barker, John Bender, Max Byrd, John D'Amico, Gregson Davis, Jay Fliegelman, Robert Folkenflik, John Loftis, John Richetti, Kevin Sharpe, and Edward Spofford. Nelee Langmuir reviewed my translations from the French (and spotted at least one embarrassing error). As research assistants at different times, Deborah Laycock and Lydia Fillingham were scrupulous and thoughtful. Paul Schacht and Colleen Redmond also gave careful attention to details in preparation of the manuscript. Librarians at Stanford University, Yale University, the British Library, and the Huntington Library responded generously to numerous appeals; of those on this long list, I want to thank William Allan, Michael Ryan, and Marjorie Wynne, in particular. Other colleagues made specific contributions that I have recorded in the notes.

For permission to quote materials in this book, I wish to thank the British Library; the James Marshall and Marie-Louise Osborn

Collection, Yale University Library; the Stanford University Libraries; and the estate of the late Sir Geoffrey Keynes.

I am grateful to the National Endowment for the Humanities for a Senior Fellowship that enabled me to begin this project, and to the American Philosophical Society for support that enabled me to travel to London and to Rome. Stanford University provided generous research support; in this connection, I am grateful to Albert Gelpi and James Rosse.

I have obligations of a different kind to those scholars whose research has made Gibbon's life and work increasingly available: in particular, the late J. E. Norton, for her edition of the letters, and Patricia B. Craddock, for her edition of *English Essays* and her biography, *Young Edward Gibbon*. Without their work, and that of others, this book would have been immeasurably more difficult to write.

To all those at the Stanford University Press, and in particular to Helen Tartar and John Feneron, I express thanks for their efficiency, good humor, and extreme tolerance for authorial anxiety.

Finally there are private obligations that escape words. To my children and to my stepdaughter, I would like to dedicate a book apiece, but I think there will not be time. To my wife, not even the obscurity of a learned language, which rescued Gibbon in different circumstances, could express my gratitude and respect. The dedication of this book to her is, in keeping with Gibbon's advice on such matters, "dictated by the heart."

W.B.C.

CONTENTS

ABBREVIATIONS

Volume and page references to *The History of the Decline and Fall of the Roman Empire*, incorporated in the text, are to J. B. Bury's revised edition (London, 1909–14; reprinted, New York, 1974).

A–F *The Autobiographies of Edward Gibbon*, ed. John Murray (London, 1896). References incorporated in the text, thus: *A*, 356. Each letter identifies a separate draft of Gibbon's autobiography; the page reference is to Murray's edition.

EE *The English Essays of Edward Gibbon*, ed. Patricia B. Craddock (Oxford, 1972).

EL Edward Gibbon, *Essai sur l'étude de la littérature* (London, 1761).

L *The Letters of Edward Gibbon*, ed. J. E. Norton (London, 1956).

M Edward Gibbon, *Memoirs of My Life*, ed. Georges A. Bonnard (London, 1966).

MW *Miscellaneous Works of Edward Gibbon, Esquire*, ed. John, Lord Sheffield (London, 1796–1815).

CHRONOLOGY

1737   27 April (old style), birth of Edward Gibbon.

1746   December, death of his mother.

1752   Enters Magdalen College, Oxford.

1753   Converted to Roman Catholicism; sent to Lausanne.

1754   Renounces Roman Catholicism.

1755   Gibbon's father remarries.

1757   Meets Suzanne Curchod.

1758   4 May, returns to England.

1760–62   Active duty in militia.

1761   *Essai sur l'étude de la littérature.*

1763–65   In Paris, Lausanne, and Italy; August 1763, meets John Baker Holroyd, later Lord Sheffield; 15 October 1764, supposed date of Gibbon's epiphany on the Capitoline Hill.

1767   Begins and then abandons a history of Swiss liberty.

1770   *Critical Observations on the Sixth Book of the Aeneid*; 12 November, his father dies.

1774   Elected Member of Parliament for Liskeard.

1776   *Decline and Fall*, Volume I.

1777   May–October, visits Paris.

1780   Loses parliamentary seat for Liskeard.

GIBBON'S SOLITUDE

ONE

INTRODUCTION

Not long ago, a magazine article about an eighty-eight-year-old woman named Fannie, living in dignified poverty on New York's upper West Side, told this story. Her granddaughter having graduated from college, Fannie wanted to get her a special present. What she chose, though far beyond her means even at a bargain price, was the *Decline and Fall*: "I think every young person should have a set."[1]

I suspect this story is true. A crumbling set of the *Decline and Fall* that I own, undated but probably from the turn of this century, is stamped here and there throughout with the name and occupation of a previous owner: "Dr. E. A. Crain, Physician and Surgeon, Missoula, Montana." To own the *Decline and Fall* was once a mark of well-bred learning. Nowadays, it has fallen into disuse, and Gibbon receives none of the attention, much less the celebratory admiration, reserved for Samuel Johnson. The more than three thousand pages of the *Decline and Fall* have joined with Gibbon's unprepossessing public image to move him off center stage in the literary drama of the age that is sometimes called Johnson's.

Gibbon should be nearer the center. The *Decline and Fall*, deeply rooted in its time and powerful in its contemporaneity, even its conventionality, confirms and establishes ingrained habits of modern thought: like other great texts, it is both summary and prophesy. The autobiography Gibbon tried to write after the *Decline and Fall* is equally formative, an experiment he did not recognize as such in a new genre that required new modes of self-creation. Could these texts have come from a writer whose inner life was impoverished, as Gibbon's is sometimes said to have been? I do not think so. This study of his work, and of its intersections with his life, places in relief the yearnings and strengths of mind that drove and sustained him. At the risk of protesting too much, I will add that the job does need doing, and to do it means bringing Gibbon's life and work together in a fashion that has not been common. On the one hand, we have had the great historian and the antagonist of Christianity. On the other, we have had the ineffectual talker, the small, fat, timid person who did not dare stand up to his father or to Samuel Johnson, the surreptitious object of fun and the explicit object of Johnsonian and Boswellian animus. It is almost as if Gibbon's shy awkwardness were the mark of moral failure in an age that valued "manly" conversation and in a later age that has valued Johnson's self-willed Christian heroism. But Gibbon was one person, not two, and heroism comes in many shapes and sizes. This book might have referred in its title, like that of Walter Jackson Bate's study of Johnson, to the achievement of Edward Gibbon.[2] That achievement, humanly speaking, was not much less than Johnson's own.

The next chapter sketches the conditions under which Gibbon lived and worked—conditions of solitude. This is not to say that he was friendless. In fact, he had long and deep friendships, with Georges Deyverdun, the young Swiss whom he first met in London and with whom he later shared a house in Lausanne, and with John Holroyd, Lord Sheffield, later his executor and editor of his autobiography. But for all his modest gregariousness, Gibbon defined his life as solitary. Notwithstanding his intimacy with Deyverdun and with Sheffield, the *Decline and Fall* was his closest companion.

The third chapter turns to his apprentice work, in which Gibbon tested his powers. On this early work the psychological foundations of the *Decline and Fall* were built; here he established his mastery. How was the inchoate register of historical fact to be brought into systematic order? How to challenge received opinion? And how might the historian then assert the authority of his own interpretation? In short, how to become a philosopher of history? These self-questionings run through the early work, and when Gibbon came to the *Decline and Fall*, he had a fair understanding of how a reticent scholar might become an authoritative historian.

Yet the *Decline and Fall* was a magisterial advance. To bring order to history, Gibbon not only had to arrange his material, he also had to station himself with respect to it, and the *Decline and Fall* depends on a careful placing of the narrator within the narrative—typically, on a high Roman promontory. This point of view has been called "Olympian," and accurately so, for Gibbon views history in a long prospect. Encouraging reflections on mutability and the insufficiency of life's enjoyments, the prospect situation enables him to preserve, though with a difference, the utterance of the traditional moralist who watches the turns of Fortune's wheel. At the same time, it allows him to exercise command. Prospects are, by convention, "commanding." Chapter 4 considers the *Decline and Fall* as prospect.

To command a prospect meant not only to see, and hence to moralize, but also to interpret. Having stationed himself on the heights, Gibbon fuses his long view with his inquiry into the human causes of Rome's fall. Here the proposition of the traditional moralist that all things pass runs counter to that of the analytic inquirer. But Gibbon avails himself of both views, overlaying the ironies of human superstition and fanaticism with those of cosmic change. This gives the *Decline and Fall* resonance. On the one hand, the vanity of human wishes arises as a matter of contingency; on the other, as a matter of necessity. Chapter 5 locates Gibbon's attack on the contingent madness of Christianity within a larger scene of cosmic ironies. Standing above the flux, Gibbon nonetheless establishes an intimate relationship to history and to others. His irony becomes meta-irony: as two kinds of irony clash, a third is generated that incorporates both.

But the solitary ironist, so good at understanding the clash of mighty opposites, does not understand nuances of character equally well. This is true of Gibbon, as of Swift before him. The ironist who stands above the flux cannot observe character closely; and when he situates himself within the range of his own irony, he does no more than confess that, if one could look closely, the ironist would be seen to share in a common human nature. If a lack of rigor in the analysis of why Rome fell makes the *Decline and Fall* a richer text, the same cannot so easily be said for its treatment of character. From the days of his apprenticeship, Gibbon thought of character as a deep and probably insoluble problem and never managed to settle on a workable theory. Nor did he ever achieve a satisfactory understanding of individual motives, whether those of Julian, whom he deeply admired, or of his own. In his early writing Gibbon toyed with the theory of the ruling passion, and he used it intermittently in the *Decline and Fall*. But the theory complicates more than it clarifies. The portrait of Julian works in spite of itself—that is, in spite of a layer of theory inhibiting the free development of Julian's character, and in spite of inconsistencies that we can see as ordinary marks of human nature but that Gibbon presents as self-contradictory. Chapter 6, then, examines his nervousness about character, on both its theoretical and practical sides, and looks at three portraits: of Julian, Mahomet, and the Empress Theodora. Of the thousands of characters in the *Decline and Fall*, Theodora may be the most spontaneous success, for in her portrait Gibbon circumvents difficulties that beset him elsewhere—difficulties that anticipate his frustrated struggle to achieve self-understanding, a matter of high artistic drama that is the subject of Chapter 7.

The posthumous history of the autobiography has made it difficult to recover its real story. Sheffield's composite version of the six drafts (the received text since its first publication in 1796) obscures Gibbon's quiet, fierce, unresolved effort to make his life into a coherent whole. In no small part the Gibbon known to history, the historian of the Roman Empire, is Sheffield's creation. Were it not for his unremitting labors, we would not think of Gibbon as having written a great autobiography; rather, we would think of him as a historian who tried to write an autobiography but failed. As published, the autobiography confirmed his reputation for complacency, obscuring the fact that the idea of writing it was a novel and courageous one. Along with Rousseau, whose *Confessions* were published in two installments in the 1780's, Gibbon may be said to have invented modern autobiography. But death interrupted him while he was still trying to understand the demands of self and self-expression.

Gibbon's story is, finally, not one of complacency but of longing. When he was sixteen he became a Catholic. During his apprentice-

Lorenzo Lotti (1490–1541), "Jonah," Chigi Chapel, Santa Maria del Popolo, Rome. Reproduced by courtesy of Alinari/Art Resource, New York.

ship, he thought of writing a biography of Sir Walter Raleigh. And while in Rome, in 1764, he gave way almost to rapture when he saw Lorenzetto's statue of Jonah and the Whale, in the Chigi Chapel of Santa Maria del Popolo (see preceding page). It was, he said, "the finest modern statue I have seen."[3] How much at odds with the usual image of Gibbon's skeptical reserve is his special fondness for this piece of statuary, in all its voluptuous formalism. In part his rapture probably derived from seeing a subversion of Christian themes: Lorenzetto's Jonah is modeled on classical representations of boys and dolphins. But this is not the whole story: this Jonah (carved, Gibbon romantically and wrongly supposed, by "a common stone-cutter under the eye of *Raphael*"[4]), sensuous, reflective to the point of melancholy, beautiful, embodies the pudgy historian's idealized version of reflective thought and is, in fact, his imaginary alter ego.

Though Gibbon became the notorious skeptic of the *Decline and Fall*, he never entirely surrendered the longings that led to his early conversion, that lay behind his early desire to write the biography of a great man, and that inspired his burst of appreciation in the presence of Lorenzetto's marble. At the end of his life, as at its beginning, Gibbon yearned to find a hero. At the same time, he experienced a deepening tranquillity in the face of pain and death. His last years even hint at a second conversion—not in the religious sense, but simply in admitting certain human hopes, no matter how quixotic, such as that of an afterlife. These "last things" are the subject of Chapter 8. In some ways the least approachable of writers, Gibbon had the gifts of dignity and courage. If analytical consistency makes the philosopher, his claims to be a philosophical historian are not well grounded. But like Hume and Voltaire, he faced death, when the time came, as the philosopher in him wished to do.

TWO

GIBBON'S SOLITUDE

The great writers of eighteenth-century England were often lonely figures, whether we think of the Augustan satirists; of a mysteriously protean figure like Defoe; of the gregariously remote Samuel Johnson, who sought out others as his defense against the demons of isolation; of the tormented apartness of mid-century writers like Collins, Cowper, and Gray[1]—or of Gibbon, in whom schoolboy shyness vied with the desire to make a grand figure on the world's stage. In the autobiography, Gibbon looked back and saw himself as silent, solitary, and far from the sounds of the world: "While coaches were rattling through Bond Street, I have passed many a solitary evening in my lodging with my books" (M, 94).[2] Bond Street, loud and fashionable, lay some blocks away from Gibbon's quiet lodgings at 7 Bentinck Street. If he heard the rattle of coaches at all, it was very faintly.[3]

At his most resolute, Gibbon gloried in solitude. Thus he manages to see something of himself in Mahomet, an "illiterate barbarian" (V, 358) whose views were never "far extended beyond the limits of the Arabian world," but a barbarian to whom the "book of nature and of man was open" (V, 358–59). Coming from a "solitary" world, Mahomet was a genius and if "conversation enriches

7

the understanding, . . . solitude is the school of genius" (V, 359–60). There is no mistaking the private meanings that Gibbon attached to the public history of the prophet of Islam. Gibbon went to the school of solitude and, immersed in his books, could echo the saying of Scipio Africanus that "I was never less alone than when by myself" (*M*, 95–96).[4]

At less euphoric moments, however, Gibbon was not invulnerable to the disquiet of solitude. Looking back to his early thirties, he compared his isolation with the situation of his more precocious and outgoing friends: "While so many of my acquaintance were married, or in parliament, or advancing with a rapid step in the various roads of honours and fortune, I stood, alone, immoveable and insignificant" (*M*, 139–40). Although he goes on to disclaim any thoughts of marriage ("the object of my terror rather than my wishes"), not being married meant being alone; loneliness was solitude's negative value. And when his old friend Deyverdun, with whom he had been sharing a house in Lausanne, died in July 1789, Gibbon found the loneliness hard to bear. Having finished the *Decline and Fall*, he no longer had that enterprise for his constant companion. In December he wrote his stepmother Dorothea that "each day I feel the comfortless solitude to which I am reduced" (*L*, III, 175). And again the following May, to Sheffield: "Since the loss of poor Deyverdun, I am *alone*: and even in paradise, solitude is painful to a social mind." Now Gibbon hungers for companionship: "When I was a dozen years younger, I *scarcely* felt the weight of a single existence amidst the crowds of London, of Parliament, of Clubs: but it will press more heavily upon me in this tranquil land, in the decline of life and with the encrease of infirmities. Some expedient, even the most desperate must be embraced to secure the domestic society of a male or female companion" (*L*, III, 191).

The most desperate course of all would have been marriage, and Gibbon never resorted to that, as he realized he would not: "But I am not in a hurry: there is time for reflection and advice" (*L*, III, 191). He takes the sting out of his pain with enforced ease and social complaisance, tactics that enabled him to find substitutes for domestic company. He found a surrogate family with his Swiss friends, the de Séverys, whose son Wilhelm he spoke and thought of as his own.[5] And he found someone to love, without the burden of obligation or the hope of requital, in the enchanting Lady Eliza-

beth Foster, traveling companion to the Duke and Duchess of Dev-
onshire, mistress to the Duke, and, years later, his wife. Two years
before he died, Gibbon wrote her an ardent letter, ending, "Adieu,
Vale, good night! but I dare not tell you how much I love you." By
which he meant, perhaps, more than he dared to seem to say.[6]

This social complaisance largely accounts for our missing, in Gibbon, the high drama of loneliness of some of his predecessors and
contemporaries. Swift imagined his life in Ireland as an exile; he
called himself "a stranger in a strange land."[7] Pope retreated to his
gardens and his grotto at Twickenham, and one of his finest poems
opens with a fierce image of exclusion and exhaustion:

> Shut, shut the door, good *John*! fatigu'd I said,
> Tye up the knocker, say I'm sick, I'm dead.[8]

Johnson's life, as recounted by that afflicted and alcoholic Scot,
James Boswell, gets much of its power from images of single-
handed struggle—Johnson as the lone gladiator fighting off the
beasts of his own overwrought imagination.[9] Set beside intensities
like these, Gibbon's life looks tame, sometimes pathologically so.
Did he not say of his doomed infatuation for Suzanne Curchod, "I
sighed as a lover: I obeyed as a son" (*M*, 85n)? Not an exclamation
to win affection. Yet that famous remark is revealing: what it shows
is not how fatuous its speaker was but how adept at defensive nuance, how careful to distance himself from pain and inadequacy,
how unwilling to risk exposure.[10] In the contradiction of two social
roles, the lover and the son, the self finds a place to hide.

Solitariness defined Gibbon from the start. The first of seven children, he alone survived infancy, and in retrospect, the death of his
siblings affected him deeply. He says in his autobiography that he
especially regretted the early death of his only sister: "The relation
of a brother and a sister, especially if they do not marry, appears to
me of a very singular nature. It is a familiar and tender friendship
with a female, much about our own age; an affection, perhaps softened by the secret influence of sex, but pure from any mixture of
sensual desire, the sole species of Platonic love that can be indulged
with truth and without danger" (*M*, 24–25). That is, he regretted
the death of the sister for whom he might safely have nurtured feelings he learned to keep in check.

But a very curious quirk of his memory implies that the loss of five brothers had an even stronger, if less easily specified, meaning in his imaginative construction of himself. So frail was his health as an infant, Gibbon says, that his father took the precaution of giving all his brothers the name Edward. In fact, however, only James Edward (baptized 15 August 1740) shared his elder brother's name. The error is not a slip of the pen. Gibbon is very definite about it: "So feeble was my constitution, so precarious my life, that, in the baptism of each of my brothers, my father's prudence successively repeated my Christian name of Edward, that in case of the departure of the eldest son, this patronymic appellation might be still perpetuated in the family" (*M*, 28). This extraordinary lapse of accuracy in the most accurate of historians cries out to be explained. One interpretation might be that, having become an only child, Gibbon repeoples the world of his youth with projected versions of himself. Lacking the company—and the rivalry—of his five brothers, he moves into the empty space they have left behind: five times over Gibbon becomes his own phantom companion.[11]

As a boy, Gibbon much preferred the company of his books to that of other children. Sickly, inept at sports, he was conscious all his days of self-enforced precocity: "the Dynasties of Assyria and Egypt were my top and cricket-ball" (*M*, 43). When he was seven, his father engaged John Kirkby as his tutor, a fact of Gibbon's history that has symbolic importance, for Kirkby was then working on *Automathes* (1745), the fictional tale of an autodidact that sustains his modest reputation still.[12] Gibbon describes it:

> It is the story of a youth the son of a ship-wrecked exile, who lives alone on a desert island from infancy to the age of manhood. A Hind is his nurse: he inherits a cottage with many useful and curious instruments; some ideas remain of the education of his two first years, some arts are borrowed from the beavers of a neighbouring lake, some truths are revealed in supernatural visions. With these helps and his own industry Automathes becomes a self taught though speechless philosopher, who had investigated with success his own mind, the Natural World, the abstract sciences, and the great principles of morality and Religion. (*M*, 32)

Kirkby drew on an Arabic original and on *Robinson Crusoe* for his story, and as Gibbon says, the results are neither original nor notable for "depth of thought or elegance of style" (*M*, 32). Yet Kirkby's student cannot have described his tutor's hero as "a self taught though speechless philosopher" without a sense of self-recognition, both because Gibbon was self-taught, despite bouts of formal schooling, and because he had become, to his humiliation, literally speechless in the arena where the age most rigorously tested powers of speech. His inability to make his maiden speech in Parliament, where he held two separate seats between 1774 and 1784, was the most conspicuous and most painful failure of his life.[13] Realizing that Kirkby's history of an autodidact coincided with his schooling of the shy young historian-to-be, Gibbon sees his own reflected image.

In the self-created and self-creating landscape of his youth, a dominant other presence was Gibbon's father, Edward Gibbon, Sr.—dominant but, like most eighteenth-century fathers, remote. When young Edward's mother died in childbirth, he was nine years old; he did not see his father for some weeks, and then only as an actor in a stagy drama of grief and loss: "I can never forget the scene of our first interview, some weeks after the fatal event; the awful silence, the room hung with black the mid-day tapers, his sighs and tears; his praises of my mother a saint in heaven, his solemn adjuration that I would cherish her memory, and imitate her virtues; and the fervour with which he kissed and blessed me as the sole surviving pledge of their loves" (*M*, 34).

No wonder this episode stuck in Gibbon's mind: it has the appearance of being put on for his benefit. Edward Gibbon, Sr., was a showman, and in this may have taught his son something about the mechanisms of self-concealment. But in most respects he was an impossible model for his reticent offspring. He was, in his frustrating way, a likable figure: "his spirit was lively, his appearance splendid, his aspect chearful, his address polite: he gracefully moved in the highest circles of society" (*M*, 26); he "was every where beloved as companion and esteemed as a man" (*M*, 27). This was the model, in one of Gibbon's several reconstructions almost fifty years later, set before young Edward's eyes.[14] He responded by settling into the consolations of study, rarely giving expression to his gathering sense of resentment. On one early occasion, however, he did give in. Remembering "my father's contest for Southampton when I must have been between three and four years old," he thinks he remembers too "my childish revenge in shouting, after being whipt, the names of his opponents . . . : but even that belief may be illusive, and I may only repeat the hearsay of a riper season" (*M*, 27).

In the retelling, Gibbon lodges rebellion in the embrace of obscurity and evidential hesitancy. To us, the importance of the episode, whether real or imagined, is transparent: naming his father's opponents, young Gibbon finds a mirror of his own antagonism. But the historian in him skirts the meaning of the episode by questioning its authenticity. Perhaps he remembers it happening. Perhaps it was recounted to him later—and if so, we wonder why: was the affront nurtured by his father as a standing reproach, or was it a case, as will occur between parents and children, of laughing about passions of the past? Or perhaps it never happened: hearsay evidence is not reliable. At a distance of fifty years, Gibbon turns away from himself, as if he feared another whipping.

By the time Gibbon converted to Roman Catholicism, in an act that seems utterly startling at first sight, his father had grown disconsolate, having experienced the death of his wife and a "growing perplexity of his affairs" that led him to bury himself "in the rural or rather rustic solitude of Buriton from which during several years he seldom emerged" (*M*, 35). No doubt he became less accessible than ever to his son, who had gone up to Oxford at fifteen, only to find its intellectual and parochial lassitude no better than what he had left behind at home. His impetuous conversion, inspired by the need for nurture that he had not received from either parent (even though, after Judith Gibbon died, he had found a loving substitute mother in his Aunt Catherine), provoked in his father an outburst of fury, and he "divulged a secret, which prudence might have suppressed"—that is to say, he let it be known that his son had turned Catholic. It is the betrayal of disclosure that Gibbon resents most: in retrospect, the skeptic stands "exposed to the reproach of inconstancy" (*M*, 61). The experience taught him a lesson, however, that he applied scrupulously thereafter: to be wary of revealing himself.

One ironic consequence of this bold conversion was to make Gibbon still more isolated. He had sinned like Adam, and "the gates of Oxford were shut against my return" (*M*, 68). If he stayed in England he would be vulnerable to the "seductions" of his newly-acquired Catholic friends, so, after much familial debate, he was shipped into exile. On 30 June 1753, he arrived in Lausanne, where he "immediately settled under the roof and tuition of Mr. Pavilliard a Calvinist Minister" (*M*, 69). Although Lausanne was a common place of resort for the English (Philip Stanhope had been sent there by his father, Lord Chesterfield, in 1746, accompanied by Edward Eliot, later to become Gibbon's cousin by marriage), and although Calvinism in the Pays de Vaud was more benign than in Geneva, it seems a curious disposition of even a difficult case: was the Calvinist Pavillard to effect a cure by administering Presbyterian medicine, thereby reclaiming the convert to the Anglican via media?[15] In any event, Gibbon found himself dropped in an alien society, like Gulliver, a lonely castaway in an incomprehensible land: "When I was thus suddenly cast on a foreign land I found myself deprived of the use of speech and of hearing; and during some weeks, incapable not only of enjoying the pleasures of conversation, but even of asking or answering a question in the common intercourse of life" (*M*, 69). Again like Gulliver, Gibbon soon became proficient in the language of his new country, so proficient that he not only thought in French but lost some of his command over English idiom, detaching himself from his origins. "I had ceased," he was to write, "to be an Englishman" (*M*, 86).

After a year and a half of Pavillard's instruction, Gibbon gave up Catholicism, thus becoming an adolescent without a country and without a religion, too—or with only the formalities of one. "The various articles of the Romish creed," he reports, "disappeared like a dream," and he took Protestant communion on Christmas day, 1754, "after a full conviction." At the same time, he reports that "it was here that I suspended my Religious enquiries," while "acquiescing with implicit belief in the tenets and mysteries which are adopted by the general consent of Catholics and Protestants" (*M*, 74). In what did Gibbon's full conviction lie? Surely in the futility of religious inquiry. Yet he is not being hypocritical: whatever else he may have come to believe, he never gave up believing in God, or at least wishing he could join the community of believers. In the midst of the protracted innuendo of Chapter 15 in the *Decline and Fall*, when he lets drop the remark that "in modern times, a latent, and even involuntary, scepticism adheres to the most pious dispositions" (II, 33), surely he recollects his own early piety. Odd though it is to think of Gibbon's as a pious disposition, it is too easy to forget the needs, arising out of loneliness, that inspired his adolescent leap into the arms of the mother church.

It would be accurate, then, to call his early conversion and subsequent "detoxification" a crisis of identity. Gibbon resolved the crisis, however, not by establishing a new foundation of the self but by submerging the self and its needs in the secure evasions of assumed roles. He finds a retrospective assurance in sighing as a lover and obeying as a son, and in the long run, his most satisfactory private resource was to be identified as the historian of the Roman Empire. Yet even the role of historian, which he cultivated, was one among others and not wholly fulfilling. He had fanciful dreams of being not only the solitary recorder of events but also a dashing participant, like his father, on the stage of the world. Living in Lausanne as a young man, he took part in the revelry of his English companions and tried his hand at gambling, though he was desperately unsuccessful.[16] Returning to England in 1758, he took up a captaincy in the Hampshire militia (his father was a major in the same regiment) and for more than two years marched aimlessly about the English countryside. Mostly he hated the business, but it nourished his fantasies—"A young mind, unless it be of a cold and languid temper, is dazzled even by the play of arms" (*M*, 115)—and these fantasies of military glory ultimately combined with the glories of being the historian: "The discipline and evolutions of a modern battalion gave me a clearer notion of the Phalanx and the Legion, and the Captain of the Hampshire grenadiers (the reader may smile) has not been useless to the historian of the Roman Empire" (*M*, 117). In the parallel march of the sentence, the autobiographical speaker distances himself from both the captain of the Hampshire grenadiers and from the historian of the Roman Empire. The roles of soldier and historian are counters in the self's solitary exchange with the world.

So was Gibbon's brief role as country squire, when he inherited the family estate at Buriton. About this role he felt much as he had about being a soldier: he was unsuited for it, found it burdensome, yet relished it. He saw it as a mark of rural sociability and usefulness: "I will not deny that my pride was flattered by the local importance of a country gentleman: the busy scene of the farm, productive of seeming plenty, was embellished in my eyes by the partial sentiment of property" (*M*, 151–52). Though he called the property "an heap of dirty acres" when he finally came to sell it (*L*, III, 137),[17] he had flirted with thoughts of doing justice to his position as a squire, had even gone so far as to buy a horse, though he hated riding, and had jokingly called himself Farmer Gibbon. In October 1771, he wrote Holroyd:

What do you mean by presuming to affirm, that I am of no use here? Farmer Gibbon of no use? *Last weak* I sold all my Hops, and I believe well, at nine Guineas a hundred to a very responsible Man. Some people think I might have got more at Weyhill Fair, but that would have been an additional expence and a great uncertainty. Our quantity has disapointed us very much but I think that besides hops for the house there will not be less than £500: no contemptible Sum of thirteen small Acres, and two of them planted last year only. *This week* I let a little Farm in Petersfield by auction, and propose raising it from £25, to 35 pr annum. and Farmer Gibbon of no use? (*L*, I, 295)

This engaging whimsy hovers between jest and earnest. Impossible as it may be to imagine the historian as Farmer Gibbon and "a very responsible Man," he tries out for the part with a certain hectic realism, talking like a man of affairs to others of the kind: nine guineas a hundred weight for hops; a decent return from thirteen acres, two of them newly planted; a farm lease in Petersfield. All this shows Gibbon aiming to master, not just to acquiesce in, the gregarious economy of husbandry: the actor masters the character he aims to play. Historian of the Empire, captain of the Hampshire militia, Farmer Gibbon, gambler, lover, son: it is a rich but inconclusive repertory.

Then there was Edward Gibbon, M.P., who announced the news of his election to Parliament in an almost identical, formulaic manner to Holroyd and to his stepmother Dorothea. To Holroyd, in November 1774: "I am sure you have generosity enough to hear with pleasure the news which I have just received: that I am elected Member of Parliament for Liskeard" (*L*, II, 39). And to his stepmother, on the same day: "I fancy Mrs. Eliot has already conveyed to you the pleasing intelligence which I received to-day, that I am elected Member for Liskeard" (*L*, II, 39). This role, however, eluded him in its most essential attribute. The pain of his parliamentary silence was that of not being able to assume one more self-concealing part (protective even if its oratorical demands would have seemed to expose him). In his humiliation he fancied himself tied down to his seat by some invisible power. He was "mutus pecus," a dumb sheep and altogether too visible.[18] If Gibbon played a number of parts, in this instance he suffered a bad case of stage fright.

Near the end of his life, however, he settled into a role that seemed to suit him—that of an éminence grise, even of a social lion, in the undemanding society of Lausanne. Playing whist, attending fêtes, striking familiar attitudes for all to see, he bequeathed his dubious reputation to history: that of the poseur, flabby of body and foolish of spirit, notwithstanding an antiquated charm.[19] Yet while he was performing this final, studied part in a provincial society, he became engaged in the last, most intriguing intellectual struggle of his life, that of trying to shape his life's history into coherent form. The irony is patent. How could Gibbon, not only the historian of the Roman Empire but the would-be man of affairs, the mute M.P., the sometime soldier, discover the chemistry of self that could make an autobiography whole? The answer is, he could not. But that is looking ahead. What matters here is the distance between the public man, the apparently self-satisfied fish in the little pool of Lausanne, and the private man, the autobiographer manqué, the player struggling to bind many parts together into one.

So protean is Gibbon and, as the gray eminence of Lausanne, so apparently comfortable in his last role, that we seldom infer subterranean currents in his mental life. To speak of his autobiographical enterprise as a struggle is accurate, given the evidence of the six drafts. Yet few signs mark the struggle: the pages flow fluently off his pen, scarcely marred by strike-outs or revisions.[20] His writing habits make an emblem of his public life: not often does a career of such accomplishment seem to be conducted so studiously on the surface. But the public life and the role-playing are not the whole story. During his years in the militia, Gibbon noticed a swelling in his groin and twice consulted surgeons about it, but he soon learned to live with it. This secret swelling became a crucial fact of his inner life.[21]

In time, the swelling grew to enormous size. As a result it was no longer secret to anyone who saw Gibbon in the tight-fitting breeches that were customary eighteenth-century dress. At the same time, because he was so fat, he could pretend the swelling did not exist, and others could see that he could not himself see it. In this he acted the part of the child who puts his hands over his eyes and pretends no one can see him. The swelling and his fatness made it possible for Gibbon to exhibit himself grotesquely while maintaining a sense of tranquil eminence. Eventually, however, in the months before his death, the condition grew worse, apparently the result of cirrhosis of the liver. At this point he could neither maintain the fiction that all was well nor avoid, after thirty years of neglect, going back to a surgeon. On 11 November 1793, he wrote Sheffield a letter with an urgent, though punning, notation at the start, "(Most private)":

I must at length undraw the veil before my state of health, though the naked truth may alarm you more than a fit of the Gout. Have you never observed through my inexpressibles a large prominency circa genitalia. It was a swelled testicle which as it was not at all painful, and very little troublesome I had strangely neglected for many years. But since my departure from SP [Sheffield Place] it has encreased (most stupendously) is encreasing and ought to be diminished. (*L*, III, 359)

Gibbon makes clear that he knows that others know of his affliction: "Have you never observed through my inexpressibles a large prominency circa genitalia?" He also knows that the reasons he gives for neglecting his ailment, that the swelling was neither painful nor troublesome, do not account for his inaction: he had strangely neglected it indeed. The swelling had, in fact, become a surrogate for his private life; he had conspired with himself to ignore its being. At the same time, it held "inexpressible" possibilities: he cherished it.

The remark that the swelling has increased stupendously, is increasing, and ought to be diminished alludes to John Dunning's parliamentary resolution of April 1780 about the power of the Crown.[22] Behind the joke lies Gibbon's half-welcome knowledge that the genitals have regal power, now asserting itself energetically after years of neglect and quiescence. And when he finally went to a surgeon, he is said to have posed a telltale riddle: Why is a fat man like a Cornish borough?[23] Not only was Gibbon very fat, but in Parliament he had represented the Cornish borough of Liskeard. Therefore, the answer to the riddle—that neither a fat man nor a Cornishman ever sees his member—asserts a distancing from the invisible part, yet at the same time recognizes intimacy, welcome or otherwise. Indeed, the identification of political and genital power belies indifference, diminishes distance. Jokey or not, Gibbon's self-exposure to Sheffield has an undertone of excitement: the tumor has increased stupendously. If fatness protected Gibbon from direct sexual awareness and experience—of his sexual life very little is to be told[24]—and if his tumor nevertheless enabled him to express a clandestine sexuality, here at last he "undraws the veil" with something close to exhilaration. Here at last he admits a companion into his most private secret.

Gibbon cherished his burden, it appears, not only as the instrument of a latent potency but also as its consequence. An operation being proposed by the surgeons, he tells Sheffield that he is not "appalled," for "if the business goes off smoothly, I shall be delivered from my burthen (it is almost as big as a small child) and walk about in four or five days with a truss" (*L*, III, 359).If the operation succeeds, it will be a kind of delivery. The swelling, which his surgeons pronounced, more or less inaccurately, to be a hydrocele, is an offspring. What is more, Gibbon at first made a revelatory slip of the pen, writing that the swelling "is almost as good as a small child." Later he crossed out "good" and above it wrote "big."[25] Probably he had in mind to say that the swelling was, in size, "as good as" being a small child. Then he realized he had said something that was more than (or not exactly what) he intended or thought he had intended. The burden of which Gibbon is to be reluctantly delivered has taken on value in a curious fantasy of giving birth: it has become a good, not just a neutral thing. To be delivered of this burden means gratification but also an end to the fantasy. The clandestine display of his huge swelling asserts a hidden generative power.

After Gibbon had visited Suzanne Curchod and her new husband, the future French minister of finance, Jacques Necker, in Paris in 1765, he wrote in mock despair to Holroyd: "Could they insult me more cruelly. Ask me every evening to summer [*sic*], go to bed and leave me alone with his wife; what an impertinent security. It is making an old lover of mighty little consequence" (*L*, I, 201).[26] Necker knew his man. Gibbon knew that Necker knew his man. The swelling in his groin, which dates from a few years before his visit to the Neckers, reassured him that even if he was of mighty little consequence as a lover, there was more to his story than could politely be told.

The swelling, entailing a fantasy of generation and the exhilaration of exposure, substituted in Gibbon's life for the experience he lacked—except, that is, in his art, an exception that in a sense is everything, for his art transfigured solitude, healing the tension between equanimity and passion, between the denial of potency and the assertion of generative power. In the first place, the *Decline and Fall*, in the familiar authorial topos, is Gibbon's offspring—and a more socially acceptable one than the swelling he so oddly cherished. This is implicit in the familiar though perhaps invented account of its origin, when he heard the Franciscans singing Vespers in the church of the Aracoeli and in his mind's eye transformed it into the Temple of Jupiter: "In my Journal the place and moment of conception are recorded," he wrote, though in fact the journal survives and neither the place nor the time is anywhere to be found; it was, he claims, "the fifteenth of October 1764, in the close of evening, as I sat musing in the Church of the Zoccolanti or Franciscan fryars, while they were singing Vespers in the Temple of Jupiter on the ruins of the Capitol" (*M*, 136).[27] Preceded by a meditation on what it takes to be a good traveler—namely, "an active indefatigable vigour of mind and body" (*M*, 135)— this account hints at self-impregnation; earlier, Gibbon had spoken of losing his "litterary maidenhead" (*M*, 103).

This allusive sexuality reaches fulfillment in the almost equally familiar set piece that celebrates the completion of the *Decline and Fall*: "I have presumed to mark the moment of conception: I shall now commemorate the hour of my final deliverance" (*M*, 180). Conception had taken place at evening; delivery takes place just before midnight, and the birth is touched by the same mixed feelings with which Gibbon greeted the surgical cutting of the tumor in his groin. Here he stage-manages the final moments of composition to coincide not only with the last hours of the day but with a symbolic fullness of the moon.[28] The mood combines relief and a sense of loss:

It was on the day or rather the night of the 27th of June 1787, between the hours of eleven and twelve that I wrote the last lines of the last page in a summer-house in my garden. After laying down my pen, I took several turns in a *berceau* or covered walk of Acacias which commands a prospect of the country the lake and the mountains. The air was temperate, the sky was serene; the silver orb of the moon was reflected from the waters, and all Nature was silent. (*M*, 180)

This set piece partakes of two complementary traditions, reflecting the separate feelings generated by Gibbon's final delivery of and from the burden of the *Decline and Fall*. One is that of the "circuit walk," common to English gardens like those of Stowe, Stourhead, and Sheffield Place, and designed to elicit, as Max Schulz has said, "the pleasurable associations" that "coincided with ritual reenactments of the return to Eden and other sacred forms of the soul's eternal pilgrimage back to its original home."[29] The other is that of the night piece, in which the soul's pathway home lies through the gates of death. Gibbon lays down his pen, cherishes prospects of freedom and fame, but then contemplates mortality and loss: "But my pride was soon humbled, and a sober melancholy was spread over my mind by the idea that I had taken my everlasting leave of an old and agreable companion, and that, whatsoever might be the future date of my history, the life of the historian must be short and precarious" (*M*, 180). The *Decline and Fall*, his offspring, has also become his closest, oldest, most agreeable companion. Its delivery, like the tapping of his swelling, deprives him of a friendship deeper than that he shared with his worldly acquaintance.[30]

If Gibbon perceived his art as generation, it was also his means of taming the vast, monstrous, and hidden in nature. Just as he finally lifted the veil on his state of health, letting Sheffield know the naked truth, so he draws away the veils and penetrates the mists—in his usual metaphors—that conceal dark events of Roman history. With its marches and countermarches, political and ecclesiastical wars, sieges, invasions, earthquakes, plagues, fires, devastation and death, the *Decline and Fall* rests on a foundation of the monstrous. Without it, Gibbon realized, he would have had no story to tell. The years of Antonine rule, in their idealized tranquillity, may have made the people of the empire happy (if not so happy as Gibbon claims); but if history is at bottom only "the register of the crimes, follies, and misfortunes of mankind," a ruler like Antoninus, pious, amiable, good, unaffected, moderate, and benevolent, furnishes "very few materials for history"—a "rare advantage" for his subjects but not for the historian (I, 84). The *Decline and Fall* depends on this paradox. For the historian, the fall of Rome is fortunate. Gibbon's talent is to endow the intrinsically dreadful with a sense of necessity, order, even serenity.

While he pacifies the monstrous, however, the historian exposes himself vicariously to its perils. It is no accident that, having painted his tranquil picture of the Antonines in the first three chapters of the *Decline and Fall*, Gibbon closes his account with an exuberant flashback to the unruly days of Tiberius, Caligula, Nero, and Domitian: "The golden age of Trajan and the Antonines had been preceded by an age of iron" (I, 86). Gibbon warms to his task with enormous relish:

It is almost superfluous to enumerate the unworthy successors of Augustus. Their unparalleled vices, and the splendid theatre on which they were acted, have saved them from oblivion. The dark unrelenting Tiberius, the furious Caligula, the stupid Claudius, the profligate and cruel Nero, the beastly Vitellius, and the timid inhuman Domitian are condemned to everlasting infamy. During fourscore years (excepting only the short and doubtful respite of Vespasian's reign), Rome groaned beneath an unremitting tyranny, which exterminated the ancient families of the republic, and was fatal to almost every virtue and every talent that arose in that unhappy period. (I, 86–87)

Such energy of feeling had no place in the Antonine world. But surely this is the real historical thing: the theater in which the emperors act out their unparalleled vices is splendid; the emperors, though condemned to infamy, are magically interesting, sketched with strong flourishes. Rome groans under their tyranny. The Antonines could in no way rival such drama.

This interchange between pacification and participation, which is the dialectic of Gibbon's inner life, finds its most dramatic expression at the very end of Chapter 3. Where we might have expected a valediction to the lost happiness of the Antonines, there comes instead an image of omnipotent empire under Tiberius, Caligula, and the rest, which makes the world a prison cell:

But the empire of the Romans filled the world, and, when that empire fell into the hands of a single person, the world became a safe and dreary prison for his enemies. The slave of Imperial despotism, whether he was condemned to drag his gilded chain in Rome and the senate, or to wear out a life of exile on the barren rock of Seriphus or the frozen banks of the Danube, expected his fate in silent despair. To resist was fatal, and it was impossible to fly. On every side he was encompassed with a vast extent of sea and land, which he could never hope to traverse without being discovered, seized, and restored to his irritated master. Beyond the frontiers, his anxious view could discover nothing, except the ocean, inhospitable deserts, hostile tribes of barbarians, of fierce manners and unknown language, or dependent kings, who would gladly purchase the emperor's protection by the sacrifice of an obnoxious fugitive. "Wherever you are," said Cicero to the exiled Marcellus, "remember that you are equally within the power of the conqueror." (I, 89–90)

The power of the *Decline and Fall* depends on its energy and violence and, equally, on its narrative containment of energy and violence. The prison cell of the world is simultaneously "safe and dreary." What is dreary for the prisoner is safe for the emperors. For the prisoner, the world is not safe but full of danger: discovery, seizure, sacrifice. But Gibbon has double vision. If in temperament he imitated the mild Stoicism of an emperor like Antoninus, in his art he exercised an ordering power like that of Antoninus's predecessors. In his art nothing escaped his will.

In 1774, as he was working on the first volume of the *Decline and Fall*, Gibbon wrote Holroyd: "Yesterday morning about half an hour after seven as I was destroying an army of Barbarians, I heard a double rap at the door and my Cornish friend was soon introduced" (*L*, II, 32). Gibbon's Cornish friend was his cousin Edward Eliot, who was about to offer him a seat in Parliament. On the one hand, then, Gibbon acts out, by writing out, the fantasy of being a great Roman commander, a Julian or a Belisarius, destroying barbarians. On the other hand, the door opens to let in his benefactor, offering him a place on the world's stage—the stage on which, like the prisoner of the emperors, he would sit in silent despair. This ironic conjunction of art and life marks Gibbon's solitude and the manner in which he overcame it.

THREE

APPRENTICESHIP AND AUTHORITY

The temptation to see life's plots as determined from the start is strong, hindsight combining with the love of design. In Gibbon's case the temptation does not seem wrong: "I *know* by experience that from my early youth, I aspired to the character of an historian" (*M*, 119).[1] Still, Gibbon arrived publicly at his theme only after numerous false starts. While on militia duty in 1761, he toyed with one subject after another: Richard I's crusade, the barons' wars against John and Henry III, the history of Edward the Black Prince, parallel lives of Henry V and the Emperor Titus. He thought of doing a biography, perhaps of Sir Philip Sidney, or the Marquis of Montrose, or, most seriously, Sir Walter Raleigh. "At length," he reports with premature relief, "I have fixed on Sir Walter Raleigh for my Hero" (*M*, 120). Playing the part of a soldier, young Gibbon is also scanning the landscape of the past for a suitably large, heroic theme. As both an adventurer and a historian, Raleigh holds a special attraction for him.[2]

Gibbon soon realized, however, that Raleigh's age had been thoroughly studied by English historians, that a biography of him would entangle its author in fierce partisan warfare, and that he appealed only to an English audience. Therefore, "I must embrace a safer and more extensive theme" (*M*, 122).[3] This meant a safer theme in two senses: it ought not to generate partisan fights; and it should be a passport to more than local fame. With these mixed desires and inhibitions at work, Gibbon shifted his sights to European history. Perhaps he would write a history of Swiss liberty; perhaps a history of Florence under the Medicis. And with Deyverdun's help he did manage to draft an introduction in French to a history of Swiss liberty.[4] But he got no farther, and his early years have about them a more than faintly troubled uncertainty. Gibbon's aspiration to the character of historian took the form of fledgling gestures toward some unpredictable flight.

Moreover, when we look at Gibbon's career without hindsight, the character and vocation of the historian seem less irrevocably stamped on him than, in time, he would claim. During his apprenticeship he was equally the man of letters, the reviewer, the literary critic, the textual scholar. Only because he reports (or invents) the story more than twenty years later, with the *Decline and Fall* already his monument, do we remember so vividly his epiphany on the Capitol in 1764. In 1761 he had published his *Essai sur l'étude de la littérature*, an immature but passionate defense of humanistic learning that, though consistent with his historical vocation, could not be said to have predicted it. In 1762 he had collected notes for a commentary on Richard Hurd's edition of Horace. In 1768 and 1769 he and Deyverdun wrote and edited two volumes of *Mémoires littéraires de la Grande-Bretagne*, a disastrously unsuccessful journal of reviews, in French and for continental readers, of current English publications.[5] And as late as 1770, when he had just begun serious work on the *Decline and Fall* and six years after his trip to Rome, Gibbon published *Critical Observations on the Sixth Book of the Aeneid*, the attack of an aspiring young David on an aging Goliath, Bishop William Warburton, and on his curious interpretation of *Aeneid* VI as representing its hero's initiation into the Eleusinian mysteries. This attack on Warburton, which Gibbon called, with some retrospective sense of puzzlement, "an accidental sally of love [for Virgil] and resentment [at Warburton's pedantic arrogance]" (*M*, 144), seems at first sight a diversion. In fact, it was a critical step forward.

In the usual view, Gibbon the historian is the product of his intellectual apprenticeship to Tacitus, Bayle, Pascal, Giannone, Montesquieu, Voltaire, and many more. This view has been documented in studies befitting, in their learning, Gibbon's own.[6] But the chart of his intellectual ancestry cannot by itself account for the sense of imperious command that sets the *Decline and Fall* apart. To understand how Gibbon came to be the historian he was, the chart of his intellectual ancestry is necessary but not sufficient. The question is not only where he gathered his materials but how he came to feel secure in asserting his authority, how he achieved his sense of mastery. In this connection, the attack on Warburton will be seen to have played a decisive part.

In any account of how Gibbon achieved his authority, four issues stand out with special clarity. First, because it anticipates the others, is the primacy of fact—the deep conviction he shared with an age that could be called the age of measurement. Chronologers, geographers, political economists, demographers, anatomists, classical historians, all were taking precise measures of the world. Their premise that truth lay on a bedrock of fact Gibbon took as his own. Second is the narrative ordering of fact in space and time. If Gibbon truly knew he would be a historian, that implies a knowledge, not merely trivial, of other vocations that were not to be his; historians have to regard, as poets do not, constraints of narrative decorum. Third is the question of how to respond to error in persons and places of authority. This question was always before Gibbon's eyes in private life, given his father's capricious ways, but there he answered it by looking away. As an apprentice to a public vocation, however, he could not avoid it. Fourth is the question of how to become not just a historian but an interpreter. The answer that emerged was not the one Gibbon explicitly believed in: it did not mean only following in the footsteps of Tacitus; rather, it meant seeing history in a long view. These interwoven concerns dominated Gibbon's apprenticeship.

History and the historian begin in fact itself, as distinguished from the place of fact in the order of history, and hence from patterns the historian imposes on it. In the "Mémoire sur la monarchie des Medes," like the Swiss history an unpublished piece from the late 1760's, Gibbon sets out to separate elemental truth from different types of falsehood in the Greek historian Ctesias, whose errors range from inventions, when he trades the character of the historian for that of the poet or rhetorician, to acceptance of doubtful traditions and misinterpretation of facts, especially of chronology. On the other side of the ledger are true historical facts ("traits vraiment historiques," *MW*, III, 3).[7] This distinction between historical truth and different versions of falsehood was routine in an age not inclined like ours to question the independence of historical data. Even so, Gibbon isolates and empowers with an anxious rigor the plainness of those facts "that bear all the marks of clarity."[8] History approaches scientific certainty to the extent that it depends on indisputable fact.

Facts also provide secure ground on which to challenge authority. They enable Gibbon to correct error in high places—which he does, in private, with unrestrained delight. One of his early unpublished performances, probably dating from 1768–69, he called the "Index Expurgatorius," thereby making himself the inquisitor of error and recording in lengthy notations factual mistakes of the famous: Cicero, Sallust, Dacier, Muratori, Addison, Warburton, Voltaire, Buffon—anyone whom he can catch in an egregious blunder. Even the briefest entries indicate how self-congratulatory, how condescending, how gleeful is the enterprise:

M. de Beaufort . . . talks & quotes so very idly about the Consulars & Correctors of Italy; as to shew, he had mighty little idea of the Constantinean Scheme. I am afraid, his quotations from the Code and Notitia are only second-hand. (*EE*, 108)

Cicero speaks . . . of Ecbatana, as the royal seat of Mithridates. I suppose it is not necessary to prove, that Ecbatana was the Capital of Media, or that Media was never a part of that prince's empire. Tully was probably but an indifferent Geographer, and the celebrated name of Ecbatana, sounded extremely well. A lesson for Criticks! (*EE*, 109)

Mr. Guthrie . . . translates Getæ by Goths; a barbarous name which was first heard of 250 years after Cicero's death. (*EE*, 109)

Whatever the constraints on Gibbon's daily life, here he lets himself go free, avenging himself on the great and uttering small cries of pedagogical triumph: "A lesson for Criticks!"

The inquisitor of factual error can always choose the ground on which to conduct the inquisition, being in possession of the truth or knowing where to find it. "When I meet Voltaire upon Grecian Roman or Asiatic ground," Gibbon says disingenuously, "I treat him with the indulgence he has so much occasion for; but we might have expected to have found him better acquainted with one of the finest writers of his own country" (*EE*, 114). The great writer whom Voltaire has gotten wrong is Pascal in the *Provinciales*, a text Gibbon claimed to have read "almost every year" (*M*, 79). In the pages of the "Index Expurgatorius," out of sight of the world, Gibbon's learning enables him to reprove magisterial figures in the academic pantheon. What could be more gratifying than treating Voltaire with such indulgence?

In its adolescent condescension and petulance, however ("adolescent" seems an accurate description even if Gibbon was already thirty), the "Index" was a step in his coming to terms with authority, the prelude to an understanding. In it, he takes aim at writers he greatly valued—Montesquieu, for example, and Buffon. He had praised Buffon as early as the *Essai sur l'étude de la littérature*. And in 1777, when he met the great man during a visit with the Neckers in Paris, "I was happy in the acquaintance of Mr de Buffon, who united with a sublime Genius, the most amiable simplicity of mind and manners" (*M*, 158). Having published the first volume of the *Decline and Fall* the year before, Gibbon now meets Buffon on something like equal terms. But in the privacy of the "Index," Buffon had appeared more often than any other writer, being treated to some very snippy commentary: "It is often to be lamented that Natural Philosophers are too little acquainted with History or the laws of historical evidence" (*EE*, 121); "M de Buffon often sacrifices truth to eloquence, and consistency to variety" (*EE*, 123); "M de Buffon seems to be a very poor Classical scholar" (*EE*, 124); "Our author who is a better Naturalist, than an Antiquarian, did not know that the vast island or peninsula of Scandinavia was considered by most of the ancients as a part of Germany" (*EE*, 126). Like a niggling and assiduous reviewer, Gibbon marches through his text with a red marker, wincing at each mistake, yet delighting, too, in discovering that authority is not immune to error. The expressing of these feelings is therapeutic. It clears the way for him to put a proper value, uncolored by resentment or resistance, on the work of others.

In the "Index," Gibbon corrects Buffon on the history of the camel. In the *Decline and Fall*, he cites the identical text, with lavish acknowledgment, for now he can afford generosity. In the first instance, Buffon has not read Diodorus Siculus carefully enough: "M.

de Buffon asserts that the camel has been so compleatly subdued by man that there remains no individuals of the species in a state of nature & freedom. This may be true enough in our times, but it was not so in those of Diodorus Siculus. That curious traveller says there were wild Camels in Arabia" (*EE*, 126). In the second instance, Gibbon celebrates the camel in almost Melvillean detail: "In the sands of Africa and Arabia the *camel* is a sacred and precious gift. That strong and patient beast of burthen can perform, without eating or drinking, a journey of several days; and a reservoir of fresh water is preserved in a large bag, a fifth stomach of the animal, whose body is imprinted with the marks of servitude. The larger breed is capable of transporting a weight of a thousand pounds; and the dromedary, of a lighter and more active frame, outstrips the fleetest courser in the race" (V, 337). In a footnote he assigns credit: "Read (it is no unpleasing task) the incomparable articles of the *Horse* and the *Camel*, in the Natural History of M. de Buffon" (V, 336n). If Gibbon the apprentice hoarded facts and was very sharp about others' mistakes, he learned, in blaming, the possibilities of praise.

This passion for fact, and something of the passion for incriminating the great, lies at the heart of the *Essai sur l'étude de la littérature*, if "lying at the heart of" does not imply too coherent a notion of this rambling text. Eventually Gibbon realized how shakily the *Essai* had been put together: "a number of remarks, and examples historical, critical, philosophical are heaped on each other without method or connection, and if we except some introductory pages, all the remaining chapters might indifferently be reversed or transposed" (*M*, 103). This is true. Still, the *Essai*, centering on the debate between "érudits" and "philosophes," consistently defends a value system reposing on historical fact against one reposing on what is perceived as forever, abstractly true. In defending the "érudits," Gibbon is shielding empirical knowledge against the onslaught of moderns who would like to consign history's array of fact to the rubbish bin in favor of geometrical and moral abstractions.

To a willfully extravagant proposal of d'Alembert, Gibbon makes a more sober yet more extraordinary counterproposal on behalf of the factual. D'Alembert had satirically expressed the hope that every century should end with a ritual incineration of history, though he allowed that some facts were "really useful" and should therefore be spared the fate of the rest, which should be burned.[9] Gibbon disagrees: "Without fear of being called by the scornful name of 'érudit,' I oppose the sentence of this enlightened but severe judge, who orders us to collect every fact at the end of a century, choose some, and commit the rest to flames."[10] No, says Gibbon, "conservons-les tous précieusement" (*EL*, 105)—let us conserve them all, and with the utmost care. Don't, he says, imitate geometers like d'Alembert. They serve a tyrannical monarch, "this imperious queen who, not content with her sovereignty, proscribes her sister sciences and declares all reasoning that does not turn on line and number as unworthy of the name."[11] Imitate not the geometers but the botanists: "Imitons les botanistes" (*EL*, 105). Not every plant is useful in medicine, but valuable properties of some may be hidden and thus may yet be discovered. In Gibbon the common sense of the humanist—not everything is known, not everything is reducible to line and number—combines with the devotion of the acolyte: let us conserve every fact.

"Imitons les botanistes." Gibbon might also have said, imitate any of those empirical scientists, including the encyclopedists, who were setting out to measure the world. He might have said, imitate the scholars who had studied the weights, moneys, and measures of the ancient world—scholars he himself had turned to with a ravenous appetite for detail. Gibbon had a natural facility for the strange language ("langue") of weights and measures (*MW*, III, 406), and twice during his apprenticeship he set about abstracting and developing data from "the dry and dark treatises of Greaves, Arbuthnot, Hooper, Bernard, Eisenschmidt Gronovius, La Barre, Freret &c" (*M*, 98). These treatises seemed dark and dry to him only in retrospect. In fact, they were springs of his learning and made him almost drunk with precision. It was even a mark of Rome's superiority to Greece that Rome had the more precise system of weights. The Greeks were a more barbarous people, neglectful of the arts, and such a people are bound to be careless about detail, "un tel peuple devoit se soucier assez peu de précision dans les poids" (*MW*, III, 416). They ordered such things better in Rome.

The gods of enumeration require absolute accuracy. How much, for example, would it have cost the emperor Sulla to reward his soldiers with money rather than, as he did, with land? Gibbon's answer, in the *Essai*, would charm the most punctilious accountant—

32,489,220 English pounds, calculated as follows: 3,000 drachmas to foot soldiers, 6,000 to cavalry soldiers and centurions, 12,000 to tribunes. Hence:

	Liv. Sterl.
282,000 légionaires à 3,000 drachmes ou 12,000 sesterces, ou 105 l. sterling chacun	28,905,000
2,820 centeniers et 14,100 cavaliers à 6000 drachmes ou 210 livres sterling chacun	3,468,600
282 tribuns à 12,000 drachmes ou l. 410 chacun	115,620

En tout   l. 32,489,220   (*EL*, 36)

Arbuthnot had gotten the equivalency wrong at only £30,705,220, having figured the drachma erroneously at 7.75 English pence. Gibbon corrects him, after "some researches that I have made" ("quelques recherches que j'aie faites"; *EL*, 37n). The equivalent should be 8.2 English pence. Late in the 1730's, in an act of civic pride, William Maitland had calculated the length of London and its suburbs, "where shortest," as "Six Miles, Three Quarters, Two hundred and Ninety-one Yards"; the length of Paris, at its greatest, as "Three *English* Miles, Seventy-seven Yards, Three Inches and a Quarter." He had also calculated London's breadth as three miles, 170 yards "and a Half"—"which is Ninety-two Yards and Thirty-four Inches broader than *Paris* is in Length."[12] Young Gibbon luxuriates in acts of such specious precision as taking the length of Paris down to the quarter inch.

If the effort to calculate the equivalence between the ancient drachma and eighteenth-century English money down to the fifth of a penny looks like an accountant's obsession, the age's struggle to organize facts on the grid of space and time is easier to understand. Geography and chronology, according to conventional wisdom, were the "eyes" of history.[13] But as Gibbon was writing, the voyages of discovery had still not opened up all the world: it was in 1779, three years after the first volume of the *Decline and Fall* appeared, that Cook was killed at Kealakekua Bay. And questions of ancient chronology, especially the reconciling of secular and sacred history, continued to vex historians. Polymathic scholars of the seventeenth century had poured their energy into studying these questions, and Gibbon had absorbed very early the conventional wisdom that without geography and chronology, history was blind. Having lost himself in a wilderness of precocious reading, he reports, "the only principle that darted a ray of light into the indigested Chaos was an early and rational application to the order of time and place" (*M*, 43). Enlightenment began with the ordering of time and place.[14]

To know the ancient world was, in the first place, to see it through the eye of geography. "The maps of Cellarius and Wells," Gibbon says, "imprinted in my mind the picture of ancient Geography" (*M*, 43). Edward Wells's *Treatise of Antient and Present Geography*, a popular school text with an accompanying set of maps that went through five editions between 1701 and 1738, announces that "the most remarkable Differences of Antient and Present Geography may be quickly discern'd by a bare Inspection or comparing of correspondent Maps." The maps then show ancient and modern Europe, Gaul and France, Pannonia and Hungary, and so on—"the most natural and easy Method," as the promotional subtitle to the maps explains, "to lead Young Students . . . into a competent Knowledge of the Geographical Science."[15] The Lockean formulation of what Gibbon learned from Wells and Christoph Keller (Cellarius),[16] whose maps "imprinted" themselves on his mind, confirms the visual stamp of his knowledge.[17] Gibbon could summon up at will the image of the Roman Empire: Dacia and Pannonia and Arabia Felix were as familiar to his mind's eye as Switzerland and Sussex. Looking out from the Capitoline in 1764, he imagined himself seeing outward to the boundaries of empire.

More crucial even than geography was chronology, with its puzzles that disturbed Gibbon's youthful sleep and its implicit narrative demands. And chronology, too, he managed to make himself see. In his adolescence he read Aegidius Strauch, professor of theology at Danzig, whose chronological treatise had been translated into English in 1699 and had drawn the praise of Locke, a philosopher not altogether friendly to learned chronology;[18] he read James Anderson's *Royal Genealogies* (1732) and Christoph Helwig's (Helvicus) *Theatrum Historicum* (1609), translated into English in 1687 after at least six editions in the original Latin; he read Ussher and the vastly popular Humphrey Prideaux on the chronology of the Old and New testaments.[19] And all "the multitude of names and dates" that he collected from this voracious reading, "I engraved . . . in a clear and indelible series" (*M*, 43). Like the map of the ancient world, the names and dates of antiquity were imprinted, or engraved, on his mind.

This prodigious talent for assimilating data encouraged Gibbon to try his hand very early at the chronologer's art: "I overleaped the bounds of modesty and use. In my childish balance I presumed to weigh the systems of Scaliger and Petavius, of Marsham and Newton which I could seldom study in the originals." And then, in this densely factual context, he produces his inspired image of a childhood spent playing with the dynasties of Assyria and Egypt, as with top and cricketball. But daytime games could become the stuff of sleepless nights: "my sleep has been disturbed by the difficulty of reconciling the Septuagint with the Hebrew computation" (*M*, 43). Chronology, like enumeration, was an obsession, and at the age of fifteen, Gibbon even turned his hand to a project he called "the Age of Sesostris." Though he claims later to have burned it (it does not survive), he maintained a wry affection for its precocity: "Unprovided with original learning, unformed in the habits of thinking, unskilled in the arts of composition, I resolved—to write a book" (*M*, 55), of which the "sole object" was to date the reign of Sesostris, supposed by different authorities to have been between a thousand and fifteen hundred years before Christ. The solution "for a youth of fifteen is not devoid of ingenuity" and, for the autobiographer, not devoid of pleasure. It involved the claim that Manetho the High Priest, compiler of an Egyptian chronology, had lied in the interest of creating a flattering lineage for the pharaoh to whom his work is dedicated. Gibbon cherishes the adolescent intuition that knowledge and experience have confirmed—namely, that "falsehood . . . is not incompatible with the sacerdotal Character" (*M*, 56). He also cherishes the memory of having seemed to solve a chronological puzzle. To solve such puzzles was to free himself from insomnia.

To see geography and chronology accurately would be the first mark of a correct historian. In the "Index Expurgatorius," Gibbon criticizes Sallust for not being "correct," his failure lying in a muddled sense both of time and of African geography:

Sallust is no very correct historian. I blame. I. His Chronology. Let any one consider the context of his history from the siege of Numantia to the Consulship of Calphurnius Bestia. . . . A fair reader can never imagine, a space of more than five or six years. There were really 22. . . . 2 His Geography. Notwithstanding his laboured description of Africa, nothing can be more confused than his Geography without either division of provinces or fixing of towns. We scarce perceive any distance, between Capsa and the river Mulucho. (*EE*, 110)

To be correct was to gain control. When Pope said, of English poets and English poetry, that "late, very late, correctness grew our care," he meant by correctness the last degree of polish and refinement, especially in matters of technique—a degree of refinement he believed that he had himself achieved.[20] Metrical precision in poetry is matched, in writing history, by exactness of time and place, the meter of history.[21] Pope aimed to be a correct poet; Gibbon, to be a correct historian, by representing accurate intervals of years and of distance.

To be sure, by the time he came to the *Decline and Fall*, Gibbon realized that some chronological questions lay beyond evidence and inquiry: "Such were my juvenile discoveries; at a riper age I no longer presume to connect the Greek, the Jewish, and the Egyptian antiquities which are lost in a distant cloud" (*M*, 56). He had also realized that, over so long a stretch of centuries, a chronological narrative would have been deadening, and he congratulates himself on having found a better way. At the same time, he is at pains to say that the neglect of chronology is only seeming: "It was not till after many designs and many tryals, that I preferred, as I still prefer, the method of groupping my picture by nations . . . and the seeming neglect of Chronological order is surely compensated by the superior merits of interest and perspicuity" (*M*, 179). Gibbon does not violate chronology; rather, he subsumes it in the interest of a clearer "picture," a sharper vision. "Perspicuity," in Johnson's first definition, is "clearness to the mind." The historian who has facts at his command may then go on to break the rules, or seem to, in the interests of a more comprehensive view.[22]

It is also true, however, that ordering facts in time and space entails a literalism that Gibbon never transcended nor ever wished to transcend. If his lot was to be a historian, it was equally not to be a poet. To be a poet would have been to risk anxiety in a world not subject to the corrections of inquiry and verification. Gibbon re-proves Ctesias, in the "Mémoire sur la monarchie des Medes," for not maintaining the distinction between history, rhetoric, and po-etry: "He often abandoned the role of the historian for that of the orator and even the poet."[23] This breaking down of generic bound-aries reflects more than a lack of aesthetic control; it reflects a failure of character.

The commitment to chronology stands directly in the way of the narrative freedom that poets claim as their imaginative prerogative. In the *Essai*, Gibbon takes up a controverted and embarrassing prob-lem—whether Virgil committed an anachronism by bringing Dido and Aeneas on stage together. The burden of Gibbon's argument, that chronology is an instrument of humane as opposed to geomet-rical learning, effectively subordinates Virgil's art to claims of his-torical accuracy. Among the modern philosophers who have not neglected humanistic learning, Gibbon says, are Gassendi, Leibniz, Boyle, and, at the head of the list, Newton, whose inclusion de-pends largely on his chronological system.[24] According to this sys-tem, to Gibbon's relief, Virgil commits no anachronism. In New-ton's system, Aeneas and Dido are contemporaries.[25] The substance of Newton's argument, which Gibbon summarizes, matters less than its side benefits. If Newton and Virgil are allies in learning, science and poetry join hands in the cause of chronological preci-sion. And like Newton after him, Virgil conscientiously aims to correct the errors of others, incorporating his view of Roman chro-nology in his text and then confirming it by the episode of Dido and Aeneas: "What art in the poet to seize the moment of Aeneas's arrival in Carthage to answer his critics in the only way that the speed of his narrative and the grandeur of his subject allowed him. He makes them understand that in his hypothesis, the meeting of Dido and Aeneas is not poetic license at all."[26]

Better yet, Virgil is not alone when he questions the usual chro-nology of the Latin kings.[27] If, says Gibbon, we only had the lost forty-four books of the historian Pompeius Trogus, that is where we would find proof of the Roman chronology according to Virgil and Newton. Virgil is no fabulist but a true historian. Gibbon takes care not to let his opinion of the poet, nor of the Aeneas-Dido epi-sode, seem to depend on matters of historical veracity: "Whoever dares criticize the Dido episode has more philosophy or less taste than I do."[28] But this precaution does not obscure the fact that Virgil rises in Gibbon's estimation not only because he is right but because the *Aeneid* has the character of a historical-chronological manifesto.[29]

That Gibbon would become a historian, committed to the ordinary order of things, rather than a poet, is equally evident from some of his early reflections on narrative strategy. Soon after publication of the *Essai*, Richard Hurd's edition of Horace's epistles to Augustus and to the Pisos (the latter known best as the *Ars Poetica*) caught Gibbon's eye, and he set about drafting a response.[30] What concerns him most is the familiar Horatian question of where to begin an epic poem: "A poet may either tell his story in the natural historical order, or rushing at once into the middle of his subject he may afterwards introduce by way of Episode the events previous to it. Which method should he observe?" Horace had answered that the epic poet should begin *in medias res*, as Homer had done in the *Odyssey*. Virgil, Milton, Voltaire (in the *Henriade*), and Fénelon (in *Télémaque*) had all done the same; and Hurd had attempted "to account for and establish" this rule, "one of the most important . . . of Epic poetry." Against this phalanx of authority Gibbon ventures in the privacy of his study "to start some objections": "many things," he says, "which have stood the test of time cannot endure that of reason." Among these, none troubled him more than the belief that good poetic strategy calls for violating the "natural historical order" (*EE*, 31): he is not comfortable with stories that begin *in medias res*. Is it an essential attribute of the poet to be able to accommodate the idea that a story might begin in the middle? That Gibbon could not do.

His first objection to Hurd is not a trivial one: "Supposing the rule founded on reason it is too vague to be easily reduced into practice." It is all very well to begin *in medias res*, but where? "Since the greatest part of the poem is to consist in a recital, where the poet himself, speaks; when is that recital to begin?" (*EE*, 31). A criterion is not easy to find—indeed, by Gibbon's account, it is impossible.

The episode of Dido and Aeneas, after all, is not Virgil's main subject; that is the founding of Rome. If such an episode properly belongs in the story at all, then "why may not Æneas's meeting Andromache in Epirus be as much a part of the principal subject as his meeting Dido at Carthage?" (*EE*, 31). If so, why not have begun the narrative with Aeneas and Andromache, an episode that Aeneas recounts to Dido in Book III? What strikes us about this is its dogged skepticism and misunderstanding. Without the security of chronological order, Gibbon is adrift. Can he really have believed that the meeting of Aeneas and the maternal Andromache would have been as good a point of departure as the meeting of Aeneas and Dido? To begin *in medias res* allows the poet to weigh the narrative, to choose an action at a moment designed to be generative, not just the first of a series. Gibbon seems not to recognize the logic of putting Dido at the beginning; it is she above all others whom Aeneas has to leave behind. In a narrative that begins *in medias res* and depends on flashbacks to sketch in the hero's prior history, the poet solves the vexed problem of origins by substituting aesthetic and psychological for chronological values.

To the extent that Gibbon attaches himself to the claims of a "natural" and complete historical order, he is not Virgil's ideal reader. In an episodical narrative, such as the story of Aeneas ("or any other epic poem" [*EE*, 31]), the reader will "ask at every pause," at least in the early going, "why the bard might not begin his Invocation from thence" (*EE*, 32). This begs the question of origins while seeming to respond to it. Gibbon assumes a narrative adequately defined by its own limits, but as he conceives the question, these limits might just as logically be breached. Why did Virgil or any other epic poet not begin from some other point outside the existing narrative? Here lies the uncertainty that beginning *in medias res* aims to cure. Attached to values of sequential fact, Gibbon overlooks claims of aesthetic order, at the same time revealing the relational character of systems that he thought (or hoped) rested on bedrock.

He raises three other objections to beginning *in medias res*. The first is that the puzzled reader, "thrown at once into the midst of the subject," experiences a sense of disorientation. To be sure, drama creates the same effect, but this is an "unavoidable defect." It is a mistake "therefore voluntarily to transfer it to another species." Second, the inevitable narrative of events that have happened before the beginning of the poem frustrates the reader who has been stirred by the opening, is anxious to learn the outcome, and therefore wants to get on with the action. By the time Aeneas's narration has ended, we have "almost forgot" (*EE*, 32) who Dido is. We lose our chronological bearings in such a narrative, which disrupts what Gibbon construes as normal psychological process: "in every operation of the mind there is a much higher delight in descending from the cause to the effect than in ascending from the effect to the cause. In the perusal of a fable it is the event we are anxious about, & our anxiety encreases or diminishes as that event is known or unknown to us" (*EE*, 33). Third, the hero's inset narrative of prior events will probably be cast (though Aeneas makes an exception) in a style less grand than the rest of the poem. Unity and order will be violated once again.

It would be wrong to suppose, faced with these rigidities, that as a literary critic Gibbon was no better than a successor to John Dennis and Thomas Rymer. They hawked the rules. Gibbon, on the contrary, is independent to a fault; his values play themselves out against a background of private anxieties and needs, and he recognizes uncertainties that critics like Dennis and Rymer knew nothing of. He knew, for example, that origins were problematic. In a commonplace book that he kept in 1755, some seven years before his notes on Hurd, he had recorded an excerpt from Voltaire on the growth of the Papacy: "Tis far from this [the Papacy in the seventh century] to the Tiara; But tis far too from the first monk who preached on the banks of the Rhine to the Electoral Bonnet, or from a chief of wandering Salians to a Roman Emperor. Every grandeur is formed by little and little and every origine is inconsiderable" (*EE*, 18).

Moreover, Gibbon had some awareness that requirements of aesthetic order clash with those of historical completeness. Hurd argues that Aeneas's (rather than Virgil's) telling of the destruction of Troy spares the poet from devoting several books to it and, in effect, from writing a different (and worse) poem to which Aeneas's wanderings would have been just an appendix. An epic poem, says Hurd, "obliges the poet to relate at full length every event he himself"—as distinct from, say, Aeneas—"relates." Gibbon replies sensibly: "I should rather think that as an Epic poem must preserve an Unity of hero, and of action Every event instead of being related at full length, need only occupy a space proportionable to it's importance and degree of connection with the principal subject" (*EE*, 34). That is to say, the poet makes comparative judgments of importance in assigning space to the events of the story. But again, if space is allocated for reasons of comparative importance, why not place as well? Why is the Dido-Aeneas episode not well situated at the start? The question, thus recast, yields the same answer as before. To have been a poet would have been to risk losing the thread of fact. If Gibbon eventually substitutes topical for strictly chronological organization in the *Decline and Fall*, he also stipulates that the age of the Antonines is the place to begin (only later worrying whether he had made the right decision) and then follows the course of empire for almost fourteen hundred years.

Beyond the mastering of fact and beyond an allegiance to spatial and temporal order, Gibbon also had to find the combination of aggressiveness and deference in the presence of authority that would enable him to weigh the claims of evidence and to carry on the quarrels that were to make his history both famous and notorious. The "Index Expurgatorius," the "Mémoire sur la monarchie des Medes," the *Essai*, the reply to Hurd, all are apprentice exercises: each shows Gibbon in an argumentative or critical mood. But the gap had to be bridged between the private shrillness of the "Index" and public blandness. On the long road Gibbon traveled in his public dealings with authority, a correspondence with the Swiss scholar Johann Jacob Breitinger is an early milestone. If the "Index Expurgatorius" marks the limits of Gibbon's private aggressiveness, the correspondence with Breitinger, twelve years before, shows how well he had learned the tropes of public deference.

Breitinger was professor of Greek and Hebrew at Zürich, more than thirty-five years Gibbon's senior, and sufficiently distinguished in learning to meet the young scholar's need for someone important on whom to test his interpretations of Latin texts, especially Justin's epitome of Pompeius Trogus, which was to figure so largely in his understanding of Virgil's chronology. Breitinger had the reputation for being generous, and his Latin seems to have been less polished than his Greek and Hebrew. What is more, he was a theologian, not a historian. Hence D. M. Low's comment that "one must sympathize with [Breitinger] in being drawn into detailed discussions of topics of ancient history, which would not be immediately familiar to him, by a persistent and unknown young man" (*L*, I, 388).[31] It is another case of the young challenger choosing the ground on which to meet the veteran.

Persistent Gibbon certainly was, and the correspondence continued over some twelve months. At first he wrote anonymously, then grew bolder and revealed his identity as that of the young man who with Pavillard had visited Breitinger some months earlier. These are the strategies of a very cautious applicant for fame, and the letters rely on formulaic bowing and scraping to authority:

Vir Praestantissime et omnibus Verae Pietatis Scientiaeque Amatoribus nunquam satis Venerande.   (*L*, I, 14)

Most eminent Sir whom all lovers of True Religion and Learning can never sufficiently venerate.   (*L*, I, 19)[32]

And:

Vir Praestantissime,
   Litteras tuas summa cum gratulatione accepi, nec satis scio quid magis admirari debeam, vel humanitatem qua studiis favisti meis, vel eruditionem ac sagacitatem quibus geminum te Aristarchum praebuisti.   (*L*, I, 25)

Most eminent Sir,
   I received your letter with the highest gratification and I hardly know what I should admire more, the kindness with which you have favoured my studies, or the learning and sagacity with which you have revealed yourself a second Aristarchus.   (*L*, I, 30)

Or again:

Vir Praestantissime,
   Semper me pudor legitimus sane remoratur quoties incipere volo. Imberbis quidam nullo inter eruditos professo nomine te rogo ut aliquando momenta quaedam temporis gravissimis tuis laboribus surripere digneris.   (*L*, I, 38)

Most eminent Sir,
   A justifiable modesty holds me back whenever I am minded to begin. I, a mere youth with no standing among scholars, am asking you to deign on occasion to steal some moments from your most serious labours.   (*L*, I, 44)

The voice speaking here might come from an epistle dedicatory to a Swiftian tale of a tub, yet there is not a hint of irony. Quite the contrary, for Gibbon argues his case seriously and tenaciously; the formulas of classical deference make tenacity possible. Barely out of his adolescence, Gibbon plays by the rules. At the same time, he is truly grateful to Breitinger:

Studia adolescentis ignoti etiam promovere laboresque ejus benigne susci-
pere caeteris equidem magnum aliquid ac operosum videri potest, tibi certe
commune ac quotidianum. Hae sunt tuae artes nobilissimae sane ac laudem
merentes aeternam. (*L*, I, 49)

To help the studies of an unknown youth and to shoulder his burdens might
well seem a big and tiresome task to others, to you it is an ordinary daily
matter. Such is your truly noble practice, and one that deserves undying
fame. (*L*, I, 53–54)

Yet even in his gratitude, he knows that beneath the mandatory po-
liteness of scholarly exchange lies the struggle between generations:

Ne te displiceat Vir Praestantissime si aliquando auserim aliter quam te di-
cere. In Nocte concubia facile est Tironi cum Veterano Milite certare. In re
incertissima mihi Tecum. (*L*, I, 30)

May it not displease you, most eminent Sir, if at times I have ventured to
disagree with you. In the darkness of the night, a recruit may contend with
a veteran, and so I with you in this most uncertain subject. (*L*, I, 34)

"In Nocte concubia" means, literally, at bedtime but more than
hints at sexual meanings; the noun "concubium" means sexual intercourse. Warfare, sexuality, and scholarship merge; the polite
struggle is to the death.

If the exchange with Breitinger and the "Index Expurgatorius"
mark extremes, the *Essai* and the commentary on Hurd show Gibbon insecurely on a middle ground. Though he has axes to grind—
with d'Alembert and the philosophes, with Hurd—he grinds them
softly. And in dedicating the *Essai* to his father, he acts out publicly
the role of dutiful son; at the age of twenty-four, already an officer
in the militia, he is still subject to paternal authority. Once he had
intended to dedicate the *Essai* to Suzanne Curchod, had in fact
drafted that dedication, commenting on the insincerity of most
modern dedications (*L*, I, 94–95). In the intervening years, his father had not exactly forbidden him to marry Suzanne but, worse
yet, had let him know that to marry her was to abandon him, to
send him to his grave before his time, to be a traitor to his country
(*L*, I, 106). His father and stepmother had taken to intercepting Suzanne's letters.[33] And his father had persuaded him, after the affair had
become a dead issue, to publish the *Essai*. Under the circumstances,
its dedication looks as if it could only be ironical, but it is not.

Like the draft dedication to Suzanne, it comments on the insincerity of other dedications of the modern kind: "No performance is, in my opinion, more contemptible than a Dedication of the common sort"—that is, a dedication to some great man who "is presented with a book, which, if Science be the subject, he is incapable of understanding; if polite Literature, incapable of tasting" (*EL*, A2r). Also like the original draft, it proposes that dedications should either be addressed to a "master of the art" or "dictated by the heart, and offered to some person who is dear to us" (*EL*, A2v–A3r). But for all its ironic possibility, Gibbon never lets down his guard when he addresses to his father words once intended for Suzanne. He owes him everything: "If I am capable of producing anything worthy the attention of the public, it is to you that I owe it; to that truly paternal care which, from the first dawnings of my reason, has always watched over my education, and afforded me every opportunity of improvement" (*EL*, A3v).

Can this really be serious? Can Gibbon mean it when he says, in the next breath, "Permit me here to express my grateful sense of your tenderness to me, and to assure you, that the study of my whole life shall be to acquit my self, in some measure, of obligations I can never fully repay" (*EL*, A3v–A4r)? Can we detect, in retrospect, not the faintest ironic resonance—in those obligations, perhaps, that young Gibbon can never fully repay? After all, he had thought, and said in the draft, that Suzanne's beauty would have softened a tyrant: "La Nature vous avait doué d'une beauté qui amollirait un Tiran" (*L*, I, 94). Now that her beauty has failed to soften parental tyranny, does Gibbon not permit himself the expression of any private resentment? I cannot find it—yet it would take only the slightest raising of an eyebrow to suggest ironic content.

In the autobiography, Gibbon blamed his father's friend David Mallett for some "foolish" advice—namely, to write the dedication in English, resulting in "a confusion of tongues which seemed to accuse the ignorance of my patron" (*M*, 105) and, incidentally, to provide evidence that this was a book dedicated, like others of the modern kind, to someone unable to understand it. In other drafts of the autobiography, Gibbon calls the mixture of English dedication and French text preposterous.[34] But can he have written the dedication with no awareness of its oddity? In fact, his father's French, despite sojourns in France, was far from strong, and Mallett probably had that embarrassment in mind. Years later, in the autobiography, Gibbon still seems bothered by his father's ineptitude in the language: "the slender knowledge which he had gained of the French language was gradually obliterated" (*M*, 17). If this was so, one may even wonder whether Edward Sr. could read, without help, the letters his son wrote in that language from Lausanne. The English dedication to the *Essai*—which Gibbon signed, abjectly, with the words, "I am, dear Sir, with the sincerest affection and regard, your most dutiful son, and faithful servant" (*EL*, A4r)— looks more than ever like a rhetorical vessel waiting to be filled.[35]

The unpublished commentary on Hurd provided no occasion for dedications nor, in the text, much beyond ordinary praise and blame. Hurd "cannot be read without improvement"; his virtues include "clearness of judgement" and "niceness of penetration"; few writers better deserve "the great, tho' prostituted name of Critic." But—inevitably, but—"like many Critics he is better qualified to instruct, than to execute"; his manner is harsh and affected, his style obscure. Gibbon rides the seesaw of praise and blame with uncomplicated skill. After this routine catalogue of merits and demerits, however, he anticipates the most formative of all his early exchanges with authority, the *Critical Observations on the Sixth Book of the Aeneid* (1770). Hurd was one of Warburton's obsequious retinue, and perhaps never more, in Gibbon's mind, than a stalking horse: "His excessive praises (not to give them a harsher name) of a certain living Critic and Divine disgust the sensible reader as much as the contempt affected for the same person by many who are very unqualified to pass a judgment upon him" (*EE*, 27). Hurd's "excessive praises" of Warburton may even have called to Gibbon's mind his own recent dedication of the *Essai* to his father. And when it came to haughtiness, Warburton could hold his own with Voltaire; when it came to petulance, with Edward Gibbon, Sr.

In every sense, then, Warburton was the opponent for whom Gibbon had been looking. He was of the right generation, born nine years before Edward Gibbon, Sr. Conveniently, by 1770 he was an extinct volcano, seventy-two years old and retired from controversy. But best of all, his learning impressed even Johnson, and he had been "the reigning Monarch of English letters" at mid-century.[36] He was therefore an opponent worth testing one's abilities on, with limited risk, provided one had the right qualifications. Possibly it was Charles Churchill, among Warburton's legion of antagonists, whom Gibbon thought unqualified to pass judgment on him: Churchill's mordant posthumous "Dedication" of his sermons to Warburton had been published in 1765, and Gibbon may have envied the scapegrace Churchill the freedom of his almost frontal assault on the tyrannical Bishop of Gloucester. In any case, less than a decade after his unpublished attack on Warburton's apprentice, Gibbon took on the master. The *Critical Observations* show him for the first time proficient at, if not yet able to sustain, the ruthlessly genteel style of intellectual warfare that in the *Decline and Fall* he would make his own.

Ultimately, Gibbon looked back at this attack on Warburton, published nine months before his father's death, with an enforced blush: "I cannot forgive myself the contemptuous treatment of a man, who, with all his faults, was entitled to my esteem; and I can less forgive, in a personal attack, the cowardly concealment of my name and character" (*M*, 146). But this retrospective guilt does not ring quite true, even if we suppose it joined to a recognition of patricidal motives. Anonymity may not have been courageous, but it enabled Gibbon to publish, and the autobiography gives a self-satisfied account of his playing David to Warburton's Goliath: "*I too*"—as well, that is, as Bishop Lowth, who had attacked Warburton in 1765—"without any private offence was ambitious of breaking a lance against the Giant's shield" (*M*, 145).

The denial that Warburton had given private offense, being true, is therefore suspicious. Why insist on the lack of private offense unless Gibbon harbors a sense that Warburton was more than a merely public enemy? If Warburton had not existed, Gibbon would have done well to invent him: "The learning and abilities of the author had raised him to a just eminence; but he reigned the Dictator and tyrant of the World of Litterature. The real merit of Warburton was degraded by the pride and presumption with which he pronounced his infallible decrees; in his polemic writings he lashed his antagonists without mercy or moderation; and his servile flatterers . . . exalting the master critic far above Aristotle and Longinus, assaulted every modest dissenter who refused to consult the oracle, and to adore the Idol" (*M*, 144–45). At the age of nineteen, Gibbon had wanted a good scholar to test intellectually and, in that way, to test himself. Now, at thirty-two, he wants a great man to treat severely, and not just in the sequestered pages of a private "Index."

David, even an anonymous David, requires Goliath. For this purpose the pseudo-papal Warburton is perfect, an exponent of priestly mysteries and manifestly resistant, in Gibbon's view, to plain historical fact.

The occasion of the *Critical Observations* was Warburton's immense *Divine Legation of Moses*, published some thirty years earlier, which had set out to prove, in Warburton's words, that paganism was instituted by "the Antient Lawgivers for the support and benefit of Society" (i.e., as an instrument of social organization) and that those initiated into the mysteries were taught, in another version of the truth, "the vanity of Polytheism, and the Unity of the First Cause" (*EE*, 134). On Warburton's account, Aeneas's descent to the underworld in Book VI was the initiation of a giver of laws; on this account, Virgil and Aeneas were of the priestly class.

This trafficking in mystery and Warburton's attempt to capture Virgil for his side infuriated Gibbon. He had, after all, enlisted Virgil in the wars of chronology, and this new combat reflects a desire to keep up that early alliance, ripened now into a treaty of mutual defence against mystery-mongers: "It is well known that he [Virgil] was a determined Epicurean; and a very natural Antipathy subsisted between the Epicureans and the Managers of the Mysteries" (*EE*, 153). What is more, Warburton's argument requires him to explain what the managers of mysteries had successfully kept hidden, and it is therefore self-implicating: "as soon as we attempt this Enquiry, the honour of the Mysteries becomes our own" (*EE*, 136). In fact, there is probably no secret at all: "I admire the discretion of the Initiated; but the best security for discretion is, the vanity of concealing that we have nothing to reveal" (*EE*, 137).

Even worse, Warburton has to suppose that Virgil was an initiate who, against all probability and all the rules, exposed what he should have kept hidden. And not only is Virgil morally at fault, he also violates the historian's obligation to stick to things as they are. According to Warburton, the events recorded in Book VI are an imitation of an imitation, a mimic descent into hell. Gibbon believes instead "that Virgil described a real, not a mimic world," "that the Scene lay in the Infernal Shades, and not in the Temple of Ceres," and that the infernal landscape of Virgil's underworld replicates "the singularity of the Cumœan Shores," with their "vast cavities, sulphureous steams, poisonous exhalations, and fiery torrents" (*EE*,

149). Virgil's underworld is not allegory but reality; and Virgil not so much a fabulist as a historian, even a geographer, who wrote about what he could see, not about what he could not. The pose of the naïf, who also believes in what he sees, not in what he does not, was often to sustain Gibbon in the *Decline and Fall*.

In the *Critical Observations*, we hear for the first time the rising inflection of innuendo. "It is well known" that Virgil was not likely to have been friendly to the managers of mystery. If we try to explain the mysteries, their "honour" becomes our own. Gibbon "admires" the "discretion" of the initiated, but the best security for that sort of discretion is the vanity of concealing the lack of anything to reveal. Far from being an initiate, Virgil is a plain man's poet, drawing on the superstitions of the people but never in league with hierarchs. Gibbon has begun to learn the rhetoric of subversion. Neither one of the public, himself, nor one of the priests, he calls Virgil "my favourite Poet" (*EE*, 151) with a sense of complicity and elation.

Watching Gibbon at work as he begins the *Critical Observations* is watching the ironist finding his way. What had been simple praise, however qualified, in Hurd's case becomes ambiguous praise in Warburton's: "The Allegorical Interpretation which the Bishop of Glocester has given of the Sixth Book of the Æneid, seems to have been very favourably received by the Public. Many writers, both at home and abroad, have mentioned it with approbation, or at least with esteem; and I have more than once heard it alledged, in the conversation of scholars, as an ingenious improvement on the plain and obvious sense of Virgil" (*EE*, 133). The public, if not exactly a straw man, is a rhetorical convenience. Awareness of the public and of the scholars whose conversation he has heard, or overheard, establishes the speaker as at once knowledgeable, judicious. A dispassionate observer and listener, he only incidentally keeps the company of mystery-mongering scholars who applaud hyperingenious improvements "on the plain and obvious sense of Virgil." The critical observer of *Critical Observations* is a wise amateur, not a professional grasping for learned obscurity.

As a "candid critic" he is also an entertaining companion, even a fellow rider to hounds: Warburton's interpretation "is not undeserving"—an arch double negative—"of the notice of a candid critic; nor can the enquiry be void of entertainment, whilst Virgil is our constant theme. Whatever may be the fortune of the chace, we are sure it will lead us through pleasant prospects and a fine country" (*EE*, 133). In the vocabulary of the time, "candid" meant well-disposed, benign; yet by 1770 its meaning of frank, or frankly critical, had begun to encroach. Gibbon's use hovers between irony and straightforwardness. But if there is a pill waiting to be swallowed here, it will be sugarcoated by the Virgilian theme and the pleasures of the chase with its agreeable prospects. No fox hunter himself, Gibbon knew how gentlemen like his father talked about their sporting pleasures. For just a moment the role of squire merges with that of critic. But Gibbon the observer also knew that the chase, for all its green prospects, often came to a violent, bloody end. If the object of the candid young critic's sporting gallop is only Virgil's true meaning, he is in pursuit of what is already "plain and obvious." Surely that would be wasting time.

Having promised fair prospects, Gibbon sets about his business, that of running Warburton to ground—as he would later run early Christianity to ground, having first promised "a candid but rational inquiry" into its "progress and establishment" (II, 1). Dangerous work in each case, and the business must be done circumspectly: "That I may escape the imputation as well as the danger of misrepresenting his Lordship's Hypothesis, I shall expose it in his own words" (*EE*, 133)—as Gibbon then does. The danger goes beyond merely misrepresenting Warburton, though it is limited by his age and infirmity. Gibbon at least likes to think he risks drawing down on himself, even under cover of anonymity, episcopal fury.

As for his lordship's hypothesis, it "is supported with singular ingenuity, dressed up with an easy yet pompous display of Learning, and delivered in a style much fitter for the Hierophant of Eleusis, than for a Modern Critic, who is observing a remote object through the medium of a glimmering and doubtful light" (*EE*, 133). Though Gibbon has partly let down his guard, after his earlier dexterities, he still plays with double meanings. "Singular" ingenuity is not necessarily misguided, and "pompous" is a word, like "candid," that had not irrevocably settled into its modern sense: Johnson's only definition of it is "splendid; magnificent; grand." To be sure, a modern critic who talks like the Hierophant of Eleusis makes a foolishly grand figure, but in a landscape of pleasing Virgilian prospects, would it not be crude and in the Warburtonian vein to register offense? The *Critical Observations* passed without reply from the aging bishop or his subalterns. In the *Decline and Fall*, where Gibbon was, though more subtle, also more bold, he would not escape so cleanly.[37] The *Critical Observations* were a last, preparatory act of authorial concealment.[38]

After these opening paragraphs, Gibbon bothers to be subtle only intermittently, and at the end of the *Critical Observations* he attaches a paragraph that declines into sarcasm at the expense of Warburton and the obsequious Hurd: "It is perhaps some such foolish fondness for Antiquity, which inclines me to doubt, whether the BISHOP OF GLOCESTER has really united the severe sense of ARISTOTLE with the sublime imagination of LONGINUS. Yet a judicious Critic (who is now, I believe, ARCHDEACON OF GLOCESTER) assures the Public, that his Patron's mere amusements have done much more than the joint labours of the two Grecians." Then the *Critical Observations* come to a lame ending (a final postscript aside) as Gibbon quotes Hurd on Warburton: "YOU HAVE NOW AT LENGTH ADVANCED CRITICISM TO ITS FULL GLORY" (*EE*, 159). Old feelings, associated with Gibbon's earlier unpublished bout with Hurd, have resurfaced in more intense form, yielding an awkward codicil to an otherwise mature performance. Soon Gibbon would turn from Hurd and Warburton to the institution they served, its mystery-mongering and its authority. His apprenticeship was nearly over.

By the time of the *Critical Observations*, then, Gibbon had learned much of what he needed to know, yet he also believed that a great historian needed to do more than register and order facts and more, even, than counter error, dogmatism, and mystery. As early as the *Essai sur l'étude de la littérature* and the "Mémoire sur la monarchie des Medes," he had sketched an image of the historian he wanted to be, "l'historien philosophe." What he was aiming at, even if he did not realize it precisely, was an image of his own established authority. The philosophic historian could choose and judge and see.[39]

What he could above all see, Gibbon supposed, were causes and effects, yet to see them was to have participated in a game of risk: "For the philosophic spirit, history is what gaming was for the Marquis of Dangeau. He saw a system, connections, coherence, where others saw only the caprices of fortune. For him, this science is one of causes and effects."[40] In the legendary Phillipe de Courcillon, Marquis de Dangeau (1643–1723), Gibbon invents another alter ego, a compensatory model for the young adventurer whose gambling in Lausanne had been so disastrous. By seeing into the causes and effects of things, the philosophic historian would win the game and also blot out the losses of the past.

But how to become such a historian? The advice of the *Essai* consists mostly of cautions: causes should be proportioned to effects, the character of an age should not be deduced from that of an individual, facts should not be wrenched to fit a hypothesis. Good advice, but not in the spirit of the Marquis de Dangeau. In fact, Gibbon's advice reduces to one recommendation: imitate Tacitus, who uses his eloquence to make visible the chain of events and who fills the soul with wisdom.[41] Even granting Gibbon's obligation to Tacitus, however, this only faintly predicts what will be most distinctive, most nearly philosophic, most authoritative in his own way of writing history. The emphasis on causality, in particular, promises more than he was to deliver: if his chapters on Christianity identify forces that speeded the decline of empire, his views of historical causation are nonetheless thin and inconsistent. Gibbon's claim to being a philosopher-historian does not rest on powers of causal analysis.

Instead, it rests on a principle of understanding and then on a principle of aesthetic organization. Intellectually, the philosopher-historian chooses facts that best fit his hypotheses, even at risk of exaggeration, and hence of danger. In his resistance to fanaticism and superstition, Gibbon overstated his case in ways he could recognize himself and had almost predicted in the "Mémoire sur la monarchie des Medes," when he wrote that the philosophic historian "will choose, among disputed facts, those that agree best with his own principles and views." These choices, though necessary, are not less perilous: "The desire to choose the facts that agree best with one's own views will make those facts seem more probable than they actually are, and the logic of the heart will only too often prevail over that of the mind."[42] The philosopher-historian will be a partisan. Is there no way, then, to mediate that partisanship? To survey fanaticism and superstition and still preserve the appearance of disinterest, what Gibbon needed was a place to stand, a point of aesthetic vantage, a safer and more extensive view.

In the *Essai*, he had had a premonition of where that place would be: namely, above the crowd and above the long flow of history. "L'esprit philosophique," he wrote, "consiste à pouvoir remonter aux idées simples; à saisir et à combiner les premiers principes" (The philosophic spirit consists in the power to go back to simple ideas, to seize and combine first principles; *EL*, 86). And here Gibbon happens, as if by chance, on the aesthetic principle that more than any other defines his narrative in the *Decline and Fall* and provides its sense of authority. There is nothing out of the ordinary about the verb "remonter": it means to go back (often to an origin); but "monter," at its most literal, means to go up, to climb, to ascend. And in these most literal meanings, "remonter" sets Gibbon's mind in motion; for now he rises to that point of vantage from which events of the *Decline and Fall* will often be seen:[43] "Le coup-d'oeil de son possesseur est juste mais en même tems étendu. Placé sur une hauteur, il embrasse une grande étendue de païs, dont il se forme une image nette et unique, pendant que des esprits aussi justes, mais plus bornés n'en découvrent qu'une partie" (The view of one who possesses 'l'esprit philosophique' is accurate but also extensive. Placed on a height, he takes in a vast stretch of countryside, forming an image both distinct and unique, while minds as accurate but more limited discern only a part; *EL*, 86). In the words of the *Essai*'s first (and unknown) English translator, not always trustworthy but in this case with a nice sense of phrase: "Situated on an eminence," the philosophic historian "takes in a wide extensive field."[44]

It is precisely this that will be, distinctively, Gibbon's kind of history—the temporal world spatially imagined, as from a high promontory. Never quite the philosopher-historian he wanted to be, Gibbon became a visionary historian. Never fully able to understand history as a linked chain of causal circumstance, he nonetheless understood it synoptically as a panorama, a long prospect that he recorded for others also to see. In Gibbon, history is spectacle, often ironic spectacle, in the theater of the world:

Quel spectacle pour un esprit vraiment philosophique de voir les opinions les plus absurdes reçues chez les nations les plus éclairées; des barbares parvenus à la connoissance des plus sublimes vérités; des conséquences vraies mais peu justes tirées des principes les plus erronés; des principes admirables qui approchoient toujours de la vérité sans jamais y conduire; le langage formé sur les idées, et les idées justifiées par le langage; les sources de la morale par-tout les mêmes; les opinions de la contentieuse métaphysique par-tout variées, d'ordinaire extravagantes; nettes seulement pendant qu'elles furent superficielles; subtiles, obscures, incertaines, toutes les fois qu'elles prétendirent à la profondeur. (*EL*, 89–90)

What a spectacle for the truly philosophic mind, to see the most absurd opinions received in the most enlightened nations; barbarians arrived at the knowledge of the most sublime truths; true consequences falsely drawn from the most erroneous principles; admirable principles that always border the truth without ever leading to it; language formed on ideas yet these ideas justified by language; the sources of morality everywhere the same; the contentious opinions of metaphysics everywhere varied, almost always extravagant; clear only when superficial; subtle, obscure, uncertain, whenever they pretend to be profound.

The history of the mind is made visible as spectacle, even the mad opinions of mankind hinting at visual reality, as if in a wild dance of personifications, a rich, fantastical confusion that the panoramic historian absorbs at a glance. Here in the *Essai* Gibbon prefigures the historian he will become. In the *Decline and Fall* he takes in a wide extensive field.

FOUR

'DECLINE AND FALL':
THE AUTHORITY OF VISION

Virginia Woolf said that the experience of reading the *Decline and Fall*, though for hours on end it seems like being "mounted on a celestial rocking horse," which "as it gently sways up and down, remains rooted to a single spot," seems at other times like riding Pegasus: "And then we turn to the book again, and to our amazement we find that the rocking-horse has left the ground; we are mounted on a winged steed; we are sweeping in wide circles through the air and below us Europe unfolds; the ages change and pass; a miracle has taken place." As we read, we seem "raised above the tumult and the chaos into a clear and rational air." And again, Gibbon's "gaze swept far horizons and surveyed the processions of the Roman Emperors."[1]

The image that Woolf lovingly decorates seems impossible to avoid in writing about Gibbon. It crops up everywhere, casually, and with a broad range of implication:

Gibbon seems to wish to avoid the imputation of telling a story: he writes as though the story were already well known and he were alluding to it or commenting on it. Everything in Gibbon is referred to the present; he gives us a telescope but still confronts us with a perspective panorama.

51

He always seeks a lofty perspective.

Throughout the work this Olympian view is so pronounced and explicit that, were it not redeemed by Gibbon's irony and humour, one might be tempted to class him with the wise man in Lucretius who takes such an odious pleasure in gazing from the shore at the sufferings of storm-tossed mariners, and looking down from the height of his intellectual serenity upon the straying footsteps of his fellow-men.

Gibbon views Roman civilization from the eminence of eighteenth-century civilization.

Looking down from the summit of a philosophic age, Gibbon may very well disdain the fleeting phantoms who lived and died in ignorant and ignoble turmoil; but we should never forget that the same Gibbon describes Tamburlaine's pyramids of human heads, the indiscriminate slaughter of hundreds of thousands of civilians, and the sacks of human ears collected by the Moguls.

It is from the ruins of the Capitol that we perceive, as from a great distance, a thousand years filled with dim shapes of men moving blindly, performing strangely, in an unreal shadowy world.[2]

Depending on the emphasis, the image may define a narrative strategy expressed in visual terms ("he gives us a telescope but still confronts us with a perspective panorama"; "he always seeks a lofty perspective"); it may define a set of cultural attitudes interpreted as hedonistic indifference or pride ("one might be tempted to class him with the wise man in Lucretius"; "from the eminence of eighteenth-century civilization"; "from the summit of a philosophic age"); or it may define a combination of narrative strategy, a Pascalian view of the human condition, and a calculated impressionism ("it is from the ruins of the Capitol that we perceive, as from a great distance, a thousand years filled with the shapes of men moving blindly, performing strangely, in an unreal shadowy world"). In fact, Gibbon's practice is as diverse as these perceptions of it.

The Olympian narrator changes character as the long story proceeds. At first the long view enables Gibbon to stand alone above the interchange of the world, to be free from constraints, to experience exhilaration—to be like a god, above the ebb and flow. His position on the heights provides him with safety as well as with a more extensive, because a panoramic, theme. In human terms this safety resembles that of the military commander who pitches camp on the highest ground. At the same time this high station, at least in the earlier parts of the history, sometimes produces the condescension that goes with separating oneself from others. Exhilaration, freedom, extensiveness are virtues of the long view, but they have their costs.

As the history plays itself out, however, the long view yields less exhilaration, less condescension, more somber reflection. Power, freedom, and godlikeness increasingly give way to a sense of transience and the humanness of human things, as solitude is offset by shared human destinies. What is more, the long view may coincide, curiously and powerfully, with microscopical precision. The critic who noticed Tamburlaine's pyramids of human heads and the Mongols' sacks of human ears caught a feature of the *Decline and Fall* that seems incompatible with long views but is not. This apparent paradox has an explanation in ordinary psychology, and perhaps also in the physiology of vision. It is Gibbon's intuition to recognize, even if the grandeur of long views turns out to be self-canceling, their curious power to capture or at least to coexist with the concreteness of nearby objects—that is, to provide a hold on reality, even the reality of severed human ears. The Mongols did not just collect ears at random; after the battle of Liegnitz in 1241, they "filled nine sacks with the right ears of the slain" (VII, 16). These are nine sacks of right ears and they are full, it seems, to overflowing. What is most powerful about Gibbon's prospect views is that he recognizes and in the long run amends their solitary, authoritarian subjectivity.

When, years later, he reconstructed the origin of the *Decline and Fall* on the Capitoline in 1764, Gibbon must have perceived the moment of its conception through the screen of the book he had written: the origin of the *Decline and Fall*, whether real or imaginary, must have fused in his memory with the scene that opens the last chapter of his last volume. In this scene he reenacts the opening of Poggio Bracciolini's *Historiae de varietate fortunae* (1447, though unpublished until the early eighteenth century), a meditation by the Renaissance humanist on the turns of Fortune's wheel that begins with an elegiac passage on the ruins of Rome as seen from the Capitol. As the historian's destination in the *Decline and Fall*, it should be in sight from the start:

In the last days of Pope Eugenius the Fourth, two of his servants, the learned Poggius and a friend, ascended the Capitoline Hill; reposed themselves among the ruins of columns and temples; and viewed from that commanding spot, the wide and various prospect of desolation. The place and the object gave ample scope for moralising on the vicissitudes of fortune, which spares neither man nor the proudest of his works, which buries empires and cities in a common grave; and it was agreed that in proportion to her former greatness the fall of Rome was the more awful and deplorable. (VII, 313)

A sense of finality brings the historian and reader, not always on intimate terms in the *Decline and Fall*, together in a last embrace. Having completed his work, Gibbon steps back and sees himself receding into history; and, sighting figures ascending the Capitoline, we recognize their ascent as like ours, too, having followed the story through its several thousands of pages. Like Gibbon and Poggio, we see ourselves brooding over history and trying to piece together its broken meanings. This is the point to which the *Decline and Fall* will lead.

Had Gibbon written the whole of the *Decline and Fall* in the manner of the opening chapters on the happy reign of the Antonines, from which the decline and fall of empire would be plotted, we might not have heard of the Olympian historian; it is only later that the magisterial outlook comes fully into play. That is partly a matter of Gibbon's finding his way stylistically, but it is not only that: the reign of the Antonines does not encourage the magisterial view. If theirs is an age unparalleled in human happiness, then there is little to be magisterial about. The prospective historian of the mountaintop defers to emperors who put the happiness of their subjects at the head of their agenda. The historian takes a place below the imperial throne.

That is to say, the age of the Antonines may have been Utopian, but like other Utopias, it was confining. In the narrative structure of the *Decline and Fall*, it creates an enclosed space from which the historian has to escape. When Gibbon applauds himself for having avoided the normal lockstep of chronological order—"It was not till after many designs and many tryals, that I preferred, as I still prefer, the method of groupping my picture by nations" (*M*, 179)— he is not thinking of these opening chapters, even though they proceed topically, not chronologically. Rather, he is thinking ahead to his habit of interspersing the advance of Christianity, the history of Persia in the fifth and sixth centuries, or the history of Mahomet within his larger frame. The scene of the opening chapters, on the contrary, precedes chronology; it is, as it were, timeless, as Utopias have in some sense to be.

Looking back, Gibbon had second thoughts about this timeless world he had created: "Should I not have given the *history* of that fortunate period which was interposed between two Iron ages?" He even doubts that decline began in the time of the Antonines: "Should I not have deduced the decline of the Empire from the civil Wars, that ensued after the fall of Nero or even from the tyranny which succeeded the reign of Augustus? Alas! I should: but of what avail is this tardy knowledge?" (*EE*, 338).[3] But certain of his doubts go deeper than historical accuracy and reflect an anti-Utopian view of Utopian fictions. It is an odd truth about the *Decline and Fall* that it comes alive only when Gibbon recapitulates the reigns of Trajan, Hadrian, Antoninus, and Marcus Aurelius; reflects once more on the happiness of the Antonine age, mourns its transience, and antic-ipates the dark future by looking back to the dark past of Tiberius, Caligula, Nero, and Domitian; and then in Chapter 4 bursts out into the movement of history and the outrages of Commodus. Finally, that is, Gibbon breaks free, into the world of time and out of the world of spatial restraints.[4]

Inseparable from the enabling fiction of the Antonine age as that period "in the history of the world during which the condition of the human race was most happy and prosperous" (I, 85–86) is the emperors' habit of fixing and maintaining geographical limits. And like the timeless perfection of Antonine society, this too constrains the historian. Hadrian drew back from the conquests of Trajan, be-coming a new and inferior god of limits by usurping the power of Terminus, who according to tradition had defied Jove—a defiance that the augurs had interpreted "as a sure presage that the boundaries of the Roman power would never recede" (I, 7). The prophecy had for a long time been self-fulfilling, but "though Terminus had re-sisted the majesty of Jupiter, he submitted to the authority of the emperor Hadrian" (I, 8). And Hadrian's successors followed his lead, persisting "in the design of maintaining the dignity of the em-pire, without attempting to enlarge its limits" (I, 9).

For territorial aggression, the Antonines substituted peace and harmony, but these are tame virtues, fatal to heroism. There is something fainthearted about the Roman spirit in these opening chapters. The Romans were not explorers because they were not seafarers: "The ambition of the Romans was confined to the land; nor was that warlike people ever actuated by the enterprising spirit which had prompted the navigators of Tyre, of Carthage, and even of Marseilles, to enlarge the bounds of the world, and to explore the most remote coasts of the ocean." The navigators of Tyre and Carthage and Marseilles were real heroes, enlarging the bounds of the world. The Romans, on the contrary, feared the ocean, to them "an object of terror rather than of curiosity" (I, 19). They tried to subdue it, enclosing the Mediterranean by empire and reducing it to a province, mare nostrum. And they hid their fear under the mask of piety: "The Romans tried to disguise, by the pretence of religious awe, their ignorance and terror" (I, 19n). Insofar as the happiness of the Antonines depended on circumspection and observing limits, Gibbon undercuts his own Utopia.

What is more, a policy of limits encourages the smug conviction that limits of empire correspond to limits of earth. Gibbon draws this moral at the end of his first chapter. Having sketched the geography of the empire, he reflects on the habit of identifying Rome with the world: "This long enumeration of provinces, whose broken fragments have formed so many powerful kingdoms, might almost induce us to forgive the vanity or ignorance of the ancients. Dazzled with the extensive sway, the irresistible strength, and the real or affected moderation of the emperors, they permitted themselves to despise, and sometimes to forget, the outlying countries which had been left in the enjoyment of a barbarous independence; and they gradually assumed the licence of confounding the Roman monarchy with the globe of the earth" (I, 29).

It is not so much the extent of empire that engenders false pride as it is the habit of overlooking lands beyond the borders. In this Gibbon seems to be arguing the case for defensive caution: not to know or care what lies beyond the limits of empire means, in the centuries that follow, not being prepared for invasion, and the *Decline and Fall* recounts the continuous erosion of boundaries. This erosion begins in the time of the Antonines, as the god Terminus yields to the Emperor Hadrian; forgetting the lands beyond the borders means renouncing the chance of movement outward. The age of the Antonines, with its long peace and uniform government, "in-

troduced a slow and secret poison into the vitals of the empire"
(I, 62). Hadrian's withdrawal reversed the course of history, and
now the empire would consume itself.

The geographically precise historian, insofar as he charts the limits of empire and seems to forget outlying lands, himself participates in these acts of enclosure. He may not confound the limits of
empire with those of earth, but he draws the map lines with a decisive hand:

> But the temper, as well as knowledge, of a modern historian require a more
> sober and accurate language. He may impress a juster image of the greatness
> of Rome by observing that the empire was above two thousand miles in
> breadth, from the wall of Antoninus and the northern limits of Dacia to
> Mount Atlas and the tropic of Cancer; that it extended in length more than
> three thousand miles, from the Western Ocean to the Euphrates; that it was
> situated in the finest part of the Temperate Zone, between the twenty-
> fourth and fifty-sixth degrees of northern latitude; and that it was supposed
> to contain above sixteen hundred thousand square miles, for the most part
> of fertile and well-cultivated land.   (I, 29–30)

The temper, knowledge, and language of the modern historian
weigh heavily not only on the fictions of the ancients but, for a
moment, on the aspiring imagination of the historian himself. Are
there not traces of ironic regret in the self-portraiture? The voice
seems a flattened echo of Fielding's in his celebrations of the mock-
heroically factual—as if Gibbon acknowledges, however faintly, the
limitations as well as the power of the factual. Mapping the limits
of Rome, the historian rolls the empire up into a sentence and pack-
ages its greatness in a numerical supposition: "it was supposed to
contain above sixteen hundred thousand square miles, for the most
part of fertile and well-cultivated land." This is the factual emphasis
of Gibbon's own apprenticeship, which he now has to transcend.

The climactic image of enclosure in the opening chapters comes
when, at their end, Gibbon looks back from the Antonines to "the
dark unrelenting Tiberius, the furious Caligula, the stupid Claudius, the profligate and cruel Nero, the beastly Vitellius, and the
timid inhuman Domitian" (I, 87). Why look back here? Narrative
logic does not require it, but the logic of feeling does. It is time to
break loose. In the days of Tiberius, Caligula, and the rest, limitation had had the aspect of fierce constraint, and the fiction that
Rome was the world contained a literal truth for enemies of the

emperor, who could nowhere escape. Discordant images fill the closing paragraph of Chapter 3: physical restraints, restrictions on the power to move, to speak, even to see. The "slave of Imperial despotism" is condemned "to drag his gilded chain in Rome and the senate, or to wear out a life of exile on the barren rock of Seriphus or the frozen banks of the Danube." He is mute, expecting his fate "in silent despair." He is hemmed in: "On every side he was encompassed with a vast extent of sea and land, which he could never hope to traverse without being discovered, seized, and restored to his irritated master." His sight fails: "Beyond the frontiers, his anxious view could discover nothing, except the ocean, inhospitable deserts, hostile tribes of barbarians, of fierce manners and unknown language, or dependent kings" (I, 90). To be beyond the frontier is to be beyond any normal experience of seeing and being seen: "his anxious view could discover nothing." To this extremity Gibbon brings the narrative as he winds up the long opening of his history. Now the historian will shake off constraint and discover how far he can see.

To move beyond, yet not to ignore limits, requires a point of vantage. In a preface to the final three volumes of the *Decline and Fall*, his labors at last over, Gibbon explains where this has been. The preface having run its valetudinary course, with nervous worrying over the question of whether the historian will ever again take up his pen, Gibbon remembers "two *verbal* remarks"—remarks, that is, about his uses of language—that he has not found any place for earlier (I, xlvii). One of these has to do with the orthography of foreign, especially of Oriental, proper names; the other, relevant here, with the prepositional "beyond": "As often as I use the definitions of *beyond* the Alps, the Rhine, the Danube, &c., I generally suppose myself at Rome, and afterwards at Constantinople: without observing whether this relative geography may agree with the local, but variable, situation of the reader or the historian" (I, xlvii–xlviii). Not only does this deceptively casual gloss make explicit what readers will recognize or intuit—the narrative centrality of Rome—but it also underlines Gibbon's visual construction of the narrative: "I generally suppose myself at Rome," and not only "at" Rome, but on a hill that enables him, in his mind's eye, to see events beyond the Alps, the Rhine, the Danube and even beyond the boundaries of empire; or to see, at least, clouds obscuring those events.[5] The place he stands on, in fact, is so high as to generate fantasies of flight, and every so often the historian takes off, Pegasus-like, the better to survey what lies far from the center. Virginia Woolf is right: "we are mounted on a winged steed; we are sweeping in wide circles through the air."

So pervasive are long views in the *Decline and Fall* that they defy enumeration; a complete tally would require noticing every occasion when the narrator speaks of events beyond the Alps, the Rhine, the Danube. Still, it is possible to capture the force of these strategies and their development. Early in the history, when the strategies are least secure, Gibbon simply points, sometimes in this direction or in that, indicating where to look and what to look for. In these instances the reader's visual training coincides with the narrator's own training in technique. As early as Chapter 2 comes a faint gesture: "If we turn our eyes towards the monarchies of Asia, we shall behold despotism in the centre and weakness in the extremities" (I, 47). But the gesture lacks the energy of visual life, as does this one: "Before we dismiss the consideration of the life and character of Diocletian, we may, for a moment, direct our view to the place of his retirement" (I, 419). Here Gibbon tells. At his frequent best, as the history goes on, he shows.

Sometimes the technique becomes cinematic, a bare description suddenly taking on visual flair as the camera's eye moves closer in: "Amid the barren deserts of Arabia, a few cultivated spots rise like islands out of the sandy ocean" (I, 329). Sometimes everything depends on the meaning of "prospect" as, in Johnson's first definition, a "view of something distant," a meaning enforced by the lurid obscurity of dark and bloody scenes or by atmospheric disturbances. Of the Saxons, Gibbon writes: "their imperfect annals afford only a dark and bloody prospect of intestine discord" (IV, 158). Of Italy under the Gothic King Theodoric: "I have descanted with pleasure on the fortunate condition of Italy; but our fancy must not hastily conceive that the golden age of the poets, a race of men without vice or misery, was realised under the Gothic conquest. The fair prospect was sometimes overcast with clouds" (IV, 208).

Prospects in the *Decline and Fall* are often overcast with clouds. Gibbon describes, for example, "the swarms of monks, who arose from the Nile, [and] overspread and darkened the face of the Christian world" (II, 339). Or he writes, of Britain's reversion to barbarism: "By the revolution of Britain, the limits of science, as well as of empire, were contracted. The dark cloud, which had been cleared by the Phoenician discoveries and finally dispelled by the arms of Cæsar, again settled on the shores of the Atlantic, and a Roman province was again lost among the fabulous islands of the Ocean" (IV, 168). Lost, that is, to Rome, and therefore to sight as well. When Coleridge complained that reading the *Decline and Fall* is like "looking through a luminous haze or fog" and that its landscape is, "as it were, exhibited by candlelight," he calls attention, though unawares, to a crucial feature of its style, for what Coleridge regards as imprecision is calculation—the result of events and characters being seen obscurely at a distance. "All," Coleridge said accurately, "is scenical," though the scene often fades behind the clouds of time.[6]

Sometimes the visual effect depends not so much on evoking a specific scene as on the vocabulary of perception and of seeing that infiltrates nooks and crannies of the history. Gibbon separates Rome's foreign wars in the fourth century into five "theatres," each open to "view": "Perhaps the method of annals would more forcibly express the urgent and divided cares of the two emperors; but the attention of the reader, likewise, would be distracted by a tedious and desultory narrative. A separate view of the five great theatres of war: I. Germany; II. Britain; III. Africa; IV. The East; and, V. The Danube; will impress a more distinct image of the military state of the empire under the reigns of Valentinian and Valens" (III, 33).

The method of annals, the chronological rehearsal of events year by year, would only express (i.e., represent or describe) the experience of the brother-emperors, Valentinian and Valens, who had divided the empire between them. Moreover, that sort of chronicle would distract and divide the attention of the reader. A view of the several theatres of war, says Gibbon, will impress a more distinct image. He creates the illusion that we are about to watch these wars. By soliciting attention, he solicits the reader to look hard. "*Attention*," Isaac Watts had said (as cited by Johnson in the *Dictionary*), "is a very necessary thing; truth doth not always strike the soul at first sight." Johnson had also cited Locke: "By attention the ideas, that offer themselves, are taken notice of, and, as it were, registered in the memory." Moreover, the impressing of images on the mind, in Locke's epistemology, is the basic process of perception; attention, the agent of that process. The difference between expressing the urgent and divided cares of the emperors and impressing a distinct image of their empire is that between verbal representation, on the one hand, and a picture that the mind can seize in its clarity, on the other. Gibbon induces his readers to believe that they see.

At the same time, long views serve a more literal purpose: Gibbon uses them regularly to observe peoples at the edges of empire or beyond. Germans, Scandinavians, Scots, all are far from the center and, assuming the spatial metaphor, can only be seen at a distance. And it is in dealing with these remote peoples that Gibbon exposes limitations uncomfortably associated with his high station. The long view sometimes condescends to the tribes of the north, and awareness of this condescension causes the edge in some descriptions of Gibbon as the Olympian historian. Yet "uncivilized" peoples were becoming objects of interest, and Gibbon shared in some measure these changing values. This mixture of condescension and nascent interest typically yields a spectator's detached pleasure. The historian of the early volumes of the *Decline and Fall* participates, not fully aware, in satisfactions compounded both of Rome's imperial grandeur and of the intellectual curiosity of the Enlightenment. Poggio's meditation on the vanity of human endeavors is still to come.

The opening of Chapter 9, called "The State of Germany till the Invasion of the Barbarians, in the Time of the Emperor Decius" (I, 230), requires a cinematic transition from the close of Chapter 8, with its view of Persian armies that "threatened, as an impending cloud, the eastern provinces of the declining empire of Rome" (I, 229). Now Gibbon turns his gaze from east to north, from Persia to Germany: "But the warlike Germans, who first resisted, then invaded, and at length overturned, the Western monarchy of Rome, will occupy a much more important place in this history, and possess a stronger, and, if we may use the expression, a more domestic, claim to our attention and regard." "Occupy a place" signifies presence, and the near synonymity of "attention" and "regard" (Johnson defines "regard" as, first, "attention as to a matter of importance") underscores the narrator's visual concentration. Abstractions take on the aura of personification: "in the rude institutions of those barbarians we may still distinguish the original principles of our present laws and manners" (I, 230).

To distinguish is to see clearly, and Gibbon acknowledges as his master a painterly Tacitus: "the Germans were surveyed by the discerning eye, and delineated by the masterly pencil, of Tacitus" (I, 230). The sense of discrepancy between a survey and a delineation, between large and small views, will be considered later in this chapter; what counts for now is the gathering visual force of the narrative and its sweeping view of German geography. On the west is the Rhine; on the south, the Danube and "a ridge of hills" called the Carpathian Mountains. To the east, the precision of natural boundaries fades into psychological phantasmagoria: "The eastern frontier was faintly marked by the mutual fears of the Germans and the Sarmatians, and was often confounded by the mixture of warring and confederating tribes of the two nations." And to the north, vision reaches its limit: "In the remote darkness of the north the ancients imperfectly descried a frozen ocean that lay beyond the Baltic Sea and beyond the peninsula, or islands, of Scandinavia" (I, 231). Remoteness and darkness make seeing difficult, but the effort to see beyond a sea and then again beyond what may be a peninsula or islands invests this study in black and white ("a frozen ocean") with the power of Romantic efforts to reach visually beyond the horizon.

Yet distance in this case highlights the difference between the historian and the German tribes. The Germans were illiterate, Yahoo-like: "the use of letters is the principal circumstance that distinguishes a civilized people from a herd of savages, incapable of knowledge or reflection" (I, 235). Without letters, "the human memory soon dissipates or corrupts the ideas intrusted to her charge; and the nobler faculties of the mind, no longer supplied with models or with materials, gradually forget their powers: the judgment becomes feeble and lethargic, the imagination languid or irregular." The man of learning, the historian on his promontory, looks down on lesser breeds: "Fully to apprehend this important truth, let us attempt, in an improved society, to calculate the immense distance between the man of learning and the *illiterate* peasant" (I, 235–36).

Gibbon's sinuous style emphasizes the sense of distance as he winds his way—"fully to apprehend this . . . truth"—toward one of his least engaging utterances: "let us attempt, in an improved society, to calculate the immense distance. . . ." A less self-conscious writer might have said, "consider the immense distance between the man of learning and the peasant." Gibbon says, let us attempt to calculate the distance from our position in an improved society, and that seems impossible to do. Our superiority is beyond calculating, for how can we measure the distance between a stable point and a point in motion? This is the situation here: the man of learning, "by reading and reflection, multiplies his own experience, and lives in distant ages and remote countries"; the illiterate peasant, "rooted to a single spot, and confined to a few years of existence, surpasses but very little his fellow-labourer the ox in the exercise of his mental faculties" (I, 236). The peasant is rooted, more like a tree than an ox, to the earth. The man of learning, as though borne through the air, covers great tracts of time and space, living in ages that are distant and countries that are remote—or, Gibbon could as well have said, in countries that are distant and ages that are remote. As a man of learning, the historian is his own exemplar, like a visiting god traveling among peasants in the remoteness of the German past.

If this long view of an illiterate peasantry shows Gibbon at his worst, a long view of Caledonia—Scotland—in Chapter 6 shows him savoring the heroic possibilities of distant and savage lands in a mood of detached exhilaration. It also shows the compensatory feelings that underlie his fondness for the heights, for he sees the Emperor Septimius Severus, who in his old age and infirmity undertook an expedition to Britain, as yet another alter ego. Like historians, emperors may have to make steep and dangerous ascents. Unlike historians, they may find little to satisfy them at the top: "The ascent to greatness, however steep and dangerous, may entertain an active spirit with the consciousness and exercise of its own powers: but the possession of a throne could never yet afford a lasting satisfaction to an ambitious mind. This melancholy truth was felt and acknowledged by Severus" (I, 138). This melancholy, Johnsonian truth may seem to threaten even the historian on his high ground, but the continuous activity of seeing, unlike passive possession of the throne, sets him apart for the time being.

Activity, especially activity at the borders, also saves emperors from ennui. The aging Severus, "distracted with the care not of acquiring, but of preserving, an empire," finds himself "satiated with power": "all his prospects of life were closed" (I, 138). Severus's situation resembles that of the Antonines: the limits of empire having been set, his prospects of life, his views of the future, are blocked. Moreover, his two sons, "the destined heirs of the empire" (I, 139), are at each other's throats. "In these circumstances the intelligence of a war in Britain, and of an invasion of the province by the barbarians of the North, was received with pleasure by Severus" (I, 140). The British war gives Severus a way to divert his quarrelsome heirs. More than that, it lets him enact in reality the visionary experience of the man of learning in a far country.

"Though the vigilance of his lieutenants might have been sufficient to repel the distant enemy" (I, 140), Severus determines to meet the Caledonian enemy himself: "Notwithstanding his advanced age (for he was above threescore), and his gout, which obliged him to be carried in a litter, he transported himself in person into that remote island, attended by his two sons, his whole court, and a formidable army" (I, 140–41). As usual, the perspective is Roman, the enemy distant, the island of Britain remote. But Severus, no historian but an aging, gouty emperor, can only cover the space between Rome and Britain in the most laborious way: by being carried on a litter. At the same time, Gibbon endows him with energy that compensates for infirmity. Though on a litter, Severus has "transported himself in person into that remote island." In the medium of Gibbon's prose, Severus finds a mobility that enables him, gout and all, almost to rival the historian. In 1772, soon after he set seriously to work on the history, Gibbon himself had suffered a first attack of the gout that troubled him intermittently for the rest of his life.[7] Severus on his litter—passing the walls of Hadrian and Antoninus, entering the enemy's country, penetrating the northern extremity of the island, and finally defeating the Caledonians with a powerful and obstinate attack—shares the historian's aspirations, though he is earthbound, timebound, and infirm; he resembles Gibbon in the weakness of the flesh, while emulating the visionary narrator who traverses space and time.

As if prompted by Severus's example, Gibbon the narrator now takes over, stopping the forward movement of the history to look back on the Caledonian past reflectively, even with longing: "This

Caledonian war, neither marked by decisive events nor attended with any important consequences, would ill deserve our attention; but it is supposed, not without a considerable degree of probability, that the invasion of Severus is connected with the most shining period of the British history or fable" (I, 141). Visual cues are sharp. Not only does the narrator invoke our attention, with its implicit fixing of a point of view, but when he refers to the most shining period of British history or legend—the period of the Ossianic tales—he hints at a chiaroscuro scene of light and shadow. That scene he goes on to draw.

Severus's Caledonian antagonist is supposed to have been the great Fingal, "whose fame, with that of his heroes and bards, has been revived in our language by a recent publication" (I, 141). The critical furor that surrounded the publication of Macpherson's Ossianic poems in the early 1760's makes Gibbon cautious.[8] But the psychology of long views also means he can afford the luxury of supposing doubtful legends to be true and of supposing, therefore, that untutored barbarism is more to be valued than Roman civilization. The long view in this case encourages the romanticizing habit, even if that habit is admitted for what it is. At such a distance clouds may intervene, and the mists that prevent certain knowledge permit hopeful dreams:

Something of a doubtful mist still hangs over these Highland traditions; nor can it be entirely dispelled by the most ingenious researches of modern criticism: but if we could, with safety, indulge the pleasing supposition that Fingal lived, and that Ossian sung, the striking contrast of the situation and manners of the contending nations might amuse a philosophic mind. The parallel would be little to the advantage of the more civilized people, if we compared the unrelenting revenge of Severus with the generous clemency of Fingal; the timid and brutal cruelty of Caracalla, with the bravery, the tenderness, the elegant genius of Ossian; the mercenary chiefs who, from motives of fear or interest, served under the Imperial standard, with the freeborn warriors who started to arms at the voice of the King of Morven; if, in a word, we contemplated the untutored Caledonians, glowing with the warm virtues of nature, and the degenerate Romans, polluted with the mean vices of wealth and slavery. (I, 141–42)

The light is indirect, rendered by adjectives that stand out like campfires in the distance. Not only is the age of Fingal a "shining" period, but the contrast between Caledonians and Romans is "striking": the Caledonians are seen "glowing with the warm virtues of nature." The light, glimpsed through Highland mists, is one to see heroes and legends by.[9]

Through this glancing celebration of the Ossianic world runs a spirit of self-conscious play. Gibbon knows that the ingenious researches of modern criticism cannot entirely dispel the Caledonian mist. Everything happens within the embrace of the conditional: "if we could, with safety, indulge the pleasing supposition that Fingal lived, and that Ossian sung." "Safety" recalls Gibbon's search for a safer subject than Raleigh and hints again at something more than the safety of factual accuracy. On the heights, the historian removes himself from dangers below. Yet heights have their dangers, too, both real and imagined, and here Gibbon flirts with them. What amuses the philosophic mind is the safe approximation of risk and a controlled, even a contrived, euphoria. The pleasure of Gibbon's narrator implies a psychology of the heights, as detachment contemplates and defeats danger.

In its early volumes, the *Decline and Fall* engages more than once in this vicarious high-flying play with legend and with danger. How did the Goths come from Scandinavia to the mainland? According to a legendary tale, Odin is supposed to have "conducted his tribe from the frontiers of the Asiatic Sarmatia into Sweden, with the great design of forming, in that inaccessible retreat of freedom, a religion and a people which, in some remote age, might be subservient to his immortal revenge; when his invincible Goths, armed with martial fanaticism, should issue in numerous swarms from the neighbourhood of the Polar circle, to chastise the oppressors of mankind" (I, 261). But a cautionary footnote, such as Gibbon often uses to bring speculation down to earth, explains that "this wonderful expedition of Odin," though it might have made the "noble groundwork" of an epic, "cannot safely be received as authentic history" (I, 261n). Then Gibbon returns to the solid ground of the factual. Though the Goths left no account of how they crossed the Baltic (none should be expected "from such unlettered barbarians"), common sense will supply what documentary evidence does not: "To cross the Baltic was an easy and natural attempt. The inhabitants of Sweden were masters of a sufficient number of large vessels with oars, and the distance is little more than one hundred miles from Carlscroon to the nearest ports of Pomerania and Prussia.

Here, at length, we land on firm and historic ground. At least as early as the Christian æra, and as late as the age of the Antonines, the Goths were established towards the mouth of the Vistula" (I, 261).

The airy speculations about Odin have been a flight of mind beyond the borders of empire. The historian, with his readers, has been carried away to the frontiers of Asiatic Sarmatia, thence to Sweden, "that inaccessible retreat of freedom" ("inaccessible" except to Odin and ourselves) from which in some remote age (an age remote, that is, from Odin's own, and implying the utter remoteness of Odin's age from ours) the Goths will swarm into the civilized world. After all this, the return to earth yields a sense of relief and ironic anticlimax: "Here, at length, we land on firm and historic ground." The Goths' migration across the Baltic was not an extraordinary feat: a mere hundred miles, and it was done. Out of such ascents into legend and such ambiguously fortunate falls into reality comes amusement for the philosophic mind.

It is this philosophic diversion that yields, as the history plays itself out, to a more somber view. Increasingly, the view from the heights involves a meditation on the transience of things and on limitations of the historical mind. Increasingly, the view from the heights turns back on itself, as the empire shrinks into a fragment, a ruin.

At the same time, dreams of power may burn momentarily brighter as the shadows of experience grow longer. In Chapter 48, which introduces the two final volumes with a survey of some sixty Byzantine emperors, a last, long synoptic view pushes to its limit the dream of the historian as a god, a superior being in whose sight many ages are like a moment gone. Yet, in this case, pushing the dream to its limit induces an opposite and equal reaction. Finally, Gibbon offers an antidote to the dream of transcendence, which turns out to have been self-canceling.

The table of contents to Chapter 48 is a curiosity, symptomatic of a grand design yet hinting at self-parody: in its unadorned list of the emperors, one after another for six centuries, chronology becomes a bauble, a plaything. Typologically, the contents anticipate the survey of the course of empire that closes the chapter. In this survey, numerical analysis ("if we compute the number and duration of the reigns, it will be found that a period of six hundred years is filled by sixty emperors," a far more rapid turnover than Newton had calculated as normal) yields to meditation, as Gibbon reflects on the insecure summits of power: "Many were the paths that led to the summit of royalty; the fabric of rebellion was overthrown by the stroke of conspiracy or undermined by the silent arts of intrigue; the favourites of the soldiers, of the people, of the senate or clergy, of the women and eunuchs, were alternately clothed with the purple; the means of their elevation were base, and their end was often contemptible or tragic" (V, 258). The downfall of monarchs clears the way for the ascendancy of historians:

A being of the nature of man, endowed with the same faculties, but with a longer measure of existence, would cast down a smile of pity and contempt on the crimes and follies of human ambition, so eager, in a narrow span, to grasp at a precarious and short-lived enjoyment. It is thus that the experience of history exalts and enlarges the horizon of our intellectual view. In a composition of some days, in a perusal of some hours, six hundred years have rolled away, and the duration of a life or reign is contracted to a fleeting moment; the grave is ever beside the throne; the success of a criminal is almost instantly followed by the loss of his prize; and our immortal reason survives and disdains the sixty phantoms of kings, who have passed before our eyes and faintly dwell in our remembrance.   (V, 258–59)

Here the observer on an eminence, taking in "a wide extensive field," acquires more than human powers. The experience of history, which is both that of the race and that of the historian, "exalts and enlarges the horizon of our intellectual view." To exalt a horizon is an odd conceit, beyond imagining; to enlarge a horizon is to give the observer peripheral vision. The narrator projects power onto the landscape, and a changed horizon provides "a being of the nature of man" with divine insight, as space expands and time contracts to a moment.

Yet is not "a being of the nature of man, endowed with the same faculties, but with a longer measure of existence" just a man, even if he lives as long as Methuselah? The normal measure of our lives, for Gibbon, defines how we are human (as Swift had implied, in different fashion, when he created the Struldbruggs), and a being with a longer measure of existence transcends normal categories. This superior being casts down a "smile of pity and contempt" on human ambition; and it is "thus" that history exalts and enlarges our horizons.

To what does "thus" refer? On the one hand, it looks ahead to the next sentence: the historian has written this chapter, covering six centuries, in "some days"; we will have read it in "some hours"; historian and readers alike have gained a longer measure of existence.[10] On the other hand, since the longer measure of existence precedes, in context, the passing of the centuries, we seem to deduce the contraction of lives and reigns from a position of prior eminence, not just from the experience of history. And when we finally reach "our immortal reason," this timeless abstraction confirms intimations that have gone before: on the other side of transience, a fleeting moment, lies a new permanence. Moreover, it is "our" immortal reason that survives. The first-person possessive, joining with the redundant but not less reassuring proposition that whatever is immortal survives, generates that brief but heady sense of command over circumstance that every reader of the *Decline and Fall* will sometimes feel.

At the same time, the passage questions its own dream. Historians and readers may not commit imperial crimes, but they are no less subject than emperors to the "follies of human ambition, so eager, in a narrow span, to grasp at a precarious and short-lived enjoyment." What is more, this ironic resonance coincides with an awareness that the dwindling of the Roman Empire means a dwindling of the horizons of the historian. The beginning of Chapter 48 expresses this self-contradictory truth. With eight hundred years still to go, Gibbon explains that he cannot afford so comprehensive a narrative as in the earlier volumes: "Should I persevere in the same course, should I observe the same measure, a prolix and slender thread would be spun through many a volume, nor would the patient reader find an adequate reward of instruction or amusement." But in fact Gibbon can no longer see the large historical picture. If he were to recount the annals of the eastern empire, "the natural connexion of causes and events would be broken by frequent and hasty transitions, and a minute accumulation of circumstances must destroy the light and effect of those general pictures which compose the use and ornament of a remote history" (V, 180). Gibbon despairs of casting any light on the history of the eastern empire, lying remotely beyond his gaze.

The erosion of empire is bringing the historian down, too: "At every step, as we sink deeper in the decline and fall of the Eastern empire, the annals of each succeeding reign would impose a more ungrateful and melancholy task." The historian's metahistorical assumption of visionary power, at the end of the chapter, compensates for a loss of historical vision. The theater is going dark: "From the time of Heraclius, the Byzantine theatre is contracted and darkened." The horizon is receding: "the line of empire, which had been defined by the laws of Justinian and the arms of Belisarius, recedes on all sides from our view." Centrality is lost: "the Roman name, the proper subject of our inquiries, is reduced to a narrow corner of Europe, to the lonely suburbs of Constantinople." The picture fades like a river that loses itself in sand: "the fate of the Greek empire has been compared to that of the Rhine, which loses itself in the sands before its waters can mingle with the ocean" (V, 180). Distances of time and place, which the historian of the western empire controlled, now prevent vision: "The scale of dominion is diminished to our view by the distance of time and place" (V, 180–81).

In this clutter of metaphors lies an extreme sense of dislocation: the speaker is neither at Rome nor at Constantinople, unless perhaps he is shut up, like the empire, in a lonely suburb. When the historian says that "the scale of dominion is diminished to our view," we literally do not know where we stand. This sense of dislocation is truer to the usual situation of the last volumes of the *Decline and Fall* than is Gibbon's retrospective claim that he places himself at Constantinople as he had at Rome. A few pages into Chapter 48, reluctant to surrender his Roman perspective, he puts the case differently: "the historian's eye shall be always fixed on the city of Constantinople" (V, 182). Gibbon had never been to Constantinople. It provided him no familiar place of geographical advantage and no centrality. The last volumes of the *Decline and Fall* act out the knowledge that "of human life the most glorious or humble prospects are alike and soon bounded by the sepulchre" (VI, 217).

Now a sense of loss replaces the detached amusement with which the historian of the western empire had cast his eye on illiterate peasants, as he awakens to the knowledge that whatever distance lies between philosophers and peasants, whatever the difference between their great and humble prospects, that distance and difference are nothing compared to those between a finite and an infinite mind. That is very nearly what Gibbon says, while writing about the Koran. He introduces the subject with philosophers and peasants, then dissolves the distinction: "The communication of ideas requires a similitude of thought and language; the discourse of a philosopher would vibrate, without effect, on the ear of a peasant; yet how minute is the distance of *their* understandings, if it be compared with the contact of an infinite and a finite mind, with the word of God expressed by the tongue or the pen of a mortal?" (V, 364–65). This would not be out of place in a discourse on the divine attributes. If the sacred text of Islam in fact turns out to be an "endless incoherent rhapsody" (V, 366), that is in part because the distance between philosopher and peasant—indeed, between historian and prophet— bears no analogy to the distance between finite and infinite. Infinite and finite minds can have no points of contact, God's word being humanly inexpressible. Yet this inexpressibility enforces the bond between philosopher and peasant.

By the time the reader reaches the last chapter, then, the ascent of the Capitoline seems a fulfillment, a coming to terms with loss. All the distant views, remote prospects, meditations from afar are gathered together in a last contemplation of ruin. The spectator "who casts a mournful view over the ruins of ancient Rome" (IV, 21); the "wandering stranger" who contemplates "with horror the vacancy and solitude of the city" and is tempted to ask, *ubi sunt*, "where is the senate, and where are the people?" (V, 33); peasants and philosophers; historians and readers—all join in a shared solitude. Poggio's meditation makes a self-reflexive commentary, embodying the power but also the limitation of long views, their ultimate melancholy, and their paradoxical subjectivity: "In the last days of Pope Eugenius the Fourth, two of his servants, the learned Poggius and a friend, ascended the Capitoline Hill; reposed themselves among the ruins of columns and temples; and viewed from that commanding spot, the wide and various prospect of desolation" (VII, 313). The scene is wonderfully staged. These last days might be the last days of apocalypse. The spectators "repose" (or "re-pose") themselves carefully, stationary figures in the setting of ruined columns and temples. They are in a commanding spot. But the prospect they command is unpeopled, a scene of desolation. Now Gibbon adapts Poggio's text, enhancing it by allusion, merging its experience with that of others, yet emphasizing the pervasiveness of vacancy and, through a syntax that relies heavily on the passive, evoking unknowable forces that affect the shape of history:

The hill of the Capitol, on which we sit, was formerly the head of the Roman empire, the citadel of the earth, the terror of kings; illustrated by the footsteps of so many triumphs, enriched with the spoils and tributes of so many nations. This spectacle of the world, how is it fallen! how changed! how defaced! The path of victory is obliterated by vines, and the benches of the senators are concealed by a dunghill. Cast your eyes on the Palatine hill, and seek, among the shapeless and enormous fragments, the marble theatre, the obelisks, the colossal statues, the porticoes of Nero's palace: survey the other hills of the city, the vacant space is interrupted only by ruins and gardens. The forum of the Roman people, where they assembled to enact their laws and elect their magistrates, is now inclosed for the cultivation of pot-herbs or thrown open for the reception of swine and buffaloes. The public and private edifices, that were founded for eternity, lie prostrate, naked, and broken, like the limbs of a mighty giant; and the ruin is the more visible, from the stupendous relics that have survived the injuries of time and fortune. (VII, 314)

What had been simple allusion, in Poggio, ripples outward. "This spectacle of the world, how is it fallen! how changed! how defaced!" amplifies a recollection of Virgil. Poggio had put the words into the mouth of his companion Antonio Lusco:

O quantum, inquit, Poggi, haec capitolia ab illis distant, quae noster Maro cecinit,
> *Aurea nunc, olim silvestribus horrida dumis.*[11]

Oh, Poggio, he said, how different are these heights from those our Virgil sung,
> *Now golden, once wild with woods and thorn.*

Gibbon, in turn, remembers Aeneas's dream of Hector on the eve of the fall of Troy, so changed from the Hector he had once known: "Quantum mutatus ab illo / Hectore." He also remembers Satan's words to Beelzebub, fallen into hell: "But O how fall'n! how chang'd / From him, who in the happy Realms of Light . . .". And Milton had remembered Isaiah: "How art thou fallen from heaven, O Lucifer, son of the morning!"[12] These allusions evoke the shared mystery of loss.

The observers on the Capitoline, in Gibbon's version, command only emptiness. Imperatives—"cast your eyes"; "seek"; "survey" —find no objects: "survey the other hills of the city, the vacant space is interrupted only by ruins and gardens." In Poggio, empty spaces ("omnia vacua") are full ("oppleta") of ruins and vines.[13] In Gibbon, vacancy is interrupted, not filled; his gardens, recalling eighteenth-century pictorial images of life being carried on in the shadows of ruin, imply that ordinary existence only interrupts mystery. What are the agencies of ruin? Though the answer turns out to be the

injuries of time and fortune, the historian resists giving these personifications an active role. They appear only at the end, their work
done. Forces of ruin hide behind the veil of Gibbon's style. The
spectacle of the world is fallen, changed, defaced; the path of victory, obliterated; the benches of senators, concealed; vacant space,
interrupted; the forum, like some eighteenth-century common
meadow, enclosed; ancient edifices lie prostrate, as though leveled
by an unknown hand. Ghostly forces that we cannot see and that
the injuries of time and fortune inadequately represent are in control. The panorama of the *Decline and Fall* represents a vacancy,
interrupted by the history of empire. "At the heart of the world
order," as Lionel Gossman has said, Gibbon discovered "a void."[14]

At the same time, the world of the *Decline and Fall* wards off
nonexistence, is always attentive to the tangible. Gibbon knew that
melancholy was a fashionable malaise, requiring countermeasures,
and he found one in the odd yet conventional association between
remote views and close-ups. If Tacitus both surveyed the Germans
with a discerning eye and at the same time delineated their society
with a masterly pencil (I, 230), he demonstrated the truth that remote and near are convergent terms: the survey is a view from afar,
the pencil drawing a view from close up, yet each implies the other.
"In the contemplation of a minute or remote object," Gibbon says
in another context, "I am not ashamed to borrow the aid of the
strongest glasses" (V, 103n). What is seen at a great distance is seen
as small; remote views naturally inspire close-ups; and this conjunction of powers Gibbon seems to have sensed in himself at an early
stage. In his journal for 8 May 1762, he gauged his own talents, on
the occasion of his twenty-fifth birthday: "the shining qualities of
my understanding are extensiveness and penetration."[15] Extensiveness and penetration are complementary.

The association of "extensiveness" and "penetration" seems to
have been a commonplace as early as Lucian, whose fanciful moon
voyage, *Icaromenippus*, uses it as the occasion of self-conscious satirical play. Borne on the right wing of an eagle and the left wing of a
vulture, Lucian's Menippus lands on the Moon and looks down
on the Earth "like Homer's Zeus, now observing the land of the
horse-loving Thracians, now the land of the Mysians," and finds
that he can see traders, soldiers, farmers, litigants, women, animals—everything. A friend thinks this "beyond belief and self-

contradictory." Since the Earth is so far away, "how is it, then, that you have suddenly turned into a Lynceus and can make out everything on earth—the men, the animals and very nearly the nests of the mosquitoes?" The answer is that Empedocles has told Menippus to flap his eagle's wing but hold his vulture's wing still and, doing so, Menippus becomes the eagle-eyed voyeur: "I saw Ptolemy lying with his sister, Lysimachus' son conspiring against his father, Seleucus' son Antiochus flirting surreptitiously with his stepmother, Alexander of Thessaly getting killed by his wife, Antigonus committing adultery with the wife of his son, and the son of Attalus pouring out the poison for him. In another quarter I saw Arsaces killing the woman, the eunuch Arbaces drawing his sword on Arsaces, and Spatinus the Mede in the hands of the guards, being dragged out of the dining-room by the leg after having had his head broken with a golden cup."[16] The detail of the golden cup, in its shiny solidity, proves Menippus really can see all: not only the secret history of kings and emperors, who need only to be named in order to be known, but the whole spectacle of common life. With a few turns of his head he sees Egyptians working the land, Phoenicians on their trading voyages, Spartans whipping themselves. The spectator on the heights has double vision.

Gibbon's narrative alternates long views and close-ups with almost cinematic intent; transitions are often pointedly sharp. No sooner has he celebrated the godlike powers that exalt and enlarge the horizon of our intellectual view than, stooping to wonder about the motives of the Byzantine emperors, exposed to "domestic perils" and without "any lively promise of foreign conquest" (V, 259), he recalls the awful death of the Emperor Andronicus. He had recounted this episode in savage detail before seeking refuge in the situation of that imaginary "being of the nature of man, endowed with the same faculties, but with a longer measure of existence" who smiles down on human ambition. The hideous experience of Andronicus, seen close up, brackets history's long view:

Instead of the decencies of a legal execution, the new monarch abandoned the criminal to the numerous sufferers whom he had deprived of a father, an husband, or a friend. His teeth and hair, an eye and a hand, were torn from him as a poor compensation for their loss; and a short respite was allowed that he might feel the bitterness of death. Astride on a camel, without any danger of a rescue, he was carried through the city, and the basest of the populace rejoiced to trample on the fallen majesty of their prince. After a thousand blows and outrages, Andronicus was hung by the feet between two pillars that supported the statues of a wolf and sow; and every hand that could reach the public enemy inflicted on his body some mark of ingenious or brutal cruelty, till two friendly or furious Italians, plunging their swords into his body, released him from all human punishment. In this long and painful agony, "Lord, have mercy upon me!" and "Why will you bruise a broken reed?" were the only words that escaped from his mouth.   (V, 257)

In *Icaromenippus*, a golden cup gives reality to experience seen from afar. Here it is the body of Andronicus, his teeth and hair and eye and hand torn from him, as if from his own reluctant grasp; the camel that carries him through the streets; the statues of wolf and sow from which he hangs by the feet; and the two swords plunged into his body. Andronicus's dismemberment, like piles of human heads and sacks of human ears, fixes the attention on the frailness but also on the reality of body and world. In his agony, Andronicus speaks like Christ in his last words, eliciting a human pity different from that of the detached observer: "Our hatred for the tyrant is lost in pity for the man" (V, 257). At the same time, the narrative implicates both narrator and readers by a memorable shift of focus. If the narrator solicits pity for Andronicus, he also signals our complicity: "Astride on a camel, without any danger of a rescue, he was carried through the city." We expect to read "without any hope of a rescue," but instead narrator and readers suddenly find themselves on the side of the monarch who abandons Andronicus, even perhaps among the ferocious mob. When he told Sheffield, early in the writing of the *Decline and Fall*, that he had been interrupted while "I was destroying an army of barbarians" (*L*, II, 32), Gibbon had jokingly played the part of a Roman hero. At the death of Andronicus, he knows it is the narrator who kills and tortures the emperor. Knowing this, Gibbon turns the tables on himself.

He does so again in a final chapter that brings him down at last from the Capitoline, into the streets of Rome, and to the courtyard of St. Peter's, in a calculated reversal of roles. Like an eighteenth-century Baedecker, Gibbon catalogues monuments that still survived in Poggio's day and then lists reasons for the destruction of so many Roman monuments. These final views of the empire are close-ups marked by his old passion for numerical precision. Poggio may have miscounted the number of public baths: "Of the number, which he rashly defines, of seven *thermæ*, or public baths, none were sufficiently entire to represent the use and distribution of the several parts" (VII, 314). The walls of Rome, ten miles in circumference, "included three hundred and seventy-nine turrets, and opened into the country by thirteen gates" (VII, 316). This continues until, in the last paragraph but one, Gibbon ponders the restoration of Rome in more recent days ("of the eleven aqueducts of the Cæsars and Consuls, three were restored") and places himself within the frame of his own customary panorama: "and the spectator, impatient to ascend the steps of St. Peter's, is detained by a column of Egyptian granite, which rises between two lofty and perpetual fountains to the height of one hundred and twenty feet" (VII, 337). Like a pilgrim-tourist, guidebook in hand, the spectator hesitates before ascending the steps of St. Peter's, caught irresolutely between Christendom and antiquity.

When he had first come to Rome in 1764, as Michel Baridon remarks, Gibbon seems not to have been drawn to St. Peter's: "La basilique Saint Pierre ne semble guère l'avoir attiré."[17] But he could not have helped remembering that in the life he had once intended to lead—that of a devout convert—St. Peter's would have been his ultimate goal. Now, if there be any doubt that spectator and historian are kin, the lines that follow dispel it: "The map, the description, the monuments of ancient Rome have been elucidated by the diligence of the antiquarian and the student; and the footsteps of heroes, the relics, not of superstition, but of empire, are devoutly visited by a new race of pilgrims from the remote, and once savage, countries of the North" (VII, 337–38). The movement of mind in the early volumes has been outward from the Roman center to the distant north. Now mind has turned inward. The historian as mock-devout pilgrim whose religion is antiquity (but not without memories of Christian belief) merges with the historian as seer. He both sees and is seen.

Gibbon has learned what he could not have fully understood when he wrote the *Essai*—namely, that even the most extensive human views are bounded. He also recognizes a last paradox of the long view. Not only does it open on still more remote horizons, not only do its distancings arise from or inspire intimate closeness, but its objectivity is born in the subjective. The very physiology of the long view is self-regarding, as Ortega y Gasset observes in a powerful though incomplete argument in "On Point of View in the Arts." Contrasting the sharp foreground and blurred background of close-ups with the "optical democracy" and lack of sharp profiles in distant vision, Ortega then makes this "decisive observation": in distant vision, as we try to "embrace the whole field" and therefore "avoid focusing the eyes as much as possible . . . we are surprised to find that the object just perceived—our entire visual field—is concave. If we are in a house the concavity is bordered by the walls, the roof, the floor. This border or limit is a surface that tends to take the form of a hemisphere viewed from within. But where does the concavity begin? There is no possibility of doubt: it begins at our eyes themselves." In turn, "what we see at a distance is hollow space as such," and the hidden object of sight in distant vision—space perhaps "interrupted," as in Gibbon, by ruins and gardens—is not far away; sight "has drawn back to the absolutely proximate." "It begins at our cornea." Its objectivity rests on an illusion.[18]

The proximate nature of pure distant vision underlies quick transitions from distant views to close-ups. These transitions, which constitute a saving move into the closeness of the external world, find no place in Ortega's scheme. At the same time, his thumbnail sketch of Western painting and philosophy helps locate Gibbon in that large panorama. Western thought, in this account, has moved from objects to surfaces to the experience of seeing to the ideas of sight—that is, from Giotto and Dante to Descartes and Velázquez, then to the Impressionists and "the philosophers of extreme positivism" whose aim was to reduce the world to "pure sensations," and finally to Cézanne and Husserl—or, in the most general terms, from objective to subjective to intrasubjective.[19] To the extent, then, that Gibbon conceptualizes himself within his history either as self-regarding narrator or as tourist-pilgrim on the streets of Rome, he reaches beyond the radical subjectivity of distant views to the intrasubjectivity concerned with contents of consciousness. At the close of the *Decline and Fall*, he puts his signature to his book: the historian recognizes himself in the tourist-pilgrim; the tourist-pilgrim recognizes himself in the historian. Neither the view down from the Capitoline nor the view up from the square of St. Peter's, neither the view from Rome nor the view to Rome, has precedence; taken together, they all constitute the human point of view.

In Gibbon as pilgrim-tourist we can recognize a version of the Romantic ironist, canceling subjective sublimities by submitting them to an alternative view.[20] What Ortega neglects is the fact that artists have sometimes intuited the paradoxes of distant vision and turned them to ironic account. But doing so requires more than ordinary skill. Gibbon's subtlety stands out beside a long view such as this one from the storehouse of eighteenth-century poetic convention:

> Mother of musings, Contemplation sage,
> Whose grotto stands upon the topmost rock
> Of Teneriff; 'mid the tempestuous night,
> On which, in calmest meditation held,
> Thou hear'st with howling winds the beating rain
> And drifting hail descend. . . .

These opening lines of Thomas Warton's *Pleasures of Melancholy* (written when he was seventeen and published in 1747, two years later) could not be more routine. The mansion of Contemplation stands impervious on a cliff: howling winds, beating rain—none of these stock atmospheric effects invades her tranquillity. A remote Olympian figure, she imitates the Epicurean gods:

> . . . secure, self-blest,
> There oft thou listen'st to the wild uproar
> Of fleets encount'ring, that in whispers low
> Ascends the rocky summit, where thou dwell'st
> Remote from man, conversing with the spheres![21]

"Secure" and "self-blest" epitomize the subjectivity of distant views. The difference between Thomas Warton and Gibbon, who also looked for safety in distance, can be expressed in Gibbon's own words: "The theologian may indulge the pleasing task of describing Religion as she descended from Heaven, arrayed in her native purity. A more melancholy duty is imposed on the historian. He must discover the inevitable mixture of error and corruption which she contracted in a long residence upon earth, among a weak and degenerate race of beings" (II, 2). Warton, the theologian of subjective contemplation and melancholy, sees the two arrayed in native purity. Gibbon knows that contemplation and melancholy, like other human feelings, are impure: he undertakes the historian's melancholy task with unmelancholy relish. In irony Gibbon expresses the knowledge that historians and philosophers on their heights, as much as kings and emperors on theirs, do not just preside over their kingdom: they also participate in the struggles of the world.

FIVE

'DECLINE AND FALL': IDEALISM, IRONY, AND "ANTONINE" SATIRE

Proceeding from the shrillness of the "Index Expurgatorius" to the slyness of the *Critical Observations*, Gibbon learned irony's subversive power. Climbing the heights in the *Decline and Fall*, then descending to St. Peter's Square and gazing back upward, he came to see how vulnerable was the ironist's apparently secure authority above the flux of history. Yet he had intimations of this knowledge almost from the start, and his irony, altogether different from that of his Augustan predecessors, is an art of continuous reflection and adjustment.

His was not an ironic age: Gibbon stands out, in the 1770's and 1780's, as virtually a unique case.[1] Johnson might be called a Christian ironist, but the Christian in him overpowers the ironist. Sterne, with whom Gibbon had some habits in common, had died in 1768. Behind lay the irony of the great Augustan writers; ahead, that of the Romantics. Once more Gibbon makes a solitary figure in the landscape, nor is his solitariness relieved by the Augustan satirists' Horatian fancy that a small band of like-minded writers might be able to drive the world before them.[2] The Augustans believed in a camaraderie of the elite. However solitary a life Swift felt he was leading in Ireland, he still subscribed to the Scriblerian alliance.[3] Gibbon had no such company.

This difference is both cause and effect of other differences that distinguish Gibbon's irony from the irony of the Augustans. Like Swift and Pope, he transposes the literary values of his own time. Like them, he seeks value at the moment he seems most directly to challenge it. But where Swift and Pope transpose the values of decorum, Gibbon transposes those of melancholy and nostalgia for a lost past. If the designation of Swift and Pope as "Augustans" has more than arbitrary convenience to recommend it (as I think it does), then Gibbon's satire might be called "Antonine."[4] The contrast between Swift and Gibbon is between ferocious energy, on the one hand, and reflective insinuation, on the other; between the beginnings of empire and its consolidation; between the domineering Augustus and the poet-emperor Hadrian, whose deathbed lyric helped prepare the twilight mood of mid-eighteenth-century England:

> Animula, vagula, blandula,
> Hospes comesque corporis
> Quae nunc abibis in loca,
> Pallidula, rigida, nudula?
> Nec ut soles dabis jocos?[5]

Matthew Prior had translated this crystalline lyric in 1703:

> Poor little, pretty, flutt'ring Thing,
>   Must We no longer live together?
> And dost Thou prune thy trembling Wing,
>   To take thy Flight Thou know'st not whither?
>
> Thy humourous Vein, thy pleasing Folly
>   Lyes all neglected, all forgot:
> And pensive, wav'ring, melancholy,
>   Thou dread'st and hop'st Thou know'st not what.[6]

And Byron tried it in 1806 when he was eighteen:

> Ah! gentle, fleeting, wav'ring sprite,
>   Friend and associate of this clay!
>   To what unknown region borne,
> Wilt thou, now, wing thy distant flight?
> No more, with wonted humour gay,
>   But pallid, cheerless, and forlorn.[7]

But neither Prior nor Byron quite catches the wistfully precise, Latin economy of Hadrian's farewell to his diminutive, vagabond spirit, a farewell that ironically sets off the perfections of the Antonine age.[8] In the marginal headings that accompany the text of the *Decline and Fall*, no sooner has Gibbon announced the "Happiness of the Romans" under the Antonines, than there follows, inescapably, "Its Precarious Nature" (I, 85–86). The precariousness of human happiness impinges on the consciousness of the Antonine world and its rulers, yielding a prescient knowledge: "A just but melancholy reflection embittered, however, the noblest of human enjoyments." To these rulers Gibbon attributes sentiments that prefigure his own: "They must often have recollected the instability of a happiness which depended on the character of a single man." Surely the Antonines, in Gibbon's view, must have feared and expected the approach of some inevitably "fatal moment" (I, 86). His irony rests on a sense of paradise as both irrevocably lost and forever being lost. As he arches his eyebrows at the spectacle of Christianity undermining the empire, Gibbon dreams of lost felicity. The irony is that the empire could not help but have been undermined.

Swift and Pope, on the contrary, do not often yearn for lost values. In their uses of mock-heroic, the old heroic world serves as a touchstone of value but is itself subject to mockery. In *Gulliver's Travels*, the fashionable theory that human beings have lost size and stature over the centuries is represented as fashionable cant.[9] Neither Swift's satire nor Pope's depends heavily on fantasies of a golden age in the past, however much it may depend, as in *Gulliver*, on fantasies of Utopian perfection. Both satirists instead construct systems of opposing values that in their collision generate new worlds. In these exercises, anger mixes with excitement. In the *Tale of a Tub*, form dissolves in chaos but then lives on in a final premonition of new birth. A phoenix arises from the ashes of decorum: the author of the *Tale* lays down his pen but anticipates the stirrings of a pulse— his own and the world's. In Swift's hoax on Partridge, Isaac Bickerstaff's avenging wit slays the foolish astrologer and then restores him to life.[10] And, at the end of the *Rape of the Lock*, silly, primping, prudish Belinda's lock is inscribed among the stars. Even Swift's late, most foreboding satires—*Gulliver's Travels* and the *Modest Proposal*—yield a manic sense of affirmation, or at least of presence. Ask any of Ireland's starving people whether they would not have thought it a great happiness to be sold for food at the age of a year and, the modest proposer implies, surely they would say yes.[11] And if Gulliver's case is more doubtful, the clash between Yahoos and Houyhnhnms producing fear, anger, disgust, shame, still Swift's eye is passionately fixed on the present, as Gibbon's was not.

Unlike his Augustan predecessors, Gibbon negotiated with authority, whether Warburton's or the Pope's. Having ridiculed Warburton in the *Critical Observations*, he repented in the autobiography: "I cannot forgive myself the contemptuous treatment of a man, who, with all his faults, was entitled to my esteem" (*M*, 146). Having subverted Christianity in the *Decline and Fall*, he ended the next-to-last chapter of his history with a *nunc dimittis*, professing a readiness to be on good terms even with the Pope of Rome.[12] Swift and Pope, on the contrary, were not born to negotiate. Often they mimic the voice of an offended victim or observer, lashing or goading his betters, and occasionally lending energy even to the wrong side of an argument. In the *Battle of the Books*, the spider, representing the moderns, abuses the errant bee, representing the ancients, who has flown into his web:

> *A Plague split you,* said he, *for a giddy Son of a Whore; Is it you, with a Vengeance, that have made this Litter here? Could you not look before you, and be d——n'd? Do you think I have nothing else to do (in the Devil's Name) but to Mend and Repair after your Arse?*

Though the spider in Swift's fable may stand for all the wrong things, his colloquial outburst makes better reading than the priggishness of the bee:

> *I am glad,* answered the *Bee, to hear you grant at least, that I am come honestly by my Wings and my Voice, for then, it seems, I am obliged to Heaven alone for my Flights and my Musick; and Providence would never have bestowed on me two such Gifts, without designing them for the noblest Ends.*[13]

In fact, the bee talks like Swift's patron and never-quite-satisfactory father figure, Sir William Temple; the scurrilous spider challenges the ponderously mellow voice of authority.[14] Swift's Drapier, attacking Wood, Walpole, and their brass coinage, plays David to the English Goliath: "I rather chose to attack this *uncircumcised Philistine* (*Wood* I mean) *with a Sling and a Stone*."[15] And Pope at Twickenham turns his "sacred Weapon" of ridicule on the "tinsel Insects" of the Court.[16] Swift and Pope confront authority fiercely, unambiguously granting its strength, which alone makes combatting it worthwhile. Gibbon makes accommodations, for history ultimately rescues the powerless. Even the absolute authority of the Roman emperors, which their enemies could nowhere escape, fades before the insistence of change.

Augustan satire anticipates Gibbon, however, in one instance— the *Dunciad*, especially the third book, with its Virgilian superstructure, its large prospect of past and future, and its miniature history of Rome's decline and fall. In Pope's other satires, as in Swift's, close-ups do most of the work: Belinda's toilet with its glittering hardware, the grotesqueries of Timon's villa, the breasts of the Brobdingnagians, children dying in the streets of Dublin, the chamber pots of Swift's pastoral nymphs—all are seen at close range. In normal Augustan practice, prospects are reserved for celebratory or elegiac occasions—the vision of a grand and harmonious future, for example, at the end of *Windsor Forest*. But when Colley Cibber arrives in the underworld of *Dunciad* III, the ghost of Elkanah Settle offers him a prospect of the coming reign of Dulness: "Then stretch thy sight o'er all her rising reign, / And let the past and future fire thy brain" (65–66).[17] This requires a place to see from. "Ascend this hill," says Settle,

> . . . whose cloudy point commands
> Her boundless empire over seas and lands.
> See, round the Poles where keener spangles shine,
> Where spices smoke beneath the burning Line,
> (Earth's wide extremes) her sable flag display'd,
> And all the nations cover'd in her shade!   (67–72)

The play of light and dark, of clouds, smoke, and intermittent brightness, all seen from a high place that commands an empire, matches that of the *Decline and Fall*. Now Settle gestures grandly east to China and the "bright blaze" (78) of fires that consumed, on an emperor's order, all the learning of the empire. He gestures south to Egypt and the burning of the Ptolomean Library by a conquering caliph ("There rival flames with equal glory rise" [80]), then looks north and sees barbarian hordes:

> The North by myriads pours her mighty sons,
> Great nurse of Goths, of Alans, and of Huns!
> See Alaric's stern port! the martial frame
> Of Genseric! and Attila's dread name!

> See the bold Ostrogoths on Latium fall;
> See the fierce Visigoths on Spain and Gaul!   (89–94)

And then he looks south again to the African shore where Mahomet assembles his conquering tribes:

> See, where the morning gilds the palmy shore
> (The soil that arts and infant letters bore)
> His conqu'ring tribes th' Arabian prophet draws,
> And saving Ignorance enthrones by Laws.
> See Christians, Jews, one heavy sabbath keep,
> And all the western world believe and sleep.   (95–100)

The position that Settle and Cibber share cannot be precisely specified. But in the presence of barbarians to the north and Mahomet's conquering tribes to the south, all roads of sight lead to Rome:

> Lo! Rome herself, proud mistress now no more
> Of arts, but thund'ring against heathen lore;
> Her grey-hair'd Synods damning books unread,
> And Bacon trembling for his brazen head.
> Padua, with sighs, beholds her Livy burn,
> And ev'n th' Antipodes Vigilius mourn.
> See, the Cirque falls, th' unpillar'd Temple nods,
> Streets pav'd with heroes, Tyber choak'd with Gods:
> 'Till Peter's keys some christ'ned Jove adorn,
> And Pan to Moses lends his pagan horn;
> See graceless Venus to a Virgin turn'd,
> Or Phidias broken, and Apelles burn'd.   (101–12)

As high priests of Dulness, Settle and Cibber see the same clouds of Vandals and swarms of Goths that darken the northern sky of the *Decline and Fall*. To the priests of Dulness, the coming of the barbarians is reason for celebration. Yet Pope overlays the sense of Dulness's impending triumph with an elegiac sense of loss: Peter's keys adorn a statue of Jove; Pan turns into Moses; the goddess of love, wittily shorn of "grace," turns into the Virgin Mary. In another context, the Roman streets paved with heroes and the river Tiber choked with gods might embody, without alteration, feelings unlike those of the priests of Dulness.

In all this, Pope hints, like Gibbon, at emptiness near the heart of things, and these intimations touch beliefs to which officially he subscribed: belief is compromised as the Western world believes and sleeps. To the image of Rome "thund'ring against heathen lore" Pope adds a note, drawn from Bayle's *Dictionary*, about Gregory's "pious rage"—a rage so fierce that he "caus'd the noble monuments of the old *Roman* magnificence to be destroyed, lest those who came to *Rome* shou'd give more attention to Triumphal Arches, &c. than to Holy Things."[18] This contains a double irony: not only did travelers like Gibbon continue to pay more attention to triumphal arches than to holy things, notwithstanding Gregory's pious devastation, but given Rome's fall, its triumphal arches might have been left as monuments to the vanity of human wishes. The old Roman magnificence, in this aspect, seems a primitive value that the ironist invokes, recognizing it as an impermanent fancy of the mind. In destroying Roman monuments, Gregory, like Dryden's Alexander, slew the slain. Here irony accommodates nostalgia while acknowledging change and loss. Like irony of every sort, it manages to have things both ways. Unlike Augustan irony generally, it does not neglect history. The *Dunciad* looks ahead to the *Decline and Fall*.

Yet Gibbon need not have read the *Dunciad* to be the historian he became. Not only was he not cut out to be a poet, he did not respond with much discrimination to the poetry of his contemporaries (he thought his friend Hayley a successor to Pope),[19] and he reserved his sense of apprenticeship for writers of prose. In irony, his master was Pascal. Without the *Provinciales* and, perhaps, the *Pensées*, Chapters 15 and 16 of the *Decline and Fall* would not have been the same. It was Pascal who taught Gibbon the art of nonviolent resistance to authority while believing at the same time in a source of authority— God in Pascal's case, history in Gibbon's—that overrode human claims.

Three books, Gibbon says, "may have remotely contributed to form the historian of the Roman Empire" (*M*, 79). One was the Abbé de la Bletterie's life of Julian the Apostate (1735), a believer's impartial biography of an antagonist. Another was Pietro Giannone's civil history of Naples (1723), which for its vigorous defense of state authority against encroachment by the papal court earned its author a life of exile and imprisonment. The third was Pascal's ferociously insinuating attack on the Jesuits. In one draft of the autobiography, Gibbon says that Pascal and Giannone had taught him "the use of irony and criticism on subjects of Ecclesiastical gravity" (*C*, 235). Probably he means to identify Pascal with "irony" and

Giannone, more blunt than ironical, with "criticism." In an earlier draft, Gibbon claims to have reread the *Provinciales* "almost every year . . . with new pleasure" and credits Pascal with having shown him how "to manage the weapon of grave and temperate irony even on subjects of Ecclesiastical solemnity" (*M*, 79).

There could hardly be a better characterization of Pascal's irony, or Gibbon's, than grave and temperate—which is itself a grave and temperate irony. Pascal taught Gibbon the art of seeming temperate; of mixing deference with doubt; of never meeting authority head-on or denying its legitimacy, but always subjecting it to the ruth-lessness of insinuation; of writing ingénu satire in which the ingénu role is a masquerade, as if the naive Gulliver and his knowing cre-ator had come together in the single rhetorical creation of an inno-cent visitor who comes to know all there is to know, a sleuth who only plays dumb. Pascal and Gibbon hone ingénu satire to a grave sharpness.

In the fifth letter of the *Provinciales*, "Louis de Montalte" writes his friend in the country, incredulous that his Jansenist acquaintance in Paris can have told him the truth; but he finds that the Jesuits convict themselves out of their own mouth:

J'ai voulu m'en instruire de bonne sorte. Je ne me suis pas fié à ce que notre ami m'en avait appris. J'ai voulu les voir eux-mêmes; mais j'ai trouvé qu'il ne m'avait rien dit que de vrai. Je pense qu'il ne ment jamais. Vous le verrez par le récit de ces conférences.[20]

I wanted to be well instructed. I did not trust what our friend had told me. I wanted to see them themselves; but I found he had told me nothing but the truth. I think he never lies. You will see this from an account of these discourses.

Patient, willing to learn, anxious to explain, reluctant to believe the unbelievable, wedded to facts—that is Montalte. Being serious and judicious, he does not make light of important matters:

Vous pensez peut-être que je raille: je le dis sérieusement, ou plutôt ce sont eux-mêmes qui le disent. . . . Je ne fais que copier leurs paroles.[21]

Perhaps you think I am joking; I say it seriously, or rather it is they them-selves who say it. . . . I do no more than copy their words.

Like the ingénu travelers of Montesquieu and Goldsmith, Montalte only reports what he sees. Unlike the Persian or Chinese visitors, however, he is an insider. Relentlessly polite, like Gibbon, his commitment to finding the truth precludes spontaneity; he calculates every gesture.

In the eleventh of the letters, the speaker addresses the Jesuit fathers directly for the first time, changing character from the inquiring ingénu, unable to believe what he hears, to the sleuth who aims to confirm and expose the truth. Having learned the facts, he announces his command over them, the slant of his rhetorical questions changing from the incredulous "can it be really true that?" to the accusatory "is it not true that?" But still Pascal modulates the voice of his speaker, however indignant, by conceding an authority, however false, to the Jesuit fathers. Paragraph after paragraph, Montalte addresses them as subordinate to superior, parishioner to priest, learner to teacher, advocate to judge, detective to suspect. Something like half the paragraphs of the eleventh letter begin with, or incorporate, an honorific address to "mes Pères": "Mes Révérends Pères"; "Ce reproche, mes Pères, est bien surprenant et bien injuste"; "Quoi! mes Pères"; "En vérité, mes Pères"; "Car, mes Pères"; "Ne prétendez donc pas, mes Pères"; "Vous voyez donc, mes Pères"; "Je m'assure, mes Pères"; "Ne trouvez-vous pas, mes Pères"; "Et je vous dirai aussi, mes Pères"; "Quoi! mes Pères" (Reverend Fathers; This charge, fathers, is very surprising and quite unjust; What! fathers; Truly, fathers; Because, fathers; Do not claim, fathers; and so on).[22] Like the false humility and false inspiration of Christianity in Gibbon's history, the false fatherhood of the Jesuits resonates through the letters as Pascal insinuates that innocence knows more than experience, youth more than age.

The theme of this eleventh letter is that raillery may be used in the war against religious error ("on peut réfuter par des railleries les erreurs ridicules"),[23] even when the errors are those of the Jesuit fathers. From this proposition, derived from patristic sources, English skeptics and some believers alike were to draw comfort, even to the point of claiming, or seeming to claim, that ridicule was a test of truth. Others protested that making sport with sacred things, even with the best intentions, was paving the road to hell.[24] The controversy had played itself out by the time Gibbon wrote, but he inherited a secular version of Pascal's belief that ridicule was a fair way of testing truth and had the license of authority. Montalte cites the example of the godly and, ultimately, the borrowed authority of God, just as Gibbon speaks with the borrowed authority of history. Both speak as agents, not principals. Mockery, says Montalte, is common among the fathers of the church; it is justified by Scripture, by the example of the greatest saints, even by that of God himself. And at the day of judgment, "la sagesse divine joindra la moquerie et la risée à la vengeance et à la fureur qui les condamnera à des supplices éternels" (divine wisdom will add mockery and derision to the vengeance and the fury that will condemn the damned to eternal torment). It is God the celestial ironist who reproached Adam after the fall, according to the church fathers, with a sharp rebuke, "*une ironie piquante*": "*Ecce Adam quasi unus ex nobis.*" In the words of the King James version: "And the Lord God said, Behold, the man is become as one of us, to know good and evil" (Genesis 3:22). God's irony, said Hugh of Saint-Victor, is an act of justice.[25] Mocking the Jesuits, Pascal is God's comrade in irony.

At the same time, irony defies certainty. Gibbon and Pascal were each caught between the will to believe and the impulse to doubt.[26] The ironic antagonist of Christianity and its ironic champion both took protection under the shelter of authority, and their worlds were marked by yearning. Gibbon satisfied some of his needs by finding a place from which to take in the panorama of history; Pascal could only imagine man without God as looking for some solid place to stand, hoping there to build a tower "qui s'élève à l'infini":

Quelque terme où nous pensions nous attacher et nous affermir, il branle et nous quitte et, si nous le suivons, il échappe à nos prises, nous glisse et fuit d'une fuite éternelle. Rien ne s'arrête pour nous. C'est l'état qui nous est naturel, et toutefois le plus contraire à notre inclination; nous brûlons du désir de trouver une assiette ferme, et une dernière base constante pour y édifier une tour qui s'élève à l'infini; mais tout notre fondement craque, et la terre s'ouvre jusqu'aux abîmes.[27]

At whatever limit we hope to take firm hold, it wavers and leaves us and, if we follow, it escapes our grasp, slips away from us, recedes in eternal flight. Nothing stops for us. This is our natural state, yet is quite contrary to our inclination; we burn with desire to find a solid foundation, a final, stable ground, there to build a tower that reaches to the infinite; but our every foundation cracks, and earth opens up to the abyss.

Man's high places, in Pascal's view, open onto new abysses of thought. And even if Gibbon believed he stood on high and solid ground when he turned to history, he never freed himself entirely from a longing for the security of lost belief. If Chapters 15 and 16 of the *Decline and Fall* could not have taken the shape they did but for Pascal's example, neither could they have taken that shape but for habits of mind that had first shown their strength in Gibbon's impetuous conversion.

Had he ever shaken off these habits entirely, Gibbon would not have needed so badly the weapon of irony. When he had taken the bait of Catholicism, he had taken it whole. Having believed that "miracles are the test of truth, and that the Church must be orthodox and pure, which was so often approved by the visible interposition of the Deity," he had fallen for "the marvellous tales, which are so boldly attested by the Basils and Chrysostoms, the Austins and Jeroms" and had embraced "the superior merits of Celibacy, the institution of the monastic life, the use of the sign of the cross, of holy oil, and even of images, the invocation of Saints, the worship of relicks, the rudiments of purgatory in prayers for the dead, and the tremendous mystery of the sacrifice of the body and blood of Christ, which insensibly swelled into the prodigy of Transubstantiation" (*M*, 59). Though Gibbon came to regard monasticism, the worship of relics, and purgatory as so much hocus-pocus, Christ's sacrifice is more than satirically "tremendous," even if the "prodigy of Transubstantiation," the doctrine of Christ's real presence in the Eucharist, mercifully transforms mystery into folly.

Gibbon also thinks that the premises of his conversion were sound: "nor was my conclusion absurd, that Miracles are the test of truth, and that the Church must be orthodox and pure, which was so often approved by the visible interposition of the Deity" (*M*, 59). Inspired by Conyers Middleton's skeptical *Free Enquiry* into the miraculous powers of the early Christians (1749), Gibbon's conversion had depended on the conviction that there was no halfway house in matters of belief, that, in Patricia B. Craddock's words, "either all miracles were false, or all were true."[28] Looking back years later, he persists in believing that if there had been miracles, they would have attested to the truth of Christianity; that a true religion would have manifested itself in miracles; that any church "so often approved by the visible interposition of the Deity" would have been the true church; and that the true church is orthodox and pure. In this respect Gibbon is less worldly than Pascal, as well as less of a fideist. He continues to imagine a world in which the ideal conditions of religion might be satisfied. This otherworldliness carries over into the opening paragraphs of Chapter 15—the most notorious he ever wrote and the touchstone of his ironic powers.

Reading or rereading these virtuoso paragraphs is an experience to be indulged without preliminaries:

A candid but rational inquiry into the progress and establishment of Christianity may be considered as a very essential part of the history of the Roman empire. While that great body was invaded by open violence, or undermined by slow decay, a pure and humble religion gently insinuated itself into the minds of men, grew up in silence and obscurity, derived new vigour from opposition, and finally erected the triumphant banner of the cross on the ruins of the Capitol. Nor was the influence of Christianity confined to the period or to the limits of the Roman empire. After a revolution of thirteen or fourteen centuries, that religion is still professed by the nations of Europe, the most distinguished portion of human kind in arts and learning as well as in arms. By the industry and zeal of the Europeans it has been widely diffused to the most distant shores of Asia and Africa; and by the means of their colonies has been firmly established from Canada to Chili, in a world unknown to the ancients.

But this inquiry, however useful or entertaining, is attended with two peculiar difficulties. The scanty and suspicious materials of ecclesiastical history seldom enable us to dispel the dark cloud that hangs over the first age of the church. The great law of impartiality too often obliges us to reveal the imperfections of the uninspired teachers and believers of the gospel; and, to a careless observer, *their* faults may seem to cast a shade on the faith which they professed. But the scandal of the pious Christian, and the fallacious triumph of the Infidel, should cease as soon as they recollect not only *by whom*, but likewise *to whom*, the Divine Revelation was given. The theologian may indulge the pleasing task of describing Religion as she descended from Heaven, arrayed in her native purity. A more melancholy duty is imposed on the historian. He must discover the inevitable mixture of error and corruption which she contracted in a long residence upon earth, among a weak and degenerate race of beings.   (II, 1–2)

In this matchless performance, the ironic objectivity of the historian's inquiry provides the most conspicuous coloration. Other, subtler colorations include: (1) the necessary, empowering fiction of original unity; (2) the successful Christian challenge to the historian's imposition of order; hence, (3) the self-regarding irony of the historian's defeat; and, (4) the opening up of seemingly closed systems of antithesis. These need to be addressed one at a time.

The ironist starts by imagining the absolute, in this case "Religion as she descended from Heaven, arrayed in her native purity." The historian might have been a theologian, had his times or temperament been different. Indeed, Gibbon the historian has imitated the theologian, describing in the age of the Antonines a social institution arrayed in its native purity, and only then telling how error and corruption find their way into the garden or, ironically, how error and corruption—and hence the principle of decline—are lodged in paradise from the start. Coming to Christianity, he turns to the same constructive fiction on which his history depends, supposing an original unity in the interest of showing how it has been dispersed. Even if he thought he believed in the happiness of Rome under the Antonines and not in the native purity of Christianity, that does not, structurally, make a crucial difference. In each case, he shapes his story in the same way.

The title of Chapter 15 sets up an interplay between original purity and its decline: "The Progress of the Christian Religion, and the Sentiments, Manners, Numbers, and Condition, of the Primitive Christians" (II, 1). The loaded words are "progress" and "primitive," and their natural order is reversed. The primitive is what, in Johnson's first definition, is "ancient; original; established from the beginning," and primitive Christianity commonly represented an absolute standard of virtue, of piety, humility, chastity, justice. It had furnished Swift, for example, with a standard of virtue, though inaccessible, in the *Argument Against Abolishing Christianity*: "I hope, no Reader imagines me so weak to stand up in the Defence of *real* Christianity; such as used in primitive Times (if we may believe the Authors of those Ages) to have an Influence upon Mens Belief and Actions: To offer at the Restoring of that, would indeed be a wild Project; it would be to dig up Foundations; to destroy at one Blow *all* the Wit, and *half* the Learning of the Kingdom; to break the entire Frame and Constitution of Things."[29] But what distinguishes Swift's from Gibbon's use of primitive Christianity is what distinguishes their irony generally. In Swift, the ancient absolute is not only inaccessible but faintly ludicrous: to try to restore it would be truly a wild project, and Swift's feelings are more fierce than melancholy; it is not even certain that we should believe the church fathers. In contrast, Gibbon's image of Religion in her primitive purity, however phantasmal, is touched by nostalgia.

If "primitive" Christians awaken the dream of original perfection, however, the progress of Christianity that has oddly preceded their appearance in the title will have put the reader on guard. "The

Progress of the Christian Religion" would normally announce Christianity's spiritual triumphs. But when progress is juxtaposed with primitive Christianity, something has gone wrong in the order of things. Not only is the normal sequence distorted but Christianity was commonly supposed to have declined in perfection rather than advanced from its primitive state, whether in the melancholy view of the noncommittal historian or in the view of the true believer. Primitive Christianity will cast only a ghostly shadow, but without that shadow, ironic nuance would be lost.

Gibbon's recourse to original purity bends his iconoclasm back into the parodic semblance of orthodox shape and explains an exculpatory footnote by his nineteenth-century editor, the Reverend Henry Hart Milman, whose curious commentary on the opening paragraphs of Chapter 15 is half false and half true. A minor poet, then a distinguished church historian, Sanskrit scholar, as well as Gibbon's editor (1838), and for the last two decades of his life (1849–68) dean of St. Paul's Cathedral, Milman seems not the likeliest of editors for the infidel historian. Yet he accurately senses Gibbon's ironic strategy:

The art of Gibbon, or at least the unfair impression produced by these two memorable chapters, consists in confounding together, in one undistinguishable mass, the *origin* and *apostolic* propagation of the Christian religion with its later progress. The main question, the divine origin of the religion, is dexterously eluded or speciously conceded; his plan enables him to commence his account, in most parts, *below the apostolic times*; and it is only by the strength of the dark coloring with which he has brought out the failings and the follies of succeeding ages, that a shadow of doubt and suspicion is thrown back on the primitive period of Christianity.

Then Milman makes a seemingly extraordinary claim, translating the ironic strategy into his own orthodox frame of values: "Divest this whole passage of the latent sarcasm betrayed by the subsequent tone of the whole disquisition, and it might commence a Christian history, written in the most Christian spirit of candor."[30]

What is curious is that Milman is not all wrong. Certainly he overlooks the elliptical premonitions of the chapter title and the fact that the "latent sarcasm" of these chapters does eventually reach back to the main question, "the divine origin of the religion." Though Gibbon mostly eludes that question, he does not altogether let it pass: "How," he asks, "shall we excuse the supine inattention of the Pagan and philosophic world to those evidences which were presented by the hand of Omnipotence, not to their reason, but to their senses?" (II, 74). How could Seneca and the elder Pliny, both great collectors of natural phenomena, have failed "to mention the greatest phenomenon to which the mortal eye has been witness since the creation of the globe" (II, 75)—namely, the three hours of "præternatural darkness" at the crucifixion?

How, indeed? But the opening paragraphs of Chapter 15 are very discreet. A candid inquiry, like Gibbon's candid treatment of War- burton, may be sharp, not benevolent; a humble religion that insin- uates itself into the minds of men may not be very humble; a useful inquiry into the progress of Christianity may be entertaining in more than one way. But these are hints, and the distinction between native purity and inevitable corruption not only looks orthodox but is the very distinction that Milman charges Gibbon with having confounded. If Gibbon does confound it, perhaps that testifies to his own situation "among a weak and degenerate race of beings," not only discovering but contributing to the mixture of error and cor- ruption that Religion has contracted like a disease. Without the fic- tion of pure origins, neither the history of the decline and fall nor the ironic story of the progress of Christianity could have been told.

If the fiction of origins is enabling but false, so is the fiction of order that the historian imposes on his narrative, and the progress of Christianity brings this truth home. Christianity spills over Ro- man boundaries of time and place, creating temporal and spatial uncertainty in the narrative and upsetting the narrator's perspective, hence his authority: "Nor was the influence of Christianity confined to the period or to the limits of the Roman empire. . . . By the industry and zeal of the Europeans it has been widely diffused to the most distant shores of Asia and Africa; and by the means of their colonies has been firmly established from Canada to Chili, in a world unknown to the ancients." The security of high places and long views fades away. The historian of the Roman Empire may know just where he stands and what the world looks like, but the historian of the progress of Christianity sees unruliness and disorder in which he is himself entangled. When Gibbon writes that "the industry and zeal of the Europeans" have carried Christianity far and wide, the idea of Europe superimposes itself on the map of empire, and the author of the *Decline and Fall*, himself one of the

Europeans, becomes remote from himself. "The most distant shores of Asia and Africa" are distant from an uncertain point, while Canada and "Chili" jar us still further loose from the sense of being safely grounded. After the fall of Rome, the world has changed shape. The existence of a new world unknown to the ancients makes it impossible to take everything in from one spot and in one glance. The flat map of empire has become round. Of course, the new world would have come into being anyway, but the pervasiveness of Christianity marks the defeat of the historian's attempt to bring all the world within view.

When Gibbon returns, then, to the heights in the second paragraph, he carries the knowledge that will dominate later volumes of the history—that of a melancholy fatality touching the historian himself, ambiguously placed within the scheme of history. Now a "dark cloud . . . hangs over the first age of the church": the historian has recaptured a commanding prospect, but of an obscure scene. He submits to sweeping laws and obligations. The "great law of impartiality" that "obliges" him to reveal the imperfections of the uninspired has the look of some Newtonian truth, mysteriously ordering the heavens. And the theologian, who may "indulge" himself, has a freedom that the historian lacks. A prisoner of duty, the historian "must" discover (i.e., uncover) corruption, itself inevitable. He cannot invent history any more than he can constrict it within the limits of his own inquiries. All this is ironically spoken, but ironists submit to such necessities.

Finally, these paragraphs display the openness of Gibbon's ironic world in parallel and antithetical constructions that seem to exhaust or enclose a range of possibilities but actually generate new ones. In the autobiography, Gibbon describes Bayle as subjecting the claims of false religion to an annihilation of opposites: "he balances the *false* Religions in his sceptical scales, till the opposite quantities, (if I may use the language of Algebra) annihilate each other" (*M*, 64–65). But this is not Gibbon's way, however much he owed to Bayle;[31] rather, it is Swift's, in whose art opposites continually dissolve in collision. In Gibbon, antitheses and parallels commonly turn out to be not quite antithetical or not quite parallel. Unlike Swift's, his ironic world is not symmetrical; or, to shift the figure back to Gibbon's own, its scales are not in balance. His world resists efforts to stabilize it, just as history resists the stabilizing efforts of the historian.

In a "candid but rational inquiry," for example, why the "but"? The antithesis is stronger than required, even if we take "candid" in its primary meaning of "well-intended." Or does "candid" mean "frank"? In these cases the inquiry seems both candid and rational. Alternatively, does "candid" hide Gibbon's real meaning of "outspokenly critical"? If so, "rational" implies a restraining force rather than a release from inhibitions of good will. The ironic relationship between being candid and being rational remains unstable: both terms are susceptible to self-contradictory interpretation in a situation of unsettling, reciprocal influence.

"Useful or entertaining" is another case in point: "this inquiry, however useful or entertaining, is attended with two peculiar difficulties." In the usual view, the useful and the pleasing were the two ends of art, though distinct from each other; hence Johnson's effort to bind them together by defining the purpose of art as "to instruct by pleasing."[32] In this case, however, "entertaining" signals duplicity. When Bishop Berkeley had spoken of "knowledge both useful and entertaining" in 1713, by "entertaining" he meant little more than "pleasing." But by the 1770's, "entertaining," like "candid" and "pompous," was a word in transition: it was coming to signify witty amusement, and Gibbon plans on some irreverent entertainment.[33] With hindsight, then, we look back to "useful." Useful for what? The usefulness of irreverent entertainment is a matter of doubt. Are the decline and fall of the Roman Empire truly just an entertainment? Perhaps what is useful is incompatible with what is entertaining, the one possibility excluding the other; certainly that would be the orthodox view. The ironic relationship between being useful and being entertaining, like that between being candid and being rational, never comes to rest.

As for the two "peculiar" (both unique and odd) difficulties that constrain the historian of the church, we anticipate their running parallel. In fact, they are strangely, even inconsistently, related. On the one hand, the historian can seldom "dispel the dark cloud that hangs over the first age of the church." On the other hand, "the great law of impartiality too often obliges us to reveal the imperfections of the uninspired teachers and believers of the gospel." If the first difficulty is the obscurity of church history, the second is an obligation to reveal things that may seem hidden by the same cloud that hangs over the first age of the church. Once more, the question of origins produces a tangle. Does the historian manage sometimes to dispel the cloud that hides the church's earliest beginnings, or does he move from obscurity to greater clarity only by proceeding to a later time? In the one case, the historian seems to have more than human powers; in the other, his powers are severely limited. Yet the alternatives, if that is what they are, are not presented as mutually exclusive but as parallel and compatible cases. We are left with neither "either/or" nor "both/and" but with an eclectic combining of the two.

Gibbon becomes still more oblique as he contemplates the imperfections of uninspired teachers and believers: "to a careless observer, *their* faults may seem to cast a shade on the faith which they professed." If there are careless observers, presumably there are careful ones, also. We suppose that, like the narrator, we belong among the careful ones. Should we conclude, therefore, that the faults of the early Christians do not cast a shade on the faith they professed? Being initiated into Gibbon's irony, we know that is wrong. But what is right? The conclusion that the faults of the uninspired do cast a shade on their faith does not seem justified, either. Why should the faults of the uninspired imply anything about a faith that is inspired? Thus far, we have careless observers and uninspired Christians. What might a careful observer make of the faith of the uninspired? Possibly, but only possibly, that inspired and uninspired are indistinguishable. In this play of antithesis, uncertainty rules, not mutual annihilation. Perhaps true inspiration and true faith exist outside the boundaries of the text, like primitive Christianity. How can we observe what we cannot see?

Finally, the theologian faces the historian, an opposition complicated by an insidious yet obscure parallelism: "But the scandal of the pious Christian, and the fallacious triumph of the Infidel, should cease as soon as they recollect not only *by whom*, but likewise *to whom*, the Divine Revelation was given. The theologian may indulge the pleasing task of describing Religion as she descended from Heaven, arrayed in her native purity. A more melancholy duty is imposed on the historian." Lurking here is this equation: pious Christian:theologian = Infidel:historian. Taken at face value, this must have given the "infidel" Gibbon surreptitious pleasure. At the same time, the relationship between pious Christian and theologian is straightforward, while the relationship between infidel and historian is, at best, accidental. If Gibbon took surreptitious pleasure in it, he must also have known its fragility, even its self-contradictoriness: historians, as historians of fact, are believers. What is more, the triumphs of infidels and historians are indeed fallacious, if measured against the spread of Christianity to Asia and Africa, Canada and Chile. If the historian's duty is to discover error and corruption, then "discover" not only means to "uncover" but also to "display," frequently with a sense of self-revelation. The enterprise of the historian, being human, mixes with error and corruption. The historian needs the theologian, dreaming of purity, as he needs primitive Christianity for a backdrop to Christianity's human failings. The seemingly closed opposition of historian and theologian turns out to be open, an opposition of incommensurables.

One critic calls the *Decline and Fall* "an ironic mock-epic": "Being the epic of the Enlightenment, the work must, of course, be an ironic mock-epic."[34] What can this mean? Surely all mock epics are ironic? Yet this characterization does not seem, on reflection, a tautology; we might call the *Dunciad* "an ironic mock-epic," too, because calling it simply a mock epic does not match up fully with the experience of the poem.[35] In its redundancy, "ironic mock-epic" captures the sense of a self-reflexive style that alternates between melancholy grandeur and microscopic fragmentation. In the *Dunciad* and the *Decline and Fall*, the mock epic, normally a vision of smallness made implausibly grand, takes on another dimension by exposing ironically the true grandeur of loss. Mock epic becomes something like true epic in an act of double negation. Where then to locate Gibbon in the larger company of ironists?

Paging through recent studies of irony, one finds him infrequently. In D. C. Muecke's *The Compass of Irony* (1969), Gibbon appears four times; in Wayne C. Booth's *A Rhetoric of Irony* (1974), twice; in Anne K. Mellor's *English Romantic Irony* (1980) and in Lilian R. Furst's *Fictions of Romantic Irony* (1984), not at all; in Peter L. Thorslev's *Romantic Contraries* (1984), which closes with a chapter on "The Open Universe and Romantic Irony," twice; in Northrop Frye's *Anatomy of Criticism* (1957), three times.[36] As an ironist, Gibbon has slipped into the category of someone to be alluded to, not attended to. Hayden White, however, whose view of Gibbon in part matches and in part clashes with mine, makes an exception to the rule.

White has mixed feelings about Enlightenment historiography: "The mode in which all of the *great* historical works of the age were cast is that of Irony, with the result that they all tend toward the form of Satire, the supreme achievement of the literary sensibility of that age." In this view, Bayle, Voltaire, Hume, and Gibbon, as well as Kant, all apprehend history as an "*unresolvable* conflict, between *eternally opposed* principles of human nature." Thus far, White and I would agree: Gibbon's irony implies, in its very syntax, the unresolvable nature of human conflicts. But White goes on to argue that historiography would have to be rescued from its dead end by Herder and by Nietzsche, with his oneiric and myth-making powers. Enlightenment historians "did not believe in their own prodigious powers of dreaming, which their Ironic self-consciousness should have set free. For them, the imagination was a threat to reason and could be deployed in the world only under the most rigorous rational constraints."[37]

It is here that White and I part company. The claim that imagination threatened reason, if used to describe Gibbon's view, I take to be wrong. Even though Gibbon was never destined to be a poet, he was no enemy to the imagination. When White says that the imagination was a threat to reason, to be deployed only under the most rigorous rational constraints, he might be Matthew Arnold sounding the cry against Dryden, Pope, and their age of prose. And leaving aside the cases of Bayle, Voltaire, and Hume, White is as much off the mark about Gibbon as Arnold was about Dryden and Pope. Like Nietzsche, though in a different fashion, Gibbon believed in his own power of dreaming. "Our imagination," he wrote in the autobiography as he set out to uncover his ancestral origins, "is always active to enlarge the narrow circle in which Nature has confined us" (*M*, 3). In the *Decline and Fall*, Gibbon strove to enlarge the narrow circle of our confined experience in an act of the imagination.

At the same time, White says accurately that the *Decline and Fall*, the "greatest achievement of sustained Irony in the history of historical literature," rests on quicksand. The fall of Byzantium, with which it ends, represented "the triumph of one fanaticism over another." The revival of learning in the Renaissance, itself a prelude to the Enlightenment, ironically depended on that same clash of fanaticisms, which in its outcome "drove scholars from Constantinople to Italy, there to disseminate the knowledge of Classical antiquity, which would ultimately serve (ironically) to overturn the Christian superstition in whose service it had been (ironically) used by the monks of the Middle Ages." This set of ironies implicates even Gibbon's own values, leading him, in White's claim, "to the same debilitating skepticism about reason itself which Hume had sought refuge from in historical studies, but which had confronted him even there, in the life of action as well as in the life of thought of all past ages."[38]

At this point aesthetic description has been supplanted by normative judgment and, indeed, by questions that have affected ethical inquiry for the last two hundred years. Is an ironic skepticism about reason necessarily debilitating? Was it debilitating in the cases of Gibbon and Hume? In one sense, perhaps trivial, the answer is no: skepticism did not prevent the writing of the *Treatise of Human Nature* or the *Decline and Fall*. Beyond that, how are we to judge a self-implicating irony? Existentialists, Marxists, ideologues, all have resisted ironic habits of thought. Ironists have largely gone their way, at once asserting and denying the value of what they do and see, seldom meeting their antagonists face-to-face. The quarrel, as a result, has had a certain spectral quality, and it is not going to be settled here. But to recognize what is at stake is the better to recognize Gibbon's place in the chronicle of modern thought.

Far from representing all that modern thought, historiographical or otherwise, would repudiate, Gibbon helped to establish habits of seeing that have become pervasive. Of those who have recently noticed his irony, Thorslev is closest to the mark, though he assumes, like White, that Bayle and Voltaire and Hume and Gibbon can all be bracketed together. Thorslev locates the sources of the open universe of Romantic irony in "the skeptical and empiricist humanism of Pierre Bayle, Voltaire, Hume, Gibbon (all of whom greatly influenced Byron), with something added of the emotional exuberance and of the self-conscious analysis that one associates with Rousseau."[39] In fact, the open universe, as a scientific hypothesis, came into being well before the Enlightenment.[40] But that is incidental. By pointing out, in effect, what a work like the *Decline and*

Fall shares with one like *Don Juan*, its insistent sublimity under-
cut by an equally insistent world-weariness, Thorslev accurately
amends the notion that Romantic irony sprang into being without
precedent.

In the long run, one might think of Gibbon's contribution to his
successors in irony as that of providing a stage setting, for he redefined the conventional properties of the theater of the world. His
stage anticipates others that come after it: "in the great cold the great
dark the air and the earth abode of stones in the great cold alas alas
in the year of their Lord six hundred and something the air the earth
the sea the earth abode of stones in the great deeps the great cold on
sea on land and in the air I resume for reasons unknown in spite of
the tennis the facts are there but time will tell."[41] This is Lucky waiting for Godot, in a monologue cited by one critic to illustrate—
indeed, to sum up—the character of cosmic irony. For all its dis-
connectedness, it is much like Gibbon. Here are rhetorical melancholy ("alas alas"), great empty spaces, long views of land and sea,
and a darkness more unrelieved than the cloudy stretches of the *Decline and Fall*, yet with its own possibilities of precision. In Beckett,
as in Gibbon, "the facts are there," however ill-assorted ("in spite
of the tennis") and however imprecisely precise ("in the year of their
Lord six hundred and something"). And in both texts, since time
will and does tell, facts finally wash away in the current of history.

I believe that the ironist should be judged according to the human
consequences of his art. Does he shut his world down to interpretation or open it up? Does not Lucky, waiting for Godot, ask the
audience to join him? Does not Gibbon, sitting on the Capitoline,
call on Poggio and us, his readers, to join him? In such cases, irony
reveals itself as the solitary's self-denying invitation to enter and care
about his world.

SIX

'DECLINE AND FALL': THE ENIGMA

OF CHARACTER

No problem stirred Gibbon's interest more than how to interpret character, and none gave him more trouble, both in the *Decline and Fall* and, later, when he tried autobiographically to understand himself. On his success in portraying character, readers are divided. Gibbon's characters, says Virginia Woolf, "are daubed in with single epithets like 'the vicious' or 'the virtuous,' and are so crudely jointed that they seem capable only of the extreme antics of puppets dangling from a string."[1] Leo Braudy, on the contrary, argues that Gibbon comes close to seeing persons as a novelist might, unencumbered by the rigidity of psychological theory: "Without a commitment to a system of historical or psychological explanation, with a commitment only to his own narrative voice and the coherence it creates, Gibbon can afford to present character in the fullness of its 'contradictions' and 'inconsistencies.' Like the later Hume, he can concentrate on character for its own sake, rather than as a precise key to the truth of public events."[2] On this account, the characters of the *Decline and Fall* reflect a "rich and flexible" outlook on human behavior.[3] The truth, I think, lies between Woolf and Braudy.[4]

On the one hand, Gibbon recognized the diversity of human nature in its twistings and turnings—Braudy's "character in the fullness of its 'contradictions' and 'inconsistencies.'" On the other hand, he would have been glad to reduce contradiction and inconsistency to coherence; from the standpoint of the systematic historian, puppets dangling from a string would have been preferable to the unpredictable people he had to handle. Gibbon was not indifferent to the claims of psychological explanation. Was there no principle of human behavior, he wondered, that would preserve multiplicity yet achieve stability, no way to fix in place Hadrian or Julian or Mahomet?

This anxiety Gibbon shared with his age. As human nature had come to seem more unmanageable and inconsistent, the desire to locate the origins of self and character had intensified, yielding, at best, the imaginative syntheses of novelists. It had also yielded the destabilizing analyses of professional philosophers like Locke and Hume, concerned with the problem of identity. And in an amateur like Pope it produced a theory of the ruling passion, which had an influence out of proportion to its virtues because it addressed a need. Gibbon had some of Pope's couplets almost by heart:

> Search then the Ruling Passion: There, alone,
> The Wild are constant, and the Cunning known;
> The Fool consistent, and the False sincere;
> Priests, Princes, Women, no dissemblers here.[5]

From Pope's verse essay on the characters of men (1734), these lines reiterate the earlier *Essay on Man* (1733):

> And hence one master Passion in the breast,
> Like Aaron's serpent, swallows up the rest.
> As Man, perhaps, the moment of his breath,
> Receives the lurking principle of death;
> The young disease, that must subdue at length,
> Grows with his growth, and strengthens with his strength:
> So, cast and mingled with his very frame,
> The Mind's disease, its ruling Passion came;
> Each vital humour which should feed the whole,
> Soon flows to this, in body and in soul.
> Whatever warms the heart, or fills the head,
> As the mind opens, and its functions spread,
> Imagination plies her dang'rous art,
> And pours it all upon the peccant part.[6]

For all its reassuring simplicity, the theory has its disturbing side: the ruling passion, by which the mysteriousness of human nature can be explained, acts like a disease. Redefine the passions to include different instincts, however, and the theory can accommodate a benevolent version of human nature, as it does in Pope's epistle on the characters of men, addressed to Viscount Cobham, in which his lordship's ruling passion turns out to be patriotism;[7] as it does in *Joseph Andrews* and *Tom Jones*, in which Adams and Allworthy represent the monochromatic passion to do good; and as it does in the portrait of an amiably eccentric humorist like Sterne's Uncle Toby. Creaky and inadequate as a theory, the notion of the ruling passion was and is in practice something of a necessity. Gibbon turned to it, sometimes hesitantly, sometimes hopefully.

When he read Hurd's edition of Horace, which contained a discourse on drama, Gibbon lingered over its treatment of character and its statement of the dramatist's, which was equally the historian's, dilemma. On the one hand, only "reason and virtue pursue a steady uniform course, while the extravagant wanderings of vice and folly are infinite" (*EE*, 41); on the other hand, even foolish characters, however volatile, have to "lay themselves open" so that we may know them (*EE*, 42). This needs to be done "in a natural manner" (*EE*, 41); they should expose themselves by acts or expressions that they do not recognize as self-revealing.

But what about the ruling passion? It exists, yet like a ghost in the machine, manifesting itself ambiguously and more often staying out of sight. Character, as telltale identity, ought not "always to appear; since it cannot always exist, but as the ruling passion is modified by others, or called forth by circumstances." It is a mistake to reduce a person to a personification: "A contrary method, tho too common, is turning a man into a single passion; a man such as nature never made, since those who are the most under the dominion of a ruling passion, act and talk upon many occasions, like the rest of mankind" (*EE*, 42). Comic characters constructed of a single passion are the kind E. M. Forster called "flat,"[8] and even in comedy, Hurd argues, characters should be more intricate. Thus construed, the ruling passion has the same advantage as that proposed by any theory of personal identity that assumes the continuity of self through time. Intuitively appealing, ruling passions or continuous selves depend on uncertain manifestations and obscure revelations. It is an error, therefore, to impose a ruling passion rather than letting it emerge as an acceptable means of binding disparate facts together. Dutifully, young Gibbon records this commonsensical lesson, although he would never find it easy to remember or to live by. Precept was one thing, practice another, and he often felt at a loss for understanding. For the puzzled observer of character, the ruling passion could be an irresistible simplification.

In some fragmentary "Hints" compiled soon after 1765, Gibbon poses miscellaneous questions: Are historians friends to virtue? What differences were there between the civil wars in France and England? And in these "Hints" questions of character arise with some urgency. Noting that Henry III of France had studied "Politicks" (i.e., the science of governing) with an Italian abbé, Gibbon blurts out impatiently: "Vanity of that Science.—Ignorance why *we* have acted—how *we* shall act—how *others* will act." Not knowing why we have ourselves behaved as we have or how we will act in the future, how can we predict what others will do? Under these conditions statecraft is less a matter of prediction than of keeping a steady course: "Our sense, eloquence secrecy &c the only principles, assisted by the confidence of others" (*EE*, 89). But the historian of statecraft cannot assent so readily to the claim that we know nothing of human motives. A few pages later the ruling passion—as though in answer to the obvious, unspoken question—bobs up again, this time in jottings collected under the general heading of "Religious Wars" (*EE*, 90).

Here Gibbon chews on questions that look forward to his treatment of Christianity ("Connection of Religion and politics. The Leaders seldom free from enthusiasm, or the followers from ambition"), and they lead him to reflect on the passions: "Other passions mix with these—Massacre of Paris owing to revenge—of Charles ix.—of Guise—of the Parisians." Questions of motive intrude on the scene of history. At this juncture, perhaps the conventional solution is right? "The ruling passion? very rare. Most passions confined to times, places, persons, circumstances—Love, Hatred, revenge envy jealosy, Vanity &c—Patriotism seldom even a passion.—Ambition generally mixed with other passions, often subservient to them—when pure as in Cæsar or Richelieu must succeed or perish—Avarice perhaps the only permanent ruling passion" (*EE*, 90). Gibbon wavers. Perhaps the ruling passion does not exist in a pure state, except in the rare ambition of Caesar or Richelieu, or in avarice, which feeds itself. After this hesitancy, it comes as something of a surprise that now Gibbon remembers and quotes Pope, though not precisely:

> Search then the ruling passion, there alon[e]
> The fools are constant, & the wise are Know[n].   (*EE*, 91)

The "wise" do not appear in the original of these lines, and it is tempting to guess that Gibbon finds himself wondering what might be the ruling passion of a wise historian. In any event, with Pope's help, character becomes solid, fixed—or so it seems. Since Gibbon makes no comment on the passage, it is possible he intends a criticism. But I doubt it: like primitive Christianity or the age of the Antonines, the ruling passion was his necessary fiction. He turns to it here, as he would in the *Decline and Fall*, almost in spite of himself, reason succumbing to need.[9]

On other occasions, however, Gibbon steers clear of ruling passions, or skirts them when he ponders the mysteries of character during his apprenticeship. These occasions happen often: in an early fragment on the Roman historian Livy (1756); in the *Essai* (1761); in an essay on the character of Brutus (1769); even, remotely, in a curious "Dissertation on the Subject of l'Homme au Masque de Fer" (1774).[10] But avoiding ruling passions does not mean avoiding uneasiness, nor does Gibbon always avoid treating character according to a model constructed on similar lines as that of the ruling passion. Whether his emphasis falls on the difficulty or on the possibility of unmasking character, the task is always problematic.

In the essay on Livy, Gibbon intends to praise the historian's handling of character; but then, as if unawares, he slides off into assertions about the elusiveness of character. How might Livy have dealt with Catullus and Cicero, Pompey and Caesar, Mark Antony and Augustus, in the lost section of his history? For one thing, he would not have made the mistake some historians do—namely, substituting hypothesis for observation of how people actually behave: "Like observers of nature, he would have realized that experience counts more than systems; and . . . he would have explained the character of a man by his actions (. . . with due precautions) rather than explaining the actions according to some preconceived idea." But now Gibbon drifts off course: "He would have seen that the character on which one bases a narrative is far from being uniform and far, I say, from being able to explain an entire life; indeed, nothing less resembles the man of yesterday than the man of today." And then he is swept away by currents of uncertainty: "Those who think they can thus explain all the motives of the actions of men (who very often do not understand themselves) have a firm opinion both of the constancy of men and of their own shrewdness, but what they should remember is . . ."[11]

What is it these unwary students of human nature ought to remember? It turns out to be some lines from Pope's epistle to Cobham—not those on the ruling passion but earlier ones that stress the mystery of character. This time Gibbon has the text in front of him, judging by the accuracy with which he cites it.

> In vain the sage, with retrospective eye,
> Would from the apparent what conclude the why,
> Infer the motive from the deed, and shew
> That what we chanced, was what we meant to do.
> Behold! if Fortune or a mistress frowns,
> Some plunge in business, others shave their crowns:
> To ease the soul of one oppressive weight,
> This quits an empire, that embroils a state:
> The same adust complexion has impell'd
> Charles to the convent, Philip to the field!
> (*MW*, III, 373)[12]

And there he lets the matter rest, turning back to expressions of regret for the loss of so much of Livy's history. Not only is character so unstable we cannot make sense of a life, we cannot understand each other from one day to the next. Motives cannot be inferred from actions. Only actions count. These volatile views match the volatility Gibbon ascribes to character itself. It can be understood; then again, it cannot.

The *Essai*, as befits its celebration of human learning, is more optimistic. Persons can be known, provided, once again, we pay attention to facts (this is one reason why facts should be held in honor) rather than imposing a system on them. In understanding character, small, hidden details tell the true story, and Alexander reveals himself in the tent of Darius if not on the field of battle. In private we see emperors stripped of false appearance, out of uniform. "On se deshabille lors qu'on espère n'être pas vû" (one gets undressed when one hopes not to be seen; *EL*, 67). Understanding character, in this view, comes close to voyeurism but is not an impossible task. Gibbon's argument in the *Essai* requires that it not be.

His argument in the "Digression on the Character of Brutus" does likewise. Like other of his early work, it challenges received opinion, in this case the view that Brutus represented "the Perfect Idea of Roman Virtue" (*EE*, 96). But what counts as evidence? The issue cannot be settled by Brutus's killing of Caesar: those who value liberty above order will think one way, whereas those who value order above liberty will think another. And though it is soon clear which side Gibbon belongs on, since he intimates that love of liberty may be only love of power and associates order with the "Calm of Reason," still he recognizes the intransigence of political attitudes. At this point he turns to intention: "in these nice Cases, where the Esteem is bestowed on the INTENTION, rather than on the ACTION, we ought to be well assured that the Intention was pure from any interested or passionate Motive; that it was not the hasty Suggestion of Resentment or Vanity, but the calm Result of consistent and well grounded Virtue, impatient of Slavery and tender of the Rights of Mankind" (*EE*, 98). What the inquirer must look for in Brutus is "the uniform Tenor of his Life" (*EE*, 99)—that is, for something like a ruling passion.

Gibbon finds in Brutus what he needs, though he does not call it a ruling passion and does not organize Brutus's character around it: he discovers avarice, that lone passion which he thought might permanently govern individual action. And, having located an instance of "unrelenting Avarice" (*EE*, 100) in the "PATRIOT ASSASSIN" (*EE*, 96), he thinks he has found something consistent in Brutus's nature. The adverse judgment of his political actions then seems to follow, though we may have trouble seeing the connection between avarice and the killing of Caesar. Gibbon plays a character witness, but for the prosecution, so as to vindicate his own politics. Contrary to his principles, he imposes system on fact. Indeed, his claim in the "Hints" that avarice is perhaps the only permanent ruling passion may derive from his interest in the difficult case of Brutus, about whom the "Hints" contain several entries. Though these come after the reflections on the ruling passion, that may not represent the sequence of Gibbon's thinking. He may have decided that avarice was a permanently ruling passion while he had before him the example, with its tendentious application, of the patriot assassin.

Everywhere, then, is uncertainty. One last mystery is that of Louis XIV's political prisoner known as the man in the iron mask. The issue of character here is to one side, but not far. Voltaire had made the mystery current, and Gibbon seems to have thought he had an original solution, though it was in fact Voltaire's as well: the man in the iron mask was the illegitimate son of Louis XIII's queen, Anne of Austria, and Cardinal Mazarin.[13] This solution Gibbon embellishes with calculated intrigue, romantic speculation, and schoolboy titillation; all of it stemming from a perception of something "blind and unaccountable" in human behavior:

> The Civil Wars which raged during the Minority of Louis XIV, arose from the blind and unaccountable attachment of the Queen to Cardinal Mazarin, whom she obstinately supported against the universal Clamor of the French Nation. The Austrian Pride perhaps and the useful Merit of the Minister might determine the Queen to brave an insolent Opposition; but a connection formed by Policy might very easily terminate in Love. The necessity of business would engage that Princess in many a secret and midnight Conference with an Italian of an agreable Person, vigorous Constitution, loose Morals and artful Address. The amazing Anecdote hinted at, in the honest Memoirs of La Porte sufficiently prove that Mazarin was capable of employing every expedient to insinuate himself into *every part* of the Royal Family. (*EE*, 207)

Faced with blind and unaccountable attachments, the luminous historian-to-be flirts with secret history. His imagination heats up with thoughts of secret midnight meetings between the Queen of France and the vigorous, loose-living, artful and sinister Cardinal. And even if mystery is brought down to earth by some salacious italics (Mazarin was able to insinuate himself into *every part* of the royal family), there is no mistaking Gibbon's eager participation in the midnight doings of the great. The offspring of this clandestine union, like the minister with his black veil in Hawthorne's story, stands for what is hidden in human nature.

It is far from these early preoccupations to the *Decline and Fall*, with its countless characters. Yet Gibbon was never to become comfortable with the enigma of character. His task requires him to come to conclusive judgments, to sum up lives. In these moments, especially in the opening volumes, he frequently abandons caution and leans on ruling passions to do the job. But he uses the theory casually. Ruling passions rule in most unsystematic ways.

Sometimes they come in pairs. The ruling passions of Hadrian's soul "were curiosity and vanity" (I, 82); "cruelty and superstition were the ruling passions of the soul of Maximin" (II, 142). The passions that rule Hadrian and Maximin seem not to run in ordinary grooves: vanity aside, they are not passions like avarice, ambition, pride, or love of country. Curiosity, cruelty, and superstition might be assimilated to some superintending passion, but are not. Psychological reduction has yielded, imperceptibly, to plain description.

Ruling passions, which are, strictly speaking, immutable, sometimes develop over time. Commodus's "cruelty, which at first obeyed the dictates of others, degenerated into habit, and at length became the ruling passion of his soul" (I, 93); in the case of Christian converts, "the desire of perfection became the ruling passion of their soul" (II, 35). Ruling passions are sometimes the product of circumstance: Constantine's "boundless ambition, which, from the moment of his accepting the purple at York, appears as the ruling passion of his soul, may be justified by the dangers of his own situation, by the character of his rivals, by the consciousness of superior merit, and by the prospect that his success would enable him to restore peace and order to the distracted empire" (II, 215). Ruling passions even vary from moment to moment and clash with one another. Julian's ruling passion is first said to be "a devout and sincere attachment for the gods of Athens and Rome" (II, 456), then "superstition and vanity" (II, 476), and finally "the love of virtue and of fame" (II, 544).

These anxious, self-contradictory attempts to be conclusive give way to resigned skepticism by the time Gibbon meditates on the motives of the sixty emperors who pass in review, with such impersonal relentlessness, in Chapter 48. Philippicus and Anastasius II, Leo IV and Nicephorus I, Nicephorus II and Nicephorus III—all march by in single file, little more than names, ghostly replicas of who they once were. But what moved them? Their empire was in decay. Why did they want to rule? "The observation that, in every age and climate, ambition has prevailed with the same commanding energy may abate the surprise of a philosopher; but, while he condemns the vanity, he may search the motive, of this universal desire to obtain and hold the sceptre of dominion" (V, 259).

Gibbon might have settled on ambition as the ruling passion of the emperors, and seems close to doing so when he talks of its "commanding" energy. But in the face of such empty spectacle, the vanity that desires a throne loses its explanatory power as vanity, the passion, is absorbed in the vanity of human wishes. Neither the hope of fame nor the desire to do good inspired the emperors: "To the greater part of the Byzantine series we cannot reasonably ascribe the love of fame and of mankind." Nor could it have been happiness they sought. In the world of Alexander, which offered the prospect of great triumphs, hope could reasonably overbalance fear; but "the peculiar infelicity of the Byzantine princes exposed them to domestic perils, without affording any lively promise of foreign conquest" (V, 259). The ruling passion of emperors who sought neither fame nor the benefit of mankind and had no realistic hope of glory can only have been the passion to rule. Lost in a tautology, ruling passions are deprived of even their fragmentary power to explain.

Yet efforts to explain character, however haphazard or resigned, amount to no more than a summary shorthand that supplements, summarizes, or contradicts individual portraits. There may be ten thousand people who appear at least once in the history, hundreds with more than walk-on parts. To select any from the number is to abridge ruthlessly. Yet it is not arbitrary to pick Julian, Mahomet, and Theodora out of the crowd. All three are flesh and blood. Each fascinates Gibbon, and in each he sees something of himself, as he had in the gouty person of Septimius Severus. Their vitality comes from energies of projection.

There are also telling differences between them. In the portraits of Julian and of Mahomet, each on a large canvas, the desire to fix character in place runs counter to Gibbon's knowledge that nothing less resembles the person we were yesterday than the person we are today. Julian and Mahomet are both inscrutable, inconsistent, yet richly so: when Gibbon tries to rigidify them in terms of a ruling passion or passions, they resist with the tenacity of life itself. Theodora, by contrast, is easier to understand: she is unburdened by ruling passions and burdened only by passion itself. If her portrait is less complete than Julian's or even Mahomet's, it is also more human, less puzzling. Unlike the problematic cases of Julian and Mahomet, Theodora triumphs over any nagging worries about why she is what she is. She may be self-contradictory, but not inexplicable. She even wins Gibbon's compassion. In his portrait of Theodora, Gibbon in fact solved, without precisely knowing it, the enigma of character.

As warrior-sage, orator, judge, and satirist, Julian the Apostate represented much that Gibbon as emperor would have wanted to be; and had Julian been called to the vocation of the historian instead of to the throne, Gibbon believes he would have achieved the fame to which the historian himself aspired:

> Whatever had been his choice of life, by the force of intrepid courage, lively wit, and intense application, he would have obtained, or at least he would have deserved, the highest honours of his profession; and Julian might have raised himself to the rank of minister, or general, of the state in which he was born a private citizen. If the jealous caprice of power had disappointed his expectations, if he had prudently declined the paths of greatness, the employment of the same talents in studious solitude would have placed, beyond the reach of kings, his present happiness and his immortal fame. (II, 455)

Not only did Gibbon cherish his own studious solitude but, beyond the reach of kings, he lingered over the hope of immortal fame. When he came near to summing up his own character, at the end of the only draft of the autobiography he finished, he glanced at the "vanity of authors who presume the immortality of their name and writing" (*M*, 189), but only after admitting, as if in an aside, his own longing for a literary afterlife and the hope "that, one day his mind will be familiar to the grandchildren of those who are yet unborn" (*M*, 188). Perhaps Julian's fatal error was not to do what Gibbon had done—"prudently" decline the paths of greatness. In that "prudently," self-directed irony mixes with relief and self-congratulation. Sometimes seeing himself in Julian, both as type and antitype, Gibbon hovers ambiguously over questions about Julian's character that also implicate himself. His portrait combines hero worship and severity.

It is Julian the hero who dominates Chapter 22, the first of three devoted to him. His secret march to challenge the Emperor Constantius, with "three thousand brave and active volunteers, resolved, like their leader, to cast behind them every hope of a retreat," becomes a heroic, even a ritual sojourn in the wilderness; and our experience of it, a secret sharing. Julian disappears into the forest where the origins of the Danube are hidden. Yet we penetrate the darkness with special powers of seeing:

> At the head of this faithful band, he fearlessly plunged into the recesses of the Marcian or black forest, which conceals the sources of the Danube; and,

for many days, the fate of Julian was unknown to the world. The secrecy of his march, his diligence and vigour, surmounted every obstacle; he forced his way over mountains and morasses, occupied the bridges or swam the rivers, pursued his direct course, without reflecting whether he traversed the territory of the Romans or of the Barbarians, and at length emerged, between Ratisbon and Vienna, at the place where he designed to embark his troops on the Danube.   (II, 434)

After eleven days on the Danube, Julian attacks and conquers Sirmium, where he is welcomed like Christ entering Jerusalem: "he was received by the joyful acclamations of the army and people; who, crowned with flowers, and holding lighted tapers in their hands, conducted their acknowledged sovereign to his Imperial residence" (II, 436).

And even though Julian may have forgotten "the fundamental maxim of Aristotle that true virtue is placed at an equal distance between the opposite vices" (II, 446), excess in him is an excess of perfection: "he could employ his hand to write, his ear to listen, and his voice to dictate; and pursue at once three several trains of ideas without hesitation and without error" (II, 442). Of course, perfection may cancel itself in the eye of the beholder, and hints of the mock-heroic can be picked up here and there. But on a first reading, the all-compelling hero easily prevails: "even faction, and religious faction, was constrained to acknowledge the superiority of his genius, in peace as well as in war; and to confess, with a sigh, that the apostate Julian was a lover of his country, and that he deserved the empire of the world" (II, 455). With this panegyric, Chapter 22 comes to an end.

In Chapter 23, the hero looks less like a god and more like a fanatic. In part because of the storm that Chapters 15 and 16 had brought down on him, in part because of his reliance on different sources, Gibbon now subjects Julian to a thrashing.[14] It is here that the emperor is first discovered in the grip of ruling passions, more characteristically the mark of error than of virtue. His "devout and sincere attachment for the gods of Athens and Rome" (II, 456) becomes, twenty pages later, "superstition and vanity" (II, 476), and the hero is lost to the enthusiast: "he was heard to declare with the enthusiasm of a missionary that if he could render each individual richer than Midas, and every city greater than Babylon, he should not esteem himself the benefactor of mankind, unless, at the same time, he could reclaim his subjects from their impious revolt against the immortal gods" (II, 476).

And even though he checks the persecuting habits of his ministers, Julian cannot disclaim all responsibility for their outrages: "when the father of his country declares himself the leader of a faction, the licence of popular fury cannot easily be restrained nor consistently punished" (II, 495). During his reign, it is said that mangled bodies of Christians "were dragged through the streets, they were pierced (such was the universal rage) by the spits of cooks and the distaffs of enraged women; and that the entrails of Christian priests and virgins, after they had been tasted by those bloody fanatics, were mixed with barley, and contemptuously thrown to the unclean animals of the city" (II, 495–96). Not many episodes in the *Decline and Fall* rival in horror this anti-mass celebrated by bloody fanatics of Julian's brief reign. Is this what history owes his superior genius?

It would seem that no amount of rational explanation—whether Gibbon's change of sources or his desire to placate the orthodox— could account for the radical break between Chapters 22 and 23, between Julian the philosopher and Julian the pagan enthusiast. Might we then have misread Chapter 22, failing to notice sufficiently moments when the heroic shades into mock-heroic? For example, Gibbon comments that Julian took Plato at his word and "justly concluded" (II, 442) that if he wished to rule, it was his duty to become like a god:

Julian recollected with terror the observation of his master Plato, that the government of our flocks and herds is always committed to beings of a superior species; and that the conduct of nations requires and deserves the celestial powers of the Gods or of the Genii. From this principle he justly concluded that the man who presumes to reign should aspire to the perfection of the divine nature; that he should purify his soul from her mortal and terrestrial part; that he should extinguish his appetites, enlighten his understanding, regulate his passions, and subdue the wild beast which, according to the lively metaphor of Aristotle, seldom fails to ascend the throne of a despot. The throne of Julian, which the death of Constantius fixed on an independent basis, was the seat of reason, of virtue, and perhaps of vanity. (II, 441–42)

"Justly" concluded? If the conduct of nations requires more than human powers, then it is logically a just conclusion that the emperor should imitate the gods. But if this is all Platonic rapture, mixed with ascetic cant, the conclusion completes a foolishly false syllogism. In that case, Julian's hopes of purifying his soul from its mortal and terrestrial part look like fanaticism, hardly different from that of the monks who spent years on top of pillars in the desert. Perhaps the throne of Julian was more the seat of vanity than of either reason or virtue. Across the brightness of his heroism passes the shadow of a final "perhaps," which is the shadow of suspicion.

Should we then revise the claim that Julian's ritual march through the dark forests of the Danube and his entry into Sirmium prefigures Christ the warrior-king? Is the parallel intended as a mock-heroic commentary on the desire that Julian shares with Christ—namely, to be a god? Between the march and the entry into Sirmium, Julian sails a fleet of captured ships down the Danube, and crowds of onlookers spread the word of his coming: "The banks of the Danube were crowded on either side with spectators, who gazed on the military pomp, anticipated the importance of the event, and diffused through the adjacent country the fame of a young hero, who advanced with more than mortal speed at the head of the innumerable forces of the West" (II, 435). "With more than mortal speed"? Surely Gibbon laughs at the hero worship of the crowd. What of his own?

Certainly he knows that the motives of heroes may not bear too close examination or may lie beyond reach. When Julian is proclaimed emperor by his troops, he goes into seclusion, "overwhelmed with real or affected grief." Then Gibbon answers his own implicit question: "the grief of Julian could proceed only from his innocence; but his innocence must appear extremely doubtful in the eyes of those who have learned to suspect the motives and the professions of princes." A sense of the historian's role—to be judicious, to search out obscure motives, not to succumb to the lure of heroes, in short, to suspect the motives and professions of princes—has overtaken Gibbon's feelings. The historian knows what the hero-worshiper does not, that Julian was "susceptible of the various impressions of hope and fear, of gratitude and revenge, of duty and of ambition, of the love of fame and of the fear of reproach." Julian was a man like other great men and just as inscrutable: "But it is impossible for us to calculate the respective weight and operation of these sentiments; or to ascertain the principles of action, which might escape the observation, while they guided or rather impelled the steps, of Julian himself" (II, 426).

The hero acts from motives that escape his own understanding. It is even unclear whether he acts or is acted upon. Obscure and inaccessible principles of action guide or perhaps impel him. If they guide him, they are in his service; if they impel him, he is in theirs. Finally, Julian's vision of the "Genius of the empire," which he takes as an omen that he should accept the purple, moves Gibbon from skepticism to frank mistrust: "The conduct which disclaims the ordinary maxims of reason excites our suspicion and eludes our inquiry. Whenever the spirit of fanaticism, at once so credulous and so crafty, has insinuated itself into a noble mind, it insensibly corrodes the vital principles of virtue and veracity" (II, 427). Here in the midst of a chapter announcing Julian's greatness appears the fanatic of Chapter 23.

Still, it is not a mistake to call the Julian of Chapter 22 a hero, however strong these crosscurrents. "Intrepid courage, lively wit, and intense application" are his attributes; "he deserved the empire of the world" (II, 455). Gibbon's books cannot be made to balance. Brilliant, even moving, his version of Julian puzzles as much as it convinces, not only because Gibbon puzzled over the springs of behavior, but because he sought a finality that character does not afford. In Gibbon's presentation, Julian the fanatic contradicts rather than coexists with the hero.[15]

Chapter 24 then aims to reconcile the two Julians in action and, finally, in death. As he makes war on Persia, questions of character fade. His ascetic virtues, "never more conspicuously displayed than in the last, and most active, period of his life" (II, 527), become instruments of valor again, not the symptoms of monastic pathology. In the end, however, a Persian traitor persuades the emperor rashly to burn his ships behind him, leaving no alternative but "death or conquest" (II, 537), and Julian is killed in a skirmish in June 363. At this point, according to both classical and Christian lore, his deathbed ought to clarify his life. Instead, it perpetuates doubt, leaving the historian with one last, unresolved question.

On the one hand, Julian dies as convention requires, employing "the awful moments with the firm temper of a hero and a sage" (II, 542). His dying speech is a model of its kind: "I accept, as a favour of the gods, the mortal stroke that secures me from the danger of disgracing a character, which has hitherto been supported by virtue and fortitude. I die without remorse, as I have lived without guilt" (II, 543). On the other hand, perhaps he has anticipated and stage-managed this last scene, composing the oration ahead of time and thereby frustrating the historian's hope of sighting character in pure form. In a footnote that catches the reader's eye at the moment before the dying emperor speaks, Gibbon issues a warning: "The character and situation of Julian might countenance the suspicion that he had previously composed the elaborate oration which Ammianus heard and has transcribed" (II, 543n). If we have looked down to the footnote and then back to Julian's words, reading the oration becomes a continuous act of interrogation. We can neither believe nor disbelieve its spontaneity. Of course, we may not think it matters whether Julian composed the speech ahead of time. But if he did, a question has cut across the deathbed scene: Are we watching prepared drama or spontaneous life?[16]

After the frustrations of such self-conscious uncertainty, the parting effort to capture Julian under the glass of a ruling passion cannot help but seem futile. This Gibbon apparently realized, for a parenthetic hesitation intercepts any sense of finality: "Such was the end of that extraordinary man, in the thirty-second year of his age, after a reign of one year and about eight months from the death of Constantius. In his last moments he displayed, perhaps with some ostentation, the love of virtue and of fame which had been the ruling passions of his life" (II, 544). Julian's ruling passions, whether "a devout and sincere attachment for the gods of Athens and Rome" or "superstition and vanity," become in eulogy love of virtue and of fame. But even if we want to accept the claim not as contradiction but as revision, Gibbon steps aside, adding "perhaps with some ostentation." Ostentation implies vanity, and Julian dying nobly exhibits, perhaps, the vanity of the pagan fanatic.

Gibbon did not attempt another character portrait on so large a scale, for reasons that may be guessed. Having described Julian at the end of Chapter 22 as one who might have been great in studious solitude, Gibbon hesitates, characteristically, but here with a sense of what such hesitations and afterthoughts may reveal about the motives of the historian: "When we inspect, with minute or perhaps malevolent attention, the portrait of Julian, something seems wanting to the grace and perfection of the whole figure. His genius was less powerful and sublime than that of Caesar; nor did he possess the consummate prudence of Augustus. The virtues of Trajan appear more steady and natural, and the philosophy of Marcus is more simple and consistent" (II, 455). If heroism requires perfection in all things, then someone can always be found who exceeds this hero or that one in this or that quality, and the historian's duty of judiciousness will always work to the detriment of heroes, as it does when Gibbon finds himself wondering whether Julian's grief was real or affected on being proclaimed emperor. Perhaps such striving to find perfection, and hence such minute attention, stems from envy or malevolence. When the study of character involves minute attention—when, in Julian's case, Gibbon looks closely at the hero—disappointment cannot help but follow, being a disappointment that is courted. Prudent self-interest dictates a less intense scrutiny.

Though he dared risk so close an encounter with character only once, the pattern of Gibbon's dealings with Julian repeats itself when he comes to Mahomet, another "extraordinary man" (V, 400) who takes up most of Chapter 50,[17] and in whom he again sees something of his own reflected image. Having imagined Julian as a solitary scholar in the study, now Gibbon remarks on Mahomet's rare "powers of eloquence" (V, 358) and defends him against charges that the Koran was not the prophet's own, just as he had defended himself against charges that the *Decline and Fall* was a "servile plagiarism":[18] "the enemies of Mahomet have named the Jew, the Persian, and the Syrian monk, whom they accuse of lending their secret aid to the composition of the Koran" (V, 359). It is in denying this charge that Gibbon names the school of his own studies: "Conversation enriches the understanding, but solitude is the school of genius; and the uniformity of a work denotes the hand of a single artist" (V, 359–60). This asserts, by indirection, what he had asserted directly elsewhere: the integrity of the *Decline and Fall*.[19] Having gone to the school of genius, both the historian of the Roman Empire and the prophet of Islam are victims of envy and malice.

Yet an analogy between the Koran and the *Decline and Fall* is extremely strange—if possible, even more so than Gibbon's imagining himself, fat, timid, and awkward, in the person of Julian the warrior-sage. Beneath the extravagance of the impersonations lies

Gibbon's aptitude at role-playing and even, perhaps, a sense of his own dividedness, for the portrait of Mahomet, like that of Julian, breaks in two.[20] On the one hand, Islam appeals to Gibbon deeply, and he expresses a sense of careful but unfeigned rapture at the sublime monotheism of the Koran (V, 361). Like Julian, Mahomet is a pagan-hero. On the other hand, as Gibbon looks more closely at the sacred text of Islam, he discovers, with the eyes of a European rationalist, irrational babble. Like Julian, Mahomet is a fanatic; like Julian, he inspires the worst in his followers. Each is a divided character. If Julian mixes heroism and mock heroism, ostentation and the love of virtue, asceticism and superstition, genius and doubtful judgment, all producing not one but a divided image, Mahomet mixes genius, "incoherent rhapsody" (V, 366), farce, asceticism, and lust, producing again not one but a divided image and an unanswerable question: "whether the title of enthusiast or impostor more properly belongs to that extraordinary man" (V, 400).[21]

In Mahomet the hero, Gibbon discovers a fellow satirist of Christianity: "the religions of the world were guilty, at least in the eyes of the prophet, of giving sons, or daughters, or companions, to the supreme God" (V, 360). The eyes of the prophet are also those of the historian, who shelters his unitarianism under the prophet's rational and sublime utterance:

The creed of Mahomet is free from suspicion or ambiguity; and the Koran is a glorious testimony to the unity of God. The prophet of Mecca rejected the worship of idols and men, of stars and planets, on the rational principle that whatever rises must set, that whatever is born must die, that whatever is corruptible must decay and perish. In the author of the universe, his rational enthusiasm confessed and adored an infinite and eternal being, without form or place, without issue or similitude, present to our most secret thoughts, existing by the necessity of his own nature, and deriving from himself all moral and intellectual perfection. These sublime truths, thus announced in the language of the prophet, are firmly held by his disciples, and defined with metaphysical precision by the interpreters of the Koran. A philosophic Atheist might subscribe the popular creed of the Mahometans: a creed too sublime perhaps for our present faculties. (V, 361–62)

Of course it is never safe, in matters of belief, to assume that Gibbon means everything he says, and his subsequent treatment of the Koran, like his version of Julian as fanatic, sends the reader back to look for a misreading. For example, are the students of the Koran who interpret its gospel with metaphysical precision not Islamic schoolmen, analyzing and dividing up the unanalyzable unity of God? Is a creed too sublime for our present faculties not too vaporously sublime to be taken seriously? Yet even if the answer to these questions is yes, Islam is not, like Christianity, absurd: it does not manufacture sons, daughters, or companions of the supreme God. When Gibbon says the Koran is a glorious testimony to the unity of God, I think he means what he says.

But the Koran is also full of nonsense and the prophet full of cant. "In the spirit of enthusiasm or vanity"—"enthusiasm" here implying sincerity—Mahomet "audaciously challenges both men and angels to imitate the beauties of a single page, and presumes to assert that God alone could dictate this incomparable performance" (V, 365–66). In the face of this lordly presumption, Gibbon reverts to his character as the European infidel:

This argument is most powerfully addressed to a devout Arabian, whose mind is attuned to faith and rapture, whose ear is delighted by the music of sounds, and whose ignorance is incapable of comparing the productions of human genius. The harmony and copiousness of style will not reach, in a version, the European infidel; he will peruse, with impatience, the endless incoherent rhapsody of fable, and precept, and declamation, which seldom excites a sentiment or an idea, which sometimes crawls in the dust and is sometimes lost in the clouds. (V, 366)

The European infidel, now an enemy equally to the prophet and to Christianity, replaces Mahomet the sublime monotheist with the religious charlatan. Mahomet's followers, like Julian's, go much farther than their leader, corrupting the sublimity of Islam into low farce. They insist on what Mahomet steered away from claiming—his power of performing miracles, including many that are ludicrous: "They believe or affirm that trees went forth to meet him; that he was saluted by stones; that water gushed from his fingers; that he fed the hungry, cured the sick, and raised the dead; that a beam groaned to him; that a camel complained to him; that a shoulder of mutton informed him of its being poisoned; and that both animate and inanimate nature were equally subject to the apostle of God" (V, 367). They celebrate his enormous, indeed undying, potency, as Gibbon reports in a deadpan footnote: "Al Jannabi . . . records his own testimony that he surpassed all men in conjugal vigour; and Abulfeda mentions the exclamation of Ali, who washed his body after his death, 'O propheta, certe penis tuus caelum versus erectus est'" (V, 404n). And they insist, when he dies, that he is not dead. "How can he be dead, our witness, our intercessor, our mediator with God? By God, he is not dead; like Moses and Jesus, he is wrapt in a holy trance, and speedily will he return to his faithful people" (V, 399). But perhaps this is a modest claim: after all, in death, the prophet's penis still points toward the heavens. If Julian was in some part to blame for the excesses of his followers, is Mahomet not in part to blame for the follies of his?

Ultimately, the portrait of Mahomet wavers more even than that of Julian, for at the end Gibbon declines to summarize it. He knows what is expected, and he knows his portrait has left open the critical question of whether the prophet was an "enthusiast" or "impostor": "At the conclusion of the life of Mahomet, it may perhaps be expected that I should balance his faults and virtues, that I should decide whether the title of enthusiast or impostor more properly belongs to that extraordinary man." But Gibbon steps aside: "Had I been intimately conversant with the son of Abdallah, the task would still be difficult, and the success uncertain: at the distance of twelve centuries, I darkly contemplate his shade through a cloud of religious incense; and, could I truly delineate the portrait of an hour, the fleeting resemblance would not equally apply to the solitary of mount Hera, to the preacher of Mecca, and to the conqueror of Arabia" (V, 400). Almost automatically, in conditions of such uncertainty, there comes a final gesture toward ruling passions: "Of his last years, ambition was the ruling passion" (V, 401). Even if that were true, it would not settle the main question.

When Gibbon writes, "could I truly delineate the portrait of an hour, the fleeting resemblance would not equally apply to the solitary of mount Hera, to the preacher of Mecca, and to the conqueror of Arabia" (V, 400), he seems to remember some lines of Pope:

> Come then, the colours and the ground prepare!
> Dip in the Rainbow, trick her off in Air,
> Chuse a firm Cloud, before it fall, and in it
> Catch, ere she change, the Cynthia of this minute.[22]

The Mahomet of an hour, the Cynthia of a minute, each is transient as a cloud. But the mood of Pope's poem on the characters of women differs radically from Gibbon's in his dealings with Julian and Mahomet. However mysterious a creature woman is, the mystery does not generate anxiety but puzzlement or, at best, appreciation. That is the case, also, with Gibbon's brilliant and mercurial Theodora.

Theodora is a woman. In the epistle on the characters of women, unlike that on the characters of men, Pope feels no obligation to locate the single passion of Narcissa or Flavia or Atossa. If men have many ruling passions, women have perhaps only two, "the Love of Pleasure, and the Love of Sway," and in the long run Pope surrenders the ruling passion as a fiction: "believe me, good as well as ill, / Woman's at best a Contradiction still."[23] Women have a license, which men do not, to contradict themselves. If Theodora, first a sexually ravenous prostitute, then Justinian's chaste empress, is inconsistent, she accommodates the male view of her sex. She also accommodates male fantasies of women as both lustful monsters and chaste mothers. A deeper consistency underlies her inconsistency: she stands for womanly contradictions as they exist in the imagination of men. This view of women accidentally yields a flexible version of human character.

Moreover, as an actress used to playing roles, Theodora appeals to the historian who had been both Farmer Gibbon and the captain of the Hampshire militia. Like her womanhood, her talent as an actress produces consistent inconsistency. The sexual extravagance of her early years is both stagy and displayed on stage: "The satirical historian [Procopius] has not blushed to describe the naked scenes which Theodora was not ashamed to exhibit in the theatre" (IV, 227), and blending prudence with prurience, Gibbon drops the curtain on her arts in his famous appeal to "the obscurity of a learned language." Even in her nakedness, Theodora exhibits not herself but theatrical scenes. And when she turns her attention to the destiny she had foreseen in a vision—that of becoming "the spouse of a potent monarch" (IV, 228)—she settles on a new part that momentarily identifies her as yet another solitary: "Conscious of her approaching greatness, she returned from Paphlagonia to Constantinople; assumed, like a skilful actress, a more decent character; relieved her poverty by the laudable industry of spinning wool; and affected a life of chastity and solitude in a small house, which she afterwards changed into a magnificent temple" (IV, 228–29).

What begins as acting and affectation, however, may become ingrained, indistinguishable from the real thing: "Her chastity, from the moment of her union with Justinian, is founded on the silence of her implacable enemies" (IV, 232). Like the happy hypocrite of Beerbohm's fable, whose ugly face becomes identical with his beautiful mask, Theodora reenacts herself.[24] Questions such as the one Gibbon posed about Julian's speech, whether it was spontaneous or prepared, do not touch her. In Theodora, spontaneity and calculation are the same.

Her unpredictable and inconsistent ways come from an ability to assume a role at will: when "the most illustrious personages of the state were crowded into a dark and sultry antichamber, and when at last, after tedious attendance, they were admitted to kiss the feet of Theodora, they experienced, as her humour might suggest, the silent arrogance of an empress or the capricious levity of a comedian" (IV, 231). The role of actress embraces both empress and comedian, and the arrogance of the empress reflects her talent at playing an imperial part. When she dies, her loss is "deplored by her husband, who, in the room of a theatrical prostitute, might have selected the purest and most noble virgin of the East" (IV, 233). But Theodora is not just a prostitute: she comprehends, theatrically, both prostitute and virgin. In her staginess Gibbon has stumbled on a metaphor of self that dissolves the paradox of character.[25]

The metaphor, freeing him from anxieties of having to judge, releases a current of human feeling. For all her ferocious sexuality and imperial cruelty, Theodora is remarkably sympathetic. Though her "strange elevation cannot be applauded as the triumph of female virtue" (IV, 226), Gibbon mistrusts those "who believe that the female mind is totally depraved by the loss of chastity" and who therefore "eagerly listen to all the invectives of private envy or popular resentment, which have dissembled the virtues of Theodora, exaggerated her vices, and condemned with rigour the venal or voluntary sins of the youthful harlot" (IV, 230). He is touched by "the sympathy of the empress for her less fortunate sisters, who had been seduced or compelled to embrace the trade of prostitution," even though truth and a sense of humor require him to report that Theodora's less fortunate sisters have mixed feelings when they find themselves collected together in a monastery from the streets and brothels of Constantinople and "devoted to perpetual confinement": "the despair of some, who threw themselves headlong into the sea, was lost in the gratitude of the penitents, who had been delivered from sin and misery by their generous benefactress." Gibbon is also touched by Theodora's disappointment at never having had a son by her "potent" monarch and having lost an infant daughter: "The wishes and prayers of Theodora could never obtain the blessing of a lawful son, and she buried an infant daughter, the sole offspring of her marriage" (IV, 232). Burying an infant daughter, wishing and praying for a son, Theodora assumes the burden of being the woman she was.

When she dies, it is for the rarest of reasons in the *Decline and Fall*—an identifiable, natural cause: "At length, in the twenty-fourth year of her marriage, and the twenty-second of her reign, she was consumed by a cancer" (IV, 233). When people die naturally in the *Decline and Fall*, the causes are usually lost to history, anonymous, impersonal. When Justinian dies three chapters later, Gibbon merely removes him from the world's stage: "If the emperor could rejoice in the death of Belisarius, he enjoyed the base satisfaction only eight months, the last period of a reign of thirty-eight and a life of eighty-three years" (IV, 459). Justinian becomes a historical statistic, dying 14 November 565, of unspecified causes. Perhaps it was a "pain in his head" (IV, 457) that killed him, but we do not know for certain. Otherwise, death in the *Decline and Fall*, if noticed at all, usually happens on the battlefield or by murder, by torture, by poison. The cancer that kills Theodora affirms, by consuming her, that she was flesh and blood. In the essay on the characters of women, Pope attributes to Martha Blount a memorable line, "Nothing so true as what you once let fall, / 'Most Women have no Characters at all.' "[26] This sounds dismissive, but to have no character could mean to be a human being—unpredictable, unclassifiable, inconsistent, oneself. By not giving Theodora a character, by letting her be her own self-contradictory person, Gibbon creates a portrait unshadowed by efforts to get at some missing, essential truth behind the veil. When he tried to write his autobiography, however, old anxieties surfaced to trouble him again.

SEVEN

THE CHARACTER OF A HISTORIAN

On 8 May 1788, Gibbon's publisher, Thomas Cadell, gave a party for him, having postponed publication of the final volumes of the *Decline and Fall* to coincide with the author's fifty-first birthday: "the double festival was celebrated by a chearful litterary dinner at Cadell's house; and I seemed to blush while they read an elegant compliment from Mr. Hayley whose poetical talent had more than once been employed in the praise of his friend" (*M*, 182). The party must have had a valedictory air, befitting the completion of so long, difficult, and successful an enterprise. Describing it, Gibbon sees himself both from within and from without. Leaving the *Decline and Fall* behind not only means deliverance from and of his burden, it also means he has fixed himself publicly in his role—historian of the Roman Empire. He becomes the object of all eyes, and his seeing merges with that of others: "I seemed to blush." He is Hayley's friend, but the honor lies more with the poet, perceived as friend of the historian Gibbon, who is celebrated in Hayley's verses as the peer of Newton and of Shakespeare (*MW*, I, 173–74n).

The company is otherwise an anonymous crowd; we know it was Cadell's party but never learn who "they" are. The reading of Hayley's poetical tribute has a curious choral aspect—"they read an elegant compliment from Mr. Hayley"—as separate voices merge into a single voice of praise. But what of the "I" who blushed, or seemed to? If the double festival celebrates the identification of writer and work, Gibbon's effort to write an autobiography, which occupied him on and off for the rest of his life, displays both his willing acceptance of that identification and another, incompatible effort to locate that "I" who seems to blush, hidden by embarrassment from the world.

Like the *Decline and Fall*, the autobiography wavers between the desire to fix character in place and the recognition that it is always subject to revision. The autobiography also aspires to a finished plot with a beginning, middle, end, and a resulting sense of completeness. Yet because it is an autobiography, a satisfactory plot cannot be found, and Gibbon eventually reaches some awareness of that truth, an awareness that is painfully achieved.

The fact that Gibbon never completed the enterprise to his own satisfaction is a historical orphan still waiting to be adequately noticed. Despite John Murray's edition of its six drafts, known for convenience as *A* through *F*, the autobiography lives on in the only way it could, as a single, coherent piece of writing. This is thanks first of all to the brilliant, though high-handed, editorial work of Sheffield, whose composite version appeared in the *Miscellaneous Works* of 1796; and, more recently, to the scholarship of Georges A. Bonnard, whose 1966 edition proceeds on the same recognition of the need for an accessible text. George Saintsbury grumbled in 1898 that "the fussy fidelity of modern literary methods will probably try in vain to substitute a chaos of rough drafts" (*M*, xiii n) for the Sheffield version. But Saintsbury need not have worried. Almost no one would willingly sacrifice the composite version. Still, the truth is that Gibbon produced little more than a chaos of rough drafts. For the student either of his life or of autobiography as a genre, this chaos is more fertile than a finished text could have been.[1]

Gibbon did not know he was undertaking an "autobiography," for the word did not then exist.[2] I have used it to describe his enterprise because, along with Rousseau, Gibbon brought the form as we know it into being, and because he found no wholly satisfactory title for it himself. At the same time, it would have surprised and probably alarmed him to learn he was engaged in a project with scarcely a precedent. When, in his second draft, he ransacks the past for predecessors, he produces a large, unruly list:

The authority of my masters, of the grave Thuanus and the philosophic Hume, might be sufficient to justify my design; but it would not be difficult to produce a long list of ancients and moderns who, in various forms, have exhibited their own portraits. . . . The lives of the younger Pliny, of Petrarch, and of Erasmus are expressed in the Epistles which they themselves have given to the World; the Essays of Montaigne and Sir William Temple bring us home to the houses and bosoms of the authors; we smile without contempt at the headstrong passions of Benvenuto Cellini, and the gay follies of Colley Cibber. The confessions of St. Austin and Rousseau disclose the secrets of the human heart; the Commentaries of the learned Huet have survived his Evangelical demonstration; and the Memoirs of Goldoni are more truly dramatic than his Italian comedies. The Heretic and the Churchman are strongly marked in the characters and fortunes of Whiston and Bishop Newton; and even the dullness of Michael de Marolles and Antony Wood acquires some value from the faithful representation of men and manners. (*B*, 104–5)

What stands out in this catalogue is that Gibbon did not really know what he was trying to do, even if he thought he knew what he was not trying to do: though Augustine is present, the names of more recent and less respectable spiritual autobiographers like Bunyan are conspicuously absent.[3] Those who do appear are a mixed lot, and Gibbon's two acknowledged masters, Thuanus and Hume, have little in common as autobiographers, although they shared with Gibbon a vocation as historians and the habit of offending authority. Jacques-Auguste de Thou (1553–1617) had attached to his history of contemporary France a self-justifying memoir that he may not have written himself.[4] Hume had written a very short, deceptively plain autobiographical essay, intended as a preface to a posthumous collection of his work and published in 1777, the year after his death.[5] Otherwise Gibbon lumps together epistles, essays, memoirs, Augustine's devotional exercise, and Rousseau's secular confessions. He does not recognize that Rousseau has radically broken with the past. Gibbon starts with an accurate, if half-formed, sense of moving about in the dark.

Of the questions that touch any autobiography, several have a special bearing on Gibbon's project. In brief, they are: What should it be called? Where and how should it begin? How should it end? And, finally, how can the autobiographer catch the essence of a life?

These are all extremely vexing questions. Should a life of oneself be called a confession? An apology? A memoir? The time had not yet come when, the imaginative and fictional content of autobiographical performances having been conceded, a writer could resort to inventive naming. The thing had somehow to be described by its name. Next, how should the autobiographer emerge on stage? In the corresponding question, how, possibly, should he exit? Louis Marin writes: "If autobiography means the writing of one's *own* life and of its outstanding events, this writing can only begin and end with two statements which are, strictly speaking, unutterable: 'I was born,' and 'I died,' and can only be constituted by a *single* infinitely reflexive statement: 'I write that I write that . . . *ad infinitum* my own life.'"[6] Getting born is difficult; dying, impossible. Augustine had solved the problem of endings by shifting the field of discourse outside the temporal realm; Rousseau (though unaware that he was at an ending), by recounting a public reading from his own narrative, thereby figuring Marin's infinitely reflexive statement. Autobiographical beginnings and endings mirror conditions of incomplete knowledge. How, then, to know the essence of oneself? I do not remember my birth. I do not know how I will behave on some future deathbed. If that knowledge is required for self-knowledge, then no summary judgment can be made. Am I, as autobiographer, the best judge of what passion most rules me—assuming that ruling passions exist? These questions tangled Gibbon, like Laocoön, in their embrace.

Autobiographical projects entail what Louis A. Renza calls "split intentionality," as the domains of public and private, of third person and first person come into perpetual collision. This means "that the project of writing about oneself to oneself is always at the beginning, is always propaedeutic in structure, and is therefore prone to an obsessive concern with method as well as a 'stuttering,' fragmented narrative appearance."[7] And in the chaos of its six drafts, no other autobiographical writing, unless we put *Tristram Shandy* in that class, better displays the conditions that limit autobiographical projects than Gibbon's. Its very incompleteness is literally that of a project always being begun again, displaying an obsessive concern with method (broadly defined) and a fragmented narrative structure.

A summary of the drafts will open up this labyrinth:

A: 39 manuscript pages, in quarto, written late in 1788 or early in 1789; consisting almost entirely of a preliminary account of Gibbon's family, though the headnote to this fragmentary "Chapter I" announces that it will take in as well "My birth in the year 1737," "My infancy," "My first education and studies." It breaks off abruptly with a sketch of William Law, spiritual advisor to Gibbon's Aunt Hester. Five pages of the original manuscript are missing.

B: 72 manuscript pages, in quarto, written soon and perhaps immediately after *A*; not divided into chapters, it ends in 1764, just before Gibbon leaves Lausanne for the trip to Italy that will result in the *Decline and Fall*.

C: 41 manuscript pages, in folio, written late in 1789 and early in 1790; divided into three "Sections," it ends in 1772 (early in Section III), with Gibbon having moved from Buriton to London after his father's death and preparing to write the *Decline and Fall*.

D: 13 manuscript pages, in folio, perhaps written late in 1790 and early in 1791; a quick sketch, it ends, like *C*, with Gibbon's move to London but also glances ahead in a final marginal notation to "Pecuniary affairs, A.D. 1770–1783."

E: 19 manuscript pages, in folio, dated "March 2, 1791"; the most complete of the drafts, not divided into chapters but with marginal notations and, for the first time, a numbered set of footnotes added sometime after 2 March 1791; it brings Gibbon's life approximately up to the time of writing, closing with premonitions of mortality.

F: 41 manuscript pages, in folio, written in 1792–93; in three chapters (the third perhaps incomplete), with numbered footnotes and 7 pages, on different paper, of additional notes; it ends with Gibbon's conversion and departure from Oxford in June 1753.

Would Gibbon have been able to complete the task? Though *F* has the appearance of trying to be a finished work, he wrote gloomily to Sheffield on 6 January 1793, while working on this last draft, "Of *the Memoirs* little has been done, and with that little I am not satisfied: they must be postponed till a mature season, and I much doubt whether the book and the author can ever see the light at the same time" (*L*, III, 312). Sheffield wrote back on 23 January: "I shall never consent to your dropping the Memoirs. Keep that work always going; but you should decide whether the book and the author are to see the light together, because it might be differently filled up according to that decision. A man may state many things in a posthumous work, that he might not in another; the latter often checks the introduction of many curious thoughts and facts."[8]

Bonnard thinks that "this may well have encouraged Gibbon to persist" (*M*, xxx). On the other hand, it may also have encouraged him to let the task go, by default, to his posthumous editor.[9] He was, after all, so uncomfortable with curious thoughts and facts about himself that in *F* he declined "to expatiate on so disgusting a topic" as the disorders of his childhood or to "imitate the naked frankness of Montagne, who exposes all the symptoms of his malady, and the operation of each dose of physic on his nerves and bowels" (*F*, 37). And in January 1793, Gibbon would have been acutely conscious that the most curious fact about himself was the huge swelling in his groin. In any event, when Sheffield's wife died in the spring, Gibbon left Lausanne to be with his friend in England, taking all the drafts with him. In August he wrote his distant cousin, the genealogist Samuel Egerton Brydges, with inquiries about their common ancestry.[10] By November he was ill. His death in January 1794 spared him any further struggles with autobiography.

Of these, finding a satisfactory title probably cost the least effort. Titles, autobiographical or otherwise, are often provisional until the end, often the last contrivance, hopeful or desperate, of an exhausted author. Still Gibbon's uncertainties about a title anticipate substantive problems. In particular, was this to be a narrative from without or from within? A split intentionality makes itself felt as he puts pen to paper. The first page of *A* is headed "Memoirs of My Own Life." But a preceding title page, probably intended as posthumous, reads: "The Memoirs of the Life of Edward Gibbon with Various Observations and Excursions by Himself." Here Gibbon remembers the case of Hume, who had called the short piece intended as a posthumous preface to his works, "My Own Life." In the event, "My Own Life" appeared separately with a title page evidently supplied by the publisher, William Strahan: *The Life of David Hume, Esq. Written by Himself.* Hume's autobiography came into the world endowed by his death with a duality of reference that is healing, not divisive: the title page fixes the life of the autobiography. Gibbon wonders, then, if Hume's solution will work for him, either as a stratagem of control or in case his own work also turns out to be posthumous.

This obligation to Hume becomes still clearer in *B*, for which Gibbon borrows the heading "My Own Life" and in which he acknowledges Hume as one of his masters. But in *B* no title page covers the awkwardness of autobiographical incompleteness. In the title of *C*, Gibbon abandons Hume's view from the inside in favor of the third person: "Memoirs of the Life and Writings of Edward Gibbon." In *D* he plunges in without benefit of a title. In *E* he goes back to "My Own Life." In *F* once again he does without a title. These comings and goings between the assertively possessive selfhood of "My Own Life," the cool objectivity of the third person, and the puzzlement or indifference of the untitled versions suggest Gibbon could never have found a good solution. To the problem of split intentionality, which he intuitively recognizes, is added the need to describe accurately what he is about to write. He could not recognize that a solution lay in a title that would seem to heal, by an act of imagination, the division between the self of ordinary experience and the other self of any autobiographical project. That knowledge, like the term "autobiography," lay ahead.

Title or no title, how to start? In the first sentence of *A*, Gibbon affects the pose of a man of leisure, at ease, looking backward: "In the fifty-second year of my age, after the completion of a toilsome and successful work, I now propose to employ some moments of my leisure in reviewing the simple transactions of a private and litterary life." Nothing could be more studiously casual, as Gibbon aims to catch himself in the elegant pose of a successful writer now at rest, intending to spend a few moments of leisure in a new but undemanding task, which he plans to execute in a "simple and familiar style," as befits the narrative of a "simple" life. Yet Gibbon has a premonition of the autobiographer's dilemma of whether or not to publish his story: "if these sheets are communicated to some discreet and indulgent friends, they will be secreted from the public eye till the author shall be removed from the reach of criticism or ridicule" (*A*, 353). On the one hand, he proposes private amusement for himself and a few friends in an easy and familiar style; on the other, he remembers the public eye. The ideal of an easy and familiar style fits the first-person "Memoirs of My Own Life"; the thought of publishing posthumously lies behind the third-person

"Memoirs of the Life of Edward Gibbon with Various Observations and Excursions by Himself."

What is more, the substance of *A*, whatever Gibbon may have intended in ease and familiarity, subordinates the private to the public image: he entangles himself in the red tape of genealogy and finally gives up altogether, perhaps even before he has managed formally to get himself born. That "perhaps" is necessary because of the five-page lacuna in the manuscript. Page 24 (the numbering is Gibbon's own) gives an account of Gibbon's grandfather and his disastrous financial involvement with the South Sea Bubble. Pages 25–30 are missing. Page 31 picks up after the death of Gibbon's mother, with the scene between young Edward and his father: "he saw me after the fatal event—the awful silence, the room hung with black, the midday tapers, his sighs and tears, his praises of my mother, whom he called a Saint in Heaven" (*A*, 378). Did Gibbon bring himself officially into existence in the space of the lacuna; or, more likely, finding himself with an indelible memory, did he merely incorporate it in the manuscript while describing his parents? And did he include something in those five pages that he did not want the world to see? The missing pages have the aura of lost beginnings.

In *B* Gibbon begins with a new problem: does he dare write an autobiography at all? Having realized in *A* that "pride of ancestry" (*A*, 354) is despised by philosophers (especially those of "plebeian" birth), if not by ordinary mortals, now he fears being thought vain: "A sincere and simple narrative of my own life may amuse some of my leisure hours, but it will expose me, and perhaps with justice, to the imputation of vanity." He worries the question nervously ("the author of an important and successful work may hope without presumption that he is not totally indifferent to his numerous readers" [*B*, 104]), then goes on to the eclectic roll call of his predecessors in autobiography, ending with a final spasm of self-vindication: "That I am the equal or superior of some of these Biographers the efforts of modesty or affectation cannot force me to dissemble." Having warded off charges of vanity, Gibbon feels free at last to bring himself into being: "I was born at Putney, in the County of Surrey, the twenty-seventh of April, OS., (the eighth of May, NS.), in the year one thousand seven hundred and thirty-seven; the first child of the marriage of Edward Gibbon, Esq., and of Judith

Porten" (*B*, 105). Then he dispatches his ancestry in a few pages and moves on to a leisurely account of his life before he left Lausanne for Italy in 1764. At this point in the writing, he received news that Deyverdun had died in Aix-les-Bains, and this put a stop to his work. When he returned to it, he went back to the start.

In *C* Gibbon senses the irresolution that has dogged his efforts and, as if to limit the autobiographical hazard of being always at a beginning, delivers himself in the first sentence. At the same time, cutting across this decisive gesture is an instinct for endless, irresolute tinkering with detail: "I was born the twenty-seventh of April, O.S. (the eighth of May, N.S.), in the year one thousand seven hundred and thirty-seven, the first child of the marriage of Edward Gibbon, Esqre, and of Judith Porten, his first wife." In *B* he had been born "at Putney." Here his birthplace drops into the fussy sentence that follows: "The place of my nativity is Putney, in the county of Surry, a pleasant village on the banks of the Thames, about four miles from London" (*C*, 211). To the information in *B* that he was the child of Judith Porten he adds the information that she was his father's first wife. These small revisions result more from anxiety than from reflective judgment, but that is why they are important. Revisions for their own sake, they are not merely accidental. The underlying source of the anxiety will emerge with more clarity in *F*.

In *D* and *E* Gibbon continues to worry about how to announce his birth. In *D*, as in *C*, it happens in the opening sentence, but he relegates the date to the margins, restores Putney to its original place (as in *B*), and places himself among a family of lost siblings: "I was born at Putney, in the County of Surry, of the marriage of Edward Gibbon, Esqre, and his first wife, Judith Porten; and was the eldest of their seven children, all of whom, except myself, died in their infancy" (*D*, 391). His brothers and his sister having died, Gibbon's life has the appearance of a mysteriously lucky accident.[11] In *E*—the only draft that he managed to bring up to the present—he gives the first paragraph to his ancestors, the second to himself: "I was born at his house [i.e., his father's house] at Putney, in Surry, the eldest child of his marriage, a marriage of inclination, with Judith Porten." Dates are once again in the margin, and the siblings who did not survive infancy occupy, with their mother, another sentence

132

that segregates death from life: "My five brothers and my sister all died in their infancy, and the premature decease of my mother (1746) left her fond husband a disconsolate widower" (*E*, 295). The lucky accident of survival matters less than the union of which Gibbon was born, "a marriage of inclination." Being the child of a love match is what counts. Gibbon searches for the meaning of his birth.

Finally, in *F*, he devotes a first chapter to his ancestors, this time without deferential bowing to philosophers who disdain pedigree. This first chapter may contain something from the missing pages of *A*, for Gibbon draws at times on his first draft and possibly does so when he looks forward, with an anticipatory glance, to his birth: "The union to which I owe my birth was a marriage of inclination and esteem" (*F*, 19). At the same time, this "marriage of inclination and esteem" revises *E*'s "marriage of inclination." Perhaps Gibbon wants to acquit his father of excessive inclination, a motive that may even lie behind the actual birth announcement in *F*, coming at the start of Chapter II: "I was born at Putney in Surry, the twenty-seventh of April. O.S., the eighth of May. N.S., in the year one thousand seven hundred and thirty-seven, within a twelfmonth of my father's marriage with Judith Porten, his first wife" (*F*, 28)— within twelve months but not within nine months of the marriage, lest anyone suppose that Edward Gibbon Sr.'s inclination had outrun his esteem. If this interpretation seems to wrench a simple statement into false significance, Gibbon bears some of the blame with his everlasting tinkering. What can he be getting at? Never has a birth announcement been so bedeviled (Tristram Shandy's again excepted) by the nervous tics of the person being born.

An answer surfaces a few pages later in *F*, for what Gibbon has wanted, it now becomes clear, is to capture accurately, completely, beyond any shadow of uncertainty, the origins of self. The fidgety changing of this and that detail in his birth announcements and the elaborate genealogy of the first draft have been gestures in that direction. He wants an autobiography that presents the entire story of himself, from the beginning, as the *Decline and Fall* had presented the entire story of Rome from the age of the Antonines. In the history he had arbitrarily solved the question of where to begin—arbitrarily and successfully, his own hindsight aside. How to achieve the same effect in his own history? That desire, in *F*, leads to an extraordinary and symptomatic passage, almost unanticipated in the earlier drafts, where Gibbon tries to recover his origins by going back to the womb, even to the moment of his own conception.

In *B* he had attributed a vague consciousness to life in the womb: "The first moment of animal life may be dated from the first pulsation of the heart in the human fœtus"; we pass nine months "in a dark and watery prison." If it is a prison, we should be conscious of its enclosing us. But in fact life in this prison is not really living at all. These nine months and the years of early infancy "must be subtracted from the period of our rational existence," and in this second draft Gibbon reluctantly concedes to oblivion what he cannot recall: "When I strive to ascend into the night and oblivion of infancy, the most early circumstance which I can connect with any known æra is my father's contest and election for Southampton. At that time (1740) I was about three years of age" (*B*, 113). The energy of his effort to recover events of his earliest childhood, as he strives to see or, as he says, to ascend into the doubly dark "night and oblivion" of infancy, indicates how reluctantly he concedes the case. But what he concedes, reluctantly or not, in *B*, he does not concede in *F*.

Now he tries somehow to recover his infancy and even his prenatal life. What has obstructed his efforts to get himself born is the lack of continuity in memory between the autobiographical narrator and the self that had come into being over fifty years before. In *F* Gibbon tries to heal that break in the structure of the self in a long and remarkable passage that Bonnard leaves out of his edition.[12] In it, Gibbon sets our imperfect lot beside that of Milton's perfect Adam, born into a state of mature consciousness:[13]

Of these public and private scenes, and of the first years of my own life, I must be indebted not to memory, but to information. Our fancy may create and describe a perfect Adam, born in the mature vigour of his corporeal and intellectual faculties.

> "As new wak'd from soundest sleep,
> Soft on the flow'ry herb I found me laid
> In balmy sweat, which with his beams the Sun
> Soon dry'd, and on the reaking moisture fed.
> Strait toward Heav'n my wond'ring eyes I turned
> And gaz'd awhile the ample sky, till rais'd
> By quick instinctive motion, up I sprung
> As thitherward endevoring, and upright

Stood on my feet; about me round I saw
Hill, dale, and shady woods, and sunny plains,
And liquid lapse of murm'ring streams; by these
Creatures that liv'd and mov'd, and walk'd or flew,
Birds on the branches warbling: all things smil'd;
With fragrance and with joy my heart o'erflow'd.
Myself I then perus'd, and limb by limb
Survey'd, and sometimes went and sometimes ran
With supple joints, as lively vigor led;
But who I was, or where, or from what cause,
Knew not: to speak I try'd and forthwith spake[,]
My tongue obey'd, and readily could name
Whate'er I saw."

It is thus that the poet has animated his statue: the Theologian must infuse a miraculous gift of science and language, the Philosopher might allow more time for the gradual exercise of his new senses, but all would agree that the consciousness and memory of Adam might proceed in a regular series from the moment of his birth. Far different is the origin and progress of human nature, and I may confidently apply to myself the common history of the whole species. Decency and ignorance cast a veil over the mystery of generations, but I may relate that after floating nine months in a liquid element, I was painfully transported into the vital air. Of a new born infant it cannot be predicated "he thinks, therefore he *is*"; it can only be affirmed "he suffers, therefore he feels." But in this imperfect state of existence I was still unconscious of myself and of the universe, my eyes were open without the power of vision, and, according to Mr. de Buffon, the rational soul, that secret and incomprehensible energy, did not manifest its presence till after the fortieth day. During the first year I was below the greatest part of the brute creation, and must inevitably have perished, had I been abandoned to my own care. Three years at least had elapsed before I acquired our peculiar privileges, the facility of erect motion, and the intelligent use of articulate and discriminating sounds. Slow is the growth of the body: that of the mind is still slower: at the age of seven years I had not attained to one half of the strength and proportions of manhood; and could the mental powers be measured with [the] same accuracy, their deficiency would be found far more considerable. The exercise of the understanding combines the past with the present; but the youthful fibres are so tender, the cells are so minute, that the first impressions are obliterated by new images; and I strive without much success to recollect the persons and objects which might appear at the time most forcibly to affect me.   (*F*, 32–34)

Since memory cannot reach back past a certain point, the historian intuitively turns to another source of data: "Of these public and private scenes, and of the first years of my own life, I must be indebted not to memory, but to information." At first we expect the information to be the sort we might search out ourselves—snapshots, so to speak, of our infancy, or recollections from those who knew us then. But not only had Gibbon no snapshots, by the time he wrote he had no father, no mother, no Aunt Catherine, no one to whom he could turn for anecdotal information. Failing that, he turns to another kind of information, that which comes from "the common history of the whole species" and from authority—in this case Buffon's, who had calculated that the rational soul, "that secret and incomprehensible energy," exists only after the fortieth day. From such information it might follow that it makes no sense to speak of a self, an "I," before the fortieth day of life, thus eliminating the need to get back to absolute beginnings. In fact, Gibbon grows more inquisitive than ever.

The sentences ring strangely when he writes that "in this imperfect state of existence I was still unconscious of myself and of the universe," and that "I . . . must inevitably have perished had I been abandoned to my own care," because they engender, in the one case, an "I" that is unconscious of itself; in the other, an unprotected self committed nonetheless to its own care. And, strangest of all, "decency and ignorance cast a veil over the mystery of generations, but I may relate that after floating nine months in a liquid element, I was painfully transported into the vital air." It is as if thoughts of his parents' domestic life had led Gibbon to a reverie on the moment of his own conception, once more like Tristram Shandy, obsessed with the coupling between Walter and Mrs. Shandy that created himself. Just before, Gibbon had written: "At home my father possessed the inestimable treasure of an amiable and affectionate wife, the constant object during a twelve years' marriage of his tenderness and esteem" (*F*, 31). Curiosity burns through the mist of decorous prose. Gibbon's father "possessed" a treasure, an "affectionate" wife who was the "constant object" of his "tenderness." Though ignorance may cast a veil over the mystery, especially that of one's own generation, it also stirs up the need to see, in the eye of the imagination, the primal scene of all primal scenes, the one that produced oneself—hence those inhibitions of "decency" that precede limitations of ignorance. Gibbon lets the reader into recesses of a warm imagination. He even tries to re-experience the event of his birth.

When he writes, "that after floating nine months in a liquid element, I was painfully transported into the vital air," does he mean he was brought with difficulty into the world? Or was the pain his mother's? Neither alternative seems correct. Rather, the pain seems to have been his own: "Of a new born infant it cannot be predicated 'he thinks, therefore he *is*'; it can only be affirmed 'he suffers, therefore he feels.' "[14] But if Gibbon affirms he was brought into the world in suffering, how does he know? The evidence cannot be more than inferential. And how does he affirm that the infant "suffers," a strong word implying not only pain but the reflexive consciousness of pain as suffering? In the effort to trace himself, Gibbon makes inferences from the common history of the species, from the observed behavior of newborn infants, from the authority of Buffon, from everything but the conscious experience that is not available to him. At every step the effort produces an ever more insistent need to go all the way back to the beginning. Gibbon still strives, "without much success," to remember what is beyond recall.[15]

Against the imperfections of human mind and memory stands the perfection of Adam. The lines from *Paradise Lost* seem to have affected Gibbon deeply: in a fragmentary note that identifies them and also puzzles over small matters of punctuation, he exclaims, "perfectly original" (*F*, 33n). Adam's unfallen state confers on him something more important than sinlessness—namely, a consciousness and memory of himself that "might proceed in a regular series from the moment of his birth" (*F*, 33). He comes into the world knowing the right questions:

> Myself I then perus'd, and limb by limb
> Survey'd, and sometimes went and sometimes ran
> With supple joints, as lively vigor led;
> But who I was, or where, or from what cause,
> Knew not.

To know who he is, Adam only has to speak. Indeed, he appears never to have not known who he was, for the question arises at the moment of speech, and at that moment, he acquires the power of naming whatever comes before him. In the logic of the situation, if not in the logic of the Christian story, this power also seems to entail the power of self-naming:[16]

> . . . to speak I try'd and forthwith spake[,]
> My tongue obey'd, and readily could name
> Whate'er I saw.

But even if Adam does not acquire the power of self-naming, the ability to name everything else carries autobiographical force, for whatever he sees becomes part of his own history. Even if he cannot know unaided the cause of his being, he can know what there is to know of his being. Adam is a lucky autobiographer.

Of course, Adam and his descendants would have had no need for autobiography if sin and death had not entered the world. Autobiography tries to anticipate death by disarming it, yet death frustrates the autobiographer, who does not ordinarily know when it will arrive nor what is yet to happen in an unfinished life. If Gibbon had repeated trouble with his birth, he only confronted the awkwardness of death once—in E, where he rushes to a conclusion, as if finally to face this most vexatious problem. Had he ever reached a conclusion again, surely it would have given him revisionary difficulties more than equal to his relentless grasping after beginnings in F. In F he wants to get the job done, to complete himself. It is the job that only death can do.

The autobiographical puzzle of mortality was one Hume had solved in "My Own Life," thanks to the conditions under which it was written, for he had an enormous advantage over Gibbon and most autobiographers: he was dying, and he knew it. Though Hume's account seems sparse and unrevealing (one reader calls it "doubly disappointing" because "it comes from the philosopher credited with helping to formulate the modern concept of the self"),[17] it is in fact a small masterpiece in the way it handles the autobiographical embarrassment of death. To watch Hume at the end of his life's story will make clear what Gibbon, not only still alive but busy thinking ahead to new projects, was up against.

"My Own Life" is dated 18 April 1776; four months later, Hume was dead. In his penultimate paragraph, he describes his last sickness ("a disorder in my bowels") and reports he is dying in philosophical fashion, tranquilly and in good spirits. He also pictures himself receding into history in a sentence with some peculiar syntax: "I consider, besides, that a man of sixty-five, by dying, cuts off only a few years of infirmities; and though I see many symptoms of my literary reputation's breaking out at last with additional lustre, I know that I had but few years to enjoy it." This is what Hume actually wrote, though the published text read: "and though I see many symptoms of my literary reputation's breaking out at last with additional lustre, I knew that I could have but few years to enjoy it."[18] In either case, an abrupt shift to the past tense—"I had," "I knew"—shows

Hume settling on his final strategy: to write himself out of existence. Now, he says, "It is difficult to be more detached from life than I am at present." And to confirm this ultimate detachment, he relegates himself at the start of the final paragraph to the historical past: "To conclude historically with my own character. I am, or rather was (for that is the style I must now use in speaking of myself, which emboldens me the more to speak my sentiments); I was, I say, a man of mild dispositions."[19]

At a stroke Hume overcomes the autobiographer's split intentionality, "I" merging with "he" at the right moment, which is that of death. It is very artful, as is the deceptive plainness of Hume's last sentence: "I cannot say there is no vanity in making this funeral oration of myself, but I hope it is not a misplaced one; and this is a matter of fact which is easily cleared and ascertained."[20] Hume accomplishes a final restoration of self in a permanent, present tense. Even in this funeral oration, the "I" survives, at last invulnerable to the shifts of time, asserting the usual dream of authorial immortality. That this should be a matter of fact, "easily cleared and ascertained," is Hume's final stroke: the skeptical philosopher, who denied an afterlife to the last, asserts the afterlife to which authors, Gibbon among them, aspire.

Coming to *E*, determined to see his story to the end and no doubt remembering Hume, Gibbon must have been apprehensive. He seems not to have worked out the ending in advance, for the last pages have an improvisational air: his attention moves about, on the lookout for a stopping point. At the same time, the text more than hints at a buried plot that might have brought the narrative to a satisfactory conclusion had fate been more kind. That buried plot, of paradise regained, would have provided a secular equivalent to Augustine's move out of the temporal world, for Lausanne, as Gibbon reconstructs the curve of his emotional life, was a lost Eden. No matter that he had gone there, at first, as if into exile; in retrospect, it becomes the haven to which he imagines himself forever wishing to return: "From my early acquaintance with Lausanne I had always cherished a secret wish that the school of my youth might become the retreat of my declining age" (*E*, 327).

For a time, Gibbon thought he had recovered paradise when he returned to Lausanne: "Britain is the free and fortunate island, but where is the spot in which I could unite the comfort and beauties of my establishment at Lausanne?" (*E*, 339). Sickness and death, however, invaded Eden: "Alas! the joy of my return and my studious ardour were soon damped by the melancholy state of my friend, Mr. Deyverdun. His health and spirits had long suffered a gradual decline; a succession of Apoplectic fits announced his dissolution, and before he expired, those who loved him could not wish for the continuance of his life" (*E*, 340). The death of Deyverdun interrupted not only work on *B* but also the invented plot of Gibbon's life. Though Lausanne still affords creature comforts, "I feel, and with the decline of years I shall more painfully feel, that I am alone in paradise" (*E*, 341). And though he has friends in Lausanne, even a substitute family in the de Séverys and their children ("I am encouraged to love the parents as a brother, and the children as a father"), whom he sees every day, "even this valuable connection cannot supply the loss of domestic society" (*E*, 341–42). One plot having failed, only one other remains: "the decline of years," now to be faced alone.

Still, Gibbon hesitates to look ahead to that decline. Disrupted by the death of Deyverdun, paradise is also disrupted by the "disorders of France," which have brought a "swarm of emigrants" (*E*, 342) to Eden and threaten even worse effects, "many individuals and some communities" being "infected with the French disease." What if the "disease" spreads to Lausanne? The possibility leads to the anticipation of action: "For myself (may the omen be averted) I can only declare that the first stroke of a rebel drum would be the signal of my immediate departure" (*E*, 343). This imaginary flight momentarily avoids bringing the autobiography to an end and, therefore, in more than the obvious sense, signifies an evasion of death. But it is a last strategy. Now Gibbon has to sum up.

Much of this summing up, with its anticipations of age and death, is best saved for the final chapter. But the end of the last paragraph of *E* stands comparison with Hume in its concern for literary immortality. What Hume accomplishes by combining a funeral oration and matter-of-factness, itself an ironic conjunction, Gibbon can accomplish only by self-referential irony that leaves everything characteristically open. "The abbreviation of time and the failure of hope," he writes, "will always tinge with a browner shade the evening of life" (*E*, 348), because time moves faster as we grow older, each year representing an increasingly small part of the whole, and because hope fails "after the middle season" of life. Yet hope does not fail for everyone: parents live on in their children, believers in their heaven, writers—if they are lucky—in their works: "In old age, the consolation of hope is reserved for the tenderness of parents, who commence a new life in their children; the faith of enthusiasts who sing Hallelujahs above the clouds, and the vanity of authors who presume the immortality of their name and writings" (*E*, 349). The consolations of parents have a basis in fact, for their children do live after them; the faith of enthusiasts is, at least, beyond empirical challenge; but authors may be radically wrongheaded in estimating their own value. In these, the last words of *E*, Gibbon submits to ironic scrutiny his own hope of authorial immortality.

If in the posthumous future Gibbon has no readers, his vanity becomes sound in the desert. If he does have readers, it was not mere vanity to hope for immortality: though the author may have been vain, his wishes were not. As we read the words on the page, Gibbon is acquitted of mistaking his own value, even though he himself could not have been certain of the outcome. He leaves to the future what Hume rhetorically settled for himself: the immortality of his name. This ending of *E* is wryly self-regarding. Such an ending would not have been in keeping with Gibbon's intention in *F* to tie up every thread. Perhaps, by the time he came to *F*, he had sensed the logic of autobiographical conclusions. Perhaps, despite his passion for completeness, he did not want to finish the task.

Finally, what self does Gibbon discover between the limits of a beginning that eludes his memory and an ending that he cannot locate? What essential role or passion lies behind the roles of farmer, soldier, historian? Though he is more assertive of a self in *F* than in the earlier drafts, the long process of self-revision, like the process of getting himself born, is one of minute rearrangement and spontaneous improvisation, all in the interest of achieving just the right nuance of character, and all yielding not one self but a company. With the capacious powers that had enabled him to compose whole paragraphs of the *Decline and Fall* in his mind and then write them down, Gibbon probably carried in his head earlier versions of the autobiography. Perhaps he also reviewed them while composing. Each new version is an overlay of what came before, a palimpsest of related selves.[21]

This self-revisionary instinct reaches out to include Gibbon's treatment of the two Edward Gibbons before him, his grandfather and his father. Each presented unsettling difficulties; whatever Gibbon was, whoever he was, he was of their line. His grandfather, successful at commerce, had become a director of the South Sea Company; it was, as his grandson calls it, a "fatal office" (*F*, 11) that brought him public disgrace and lost him one fortune, though he went on to make another. As for his feckless, overbearing, engaging father, even more than most fathers he was a problem to be solved for the son who had to come to terms with him and with his memory. How would the autobiographer judge these forebears?

For his role in the South Sea debacle, Gibbon's grandfather had been fined a substantial part of his wealth, more than ninety-six thousand pounds. But he evidently managed to set some money aside, safely out of reach. If so, what should history, or a grandson, think? In *E* Gibbon ignores the question, but on four other occasions he ranges from neutral reporting of suspicions to anxiety and, finally, to a blustery justification of fraud:

It is suspected that he had found means to elude the impending stroke by prævious settlements and secret conveyance, and at the time of his death . . . he could not be less opulent than he had been before the South Sea Calamity. (*B*, 109)

Some part of my grandfather's fortune was legally and, perhaps, honestly secured by prævious settlements and conveyances. (*C*, 215)

Yet something had been secreted by his foresight. (*D*, 391)

Against irresistible rapine the use of fraud is almost legitimate; in the dexterous anticipation of a conveyance some fragments of property might escape: debts of honour will not be annulled by any positive law; and the frequent imposition of oaths had enlarged and fortified the Jacobite conscience. (*F*, 16)

In *B* Gibbon reports an allegation; in *C* he nervously hopes his grandfather's action was legal and honest; in *D* the action is secret but at least foresighted; in *F* it is fraudulent but defensible by reason of Parliament's rapacity and because his grandfather's Jacobite conscience had become inured to the breaking of oaths. In *F*, that is, Gibbon admits everything and palliates it, too.

More deeply lodged, and equally symptomatic, is a nervousness about his grandfather's social standing. Six times he introduces the first Edward Gibbon, each time knowing he will have to deal with the South Sea scandal, each time wondering what the private, solitary historian should make of this public, entrepreneurial man:

Were I possessed of the books and papers of my grandfather, Edward Gibbon, I should not feel much pleasure in stating the balance of his accounts, or the progress of his fortune. Yet he moved in an higher sphere than his two predecessors of commercial and even of political life.   (*A*, 374)

My grandfather, Edward Gibbon, a man of sense and business, was of some note in the political as well as the commercial World, and under Lord Oxford's administration he exercised the office of one of the Commissioners of the Customs near four years, till the death of Queen Anne.   (*B*, 108)

My grandfather, Edward Gibbon, was of some note in the commercial and even the political World. In the four last years of Queen Anne (1710–1714) he exercised the office of one of the Commissioners of the Customs; the Ministers often consulted him on subjects of trade and finances, which he understood, according to the testimony of Lord Bolingbroke, as deeply as any man in England.   (*C*, 214)

My grandfather, a man of sense and spirit, was a Commissioner of the Customs in the last Tory Ministry of Queen Anne, and was afterwards chosen one of the Directors of the South sea company.   (*D*, 391)

My grandfather, Edward Gibbon, was Commissioner of the Customs (1710–1714) and a Director of the South Sea Company.   (*E*, 294)

The successful industry of my grandfather raised him above the level of his immediate ancestors.   (*F*, 10)

Should the boisterous, commercial story of this Edward Gibbon be of any interest to his fastidious, intellectual grandson, whose first introduction of him is condescending ("I should not feel much pleasure in stating the balance of his accounts, or the progress of his fortune")? Was he a man of consequence, at home in the political world, consulted by ministers, admired by Bolingbroke, a man of sense and spirit? Or was he just a man of business? Was his part in the South Sea disaster the one episode that mattered in his life or an incidental accident?

Gibbon's father puzzles him as much as his grandfather. Five times his father comes onstage, his first appearance in *A* evidently having taken place in the pages now missing. Each time occasions a character sketch. But was the second Edward Gibbon thoughtless or a man of integrity? Was the important thing his social grace or his improvidence? In *B* he recklessly but cheerfully turns away from the mercantile profession of his ancestors:

His education was liberal, at Westminster School, and at Emanuel College in the University of Cambridge; and he was afterwards permitted to visit Paris, and some parts of France and Italy. On his return home the gay youth despised the mercantile profession of his ancestors, and after his father's death he enjoyed, and perhaps abused, the gifts of independence and fortune. He was twice chosen a Member of Parliament.   (*B*, 110)

In *C* cheerfulness yields to unhappiness:

My father, Edward Gibbon, born in the year 1707, was introduced into the World with the advantage of Academical institution, foreign travel, and a seat in Parliament; but had he been confined, like his ancestors, to a mercantile counter, his life might have been happier, and my situation would be more opulent.   (*C*, 216–17)

In *D* Gibbon's father opposes Walpole strenuously though (like his son in Parliament) silently and, whatever his unhappiness, is again of a gay temper:

My father, who was born in the year 1707, enjoyed the advantages of Academical education and foreign travel; he successively represented in Parliament the borough of Petersfield (1734) and the town of Southampton (1740); and gave a strenuous though silent support to the Tory opposition against Sir Robert Walpole and the Pelhams. Had he trod in the mercantile path of his predecessors, he would have been an happier, and I might be a richer man. But his temper was gay, his life was dissipated.   (*D*, 392)

In *E* he becomes a hard-drinking Tory, if not a Jacobite, who grows wiser as he grows older:

My father, Edward Gibbon (born in 1707), enjoyed the advantages of education and travel, and successively represented in Parliament the borough of Petersfield (1734) and the town of Southampton (1740). In the opposition to Sir Robert Walpole and the Pelhams he was connected with the Tories— shall I say the Jacobites? With them he gave many a vote, with them he drank many a bottle. But the prejudices of youth were gradually corrected by time, temper, and good sense.   (*E*, 294)

Finally, in *F*, when Gibbon attempts a larger portrait, his father achieves almost heroic sociability:

My father, Edward Gibbon, was born in October, 1707; at the age of thirteen he could scarcely feel that he was disinherited by act of parliament; and as he advanced towards manhood new prospects of fortune opened on his view. . . . My father resided some time at Paris to acquire the fashionable exercises; and, as his temper was warm and social, he indulged in those pleasures for which the strictness of his former education had given him a keener relish. (*F*, 17–18)

The World was open before him: his spirit was lively, his appearance splendid, his aspect chearful, his address polite; he gracefully moved in the highest circles of society. . . . Yet such was the pleasing flexibility of his temper, that he could accommodate himself with ease and almost with indifference to every class—to a meeting of Lords or farmers, of Citizens or Foxhunters; and without being admired as a wit, Mr. Gibbon was everywhere beloved as companion and esteemed as a man. (*F*, 31–32)

Sociable as he is, however, a vindictive streak cuts across Edward Gibbon Sr.'s sunny disposition, and his political principles are compromised by motives of private revenge. It is as if, deep in Gibbon's mind, there lodged the metaphor of the hunt that had initiated his career as Warburton's mature combatant in the wars of intellect:

Without acquiring the fame of an orator or statesman, he eagerly joyned in the great opposition which, after a seven years' chace, hunted down Sir Robert Walpole, and, in the pursuit of an unpopular Minister, he gratified a private revenge against the oppressor of his family in the South-sea persecution. (*F*, 19)

And as good nature succumbs to extravagance, extravagance leads to disaster:

But, in the pursuit of pleasure, his happiness, alas! and his fortune were gradually injured. Œconomy was superseded by fashion; his income proved inadequate to his expence; his house at Putney, in the neighbourhood of London, acquired the dangerous fame of hospitable entertainment; against the more dangerous temptation of play he was not invulnerable, and large sums were silently precipitated into that bottomless pit. Few minds have sufficient ressources to support the weight of idleness; and had he continued to walk in the path of mercantile industry, my father might have been a happier, and his son would be a richer, man. (*F*, 32)

In this palimpsest, we think we see the second Edward Gibbon clearly, but his son sees him, like Julian, as both fatally attractive and fatally flawed, a man divided; and, like his son, a man of many roles, at ease among lords, farmers, citizens, and foxhunters. Had he continued to walk in the mercantile path, his son would have been not only richer but more clear about his origins.

If the two Edward Gibbons who preceded the historian were each a moral puzzle, the historian was equally a puzzle to himself, especially when it came to reliving that critical stretch of his life at Oxford during which his conversion determined, in its peculiar way, his future. The conversion is lodged in his mind as he recounts his petty indiscretions. Were these indiscretions to be charged against his own moral account, or were they to be excused by the lassitude of the institution and the unproductive idleness it seemed to have forced on him?

For my own part, the want of occupation and experience soon led me into some irregularities of bad company, late hours, and improper expence. (*B*, 127)

Idleness and inexperience soon led me into some disorders of late hours, bad company, and improper expence. (*C*, 226)

The idleness of a boy was easily betrayed into some irregularities of company and expence. (*D*, 395)

The want of experience, of advice, and of occupation soon betrayed me into some improprieties of conduct, ill-chosen company, late hours, and inconsiderate expence. (*F*, 81–82)

In each version, Gibbon makes the same point: at Oxford he went without supervision or advice. Beyond that, was he idle, like the idle apprentice, or did he merely want occupation? Was he "betrayed" by himself or by others? How much blame should be assigned to those who should have acted in loco parentis? How much to himself?

Late hours, bad company, and improper expense only anticipate the real issue, however. Five times Gibbon reenacts the trauma of the conversion. The first three times he represents himself as the passive plaything of fate. His curiosity finds itself "directed" toward theological disputes. Popish books "unluckily" fall into his hands, or "accident" throws them his way. He is removed from himself, only believing that he believes. Then, on a fourth try, he becomes a lost pilgrim, stumbling through the wood of controversy without master or guide, but under his own power of movement. And in the final draft he manages, though hesitantly, to paint himself as an adolescent hero, albeit so naive as to advance into combat without armor:

Without guide or preparation, my idle curiosity was unluckily directed to the study of the disputes between the Protestants and the Papists; and I soon persuaded myself that victory and salvation were on the side of the Church of Rome.   (*B*, 128)

Some Popish books unluckily fell into my hands: I was bewildered in the maze of controversy, and my understanding was oppressed by their specious arguments, till I believed that I believed in the stupendous mysteries and infallible authority of the Catholic Church.   (*C*, 227)

Accident threw into my hands, and curiosity tempted me to peruse, some Popish treatises of Controversy. I read till I was deluded by the specious sophistry, till I believed that I believed all the tremendous mysteries of the Catholic creed.   (*D*, 395)

Without a master or a guide, I unfortunately stumbled on some books of Popish controversy.   (*E*, 296)

The blind activity of idleness urged me to advance without armour into the dangerous mazes of controversy, and at the age of sixteen I bewildered myself in the errors of the Church of Rome.   (*F*, 84)

Each time Gibbon has to report the fact, he also has to make some judgment about his action. Should he be embarrassed about his youthful folly or proud of having done what his conscience told him was right?

If I now smile or blush at the recollection of my folly, I may derive some countenance from the example of Chillingworth and Bayle, who, at a riper age, were seduced by similar sophistry to embrace the same system of superstition.   (*B*, 129)

I honestly obeyed the dictates of conscience, and should I be taxed with levity and rashness, I can plead the respectable examples of Chillingworth and Bayle.   (*C*, 228–29)

And my folly may be excused by the examples of Chillingworth and Bayle, whose acute understandings were seduced at a riper age by the same arguments.   (*D*, 395)

Nor is it a matter of reproach that a boy should have believed that he believed, etc. I was seduced like Chillingworth and Bayle, and, like them, my growing reason soon broke through the toils of sophistry and superstition.   (*E*, 296–97)

For my own part, I am proud of an honest sacrifice of interest to conscience; I can never blush if my tender mind was entangled in the sophistry that seduced the acute and manly understandings of CHILLINGWORTH and BAYLE, who afterwards emerged from superstition to scepticism.   (*F*, 88–89)

In his retrospective self-judgments, Gibbon executes a 180-degree turn. In *B* he turns red at his "folly." In *C* he says he honestly obeyed his conscience. In *D* he excuses what he again calls his folly. In *E* he denies that what he did was a matter of reproach. In *F* he takes pride in having sacrificed interest to conscience: now he "can never blush" to have been caught in the same snares as those that entangled the "acute and manly" understandings of Chillingworth and Bayle.

The collected evidence indicates something of Gibbon's state of mind as he started working on *F*, hopeful that it would be his last try. In *F* he will put as good a face on as much of the evidence as he can. His grandfather's shady dealings will be a reasonable response to excesses of parliamentary authority; his father will be a "beloved" companion, however imprudent; his own indiscretions at Oxford will result not from idleness but from inexperience, lack of advice, and lack of occupation; his conversion will be an occasion for pride. Not only does Gibbon want to bring his task to completeness in *F*, he also wants to show himself and his forebears in the best light he can.

Yet he has not redefined his task for the better, because what he intends in *F* is less autobiography than apology. He aims at the same psychological decisiveness that he seeks in summary efforts to impale emperors on the pin of a ruling passion. Aiming at self-justification, Gibbon aims also at certainty. Perhaps this is another reason why, as he worked on this last draft, he found himself doubting that the job could be finished. His desire for completeness had already produced the awkward effort to trace himself back to the womb, and it might also have produced the inescapably greater awkwardness of trying to apprehend his own death. But perhaps Gibbon also came to see that the effort to flatten autobiography into apology could only be damaging to the real life of the subject, just as he knew, with at least half his mind, that spearing Julian or Hadrian or Mahomet on a ruling passion damaged their human richness. Perhaps Gibbon broke off in *F* because he realized that an apology would do the autobiographer, and the historian, an injustice.

What is more, a curve runs through these drafts that moves against the one toward self-assurance and finality. It was in *B* that Gibbon pronounced, with unusual assertiveness, that not only had he aspired to be a historian from the start but that he knows this beyond dispute: "Without engaging in a metaphysical or rather verbal dispute, I *know*, by experience, that from my early youth I aspired to the character of an historian" (*B*, 193). Readers of the composite autobiography remember this apparent firmness and resolute sense of self. Virginia Woolf, for one, remembers the italics: "But miracle is not a word to use in writing of Gibbon. If miracle there was it lay in the inexplicable fact which Gibbon, who seldom stresses a word, himself thought worthy of italics: '. . . I *know* by experience, that from my early youth I aspired to the character of an historian.' "[22]

But Gibbon never repeated the italics or the claim to have known his destiny so well. In *C* he says: "After the publication of my Essay, I revolved the plan of a second work; and a secret Genius might whisper in my ear that my talents were best qualified to excell in the line of historical composition" (*C*, 258). In *D* he remembers that he had also aspired to write biography: "I resolved to embrace some design of history or biography, to which, even from my childhood, I had been prompted by a secret instinct" (*D*, 403). And in *E* he does not mention the historian's secret calling: "After this first experiment, I meditated some historical composition" (*E*, 301). The historian of the Roman Empire, having carved himself in stone, then chips away at the hardness of the image. After assuming the character of a historian, he modestly dismantles it in favor of one that is less grand. Like other mortals with ordinary hopes, he dreams of "some historical composition." It is disingenuous to put the case that way, but human. Had he ever reached this juncture in *F*, what he might have written would probably have been more assured and less compelling.

Looking back, Gibbon also realized that his character as a historian depended in part on the lucky accident of his birth that had provided him with enough money to live comfortably but not enough to encourage complacency or self-indulgence. Four times he ponders this good fortune, and in doing so subjects the monolithic character of a historian, once again, to a sea change:

Yet I am tempted to glance in a few words on the state of my private circumstances, as I am persuaded that had I been more indigent or more wealthy, I should not have possessed the leisure or the perseverance to prepare and execute my voluminous history. (*B*, 155)

Yet I may believe, and even assert, that in circumstances more indigent or more wealthy, I should never have accomplished the task, or acquired the fame, of an historian. (*C*, 292)

Yet I am disposed to believe that the mediocrity of my life and fortune, above poverty and below riches, has powerfully contributed to the application and success of the historian.   (*D*, 414)

Perhaps the golden mediocrity of my fortune has contributed to fortify my application.   (*E*, 347)

In *B* Gibbon is rather portentously the author of a voluminous history. In *C* he becomes "an historian." In *D* he becomes "the historian," but ambiguously so: is he the historian of the Roman Empire, or just any historian? We could take it either way. In *E* he is an ordinary laborer in the vineyard of history. Again the curve runs, though unevenly, in the direction of modest utterance—even deconstruction. And here the role of the historian depends upon the possibility of being a man of leisure.

   In three of the drafts, Gibbon then goes on to generalize his case with rare consistency, still pondering his role as his father's more than moderately lucky, moderately well-to-do son. He claims a station midway between that of "gentleman" and that of "author" or "writer":

Few works of merit and importance have been executed either in a garret or a palace. A gentleman, possessed of leisure and independence, of books and talents, may be encouraged to write by the distant prospect of honour and reward; but wretched is the author, and wretched will be the work, where daily diligence is stimulated by daily hunger.   (*C*, 292)

Few books of merit and importance have been composed either in a garret or a palace. A lofty station and superfluous estate are too closely connected with the cares, the pleasures, and the vanities of the world; while the Genius of indigence will be depressed and occupied by the humble labours of some necessary calling. The distant hope of honour and reward may excite the industry of a liberal mind, but wretched is the author and wretched will be the work where daily diligence is stimulated by daily hunger.   (*D*, 414–15)

Few books of merit and importance have been composed either in a garret or a palace. A Gentleman, possessed of leisure and competency, may be encouraged by the assurance of an honourable reward; but wretched is the writer, and wretched will be the work, where daily diligence is stimulated by daily hunger.   (*E*, 347)

Like a gentleman of leisure and talent, Gibbon looked forward to the distant prospect of honor and reward. Yet he prided himself, too, on his daily diligence. If anywhere in his autobiography, it is in this double role—Gibbon the writer, Gibbon the gentleman—that we catch a glimpse of his most consistent self.

Had Gibbon ever finished the autobiography to his satisfaction, the odds are that he would have destroyed the manuscripts, just as he seems to have destroyed drafts of the *Decline and Fall*.[23] That would have been a sad loss. His failure to flatten out the psychological terrain of which the autobiographical drafts are so full a chart is history's good fortune. Saintsbury to the contrary, Gibbon's autobiography—that is, his true story—lies in a chaos of rough drafts. A necessary labor of love, Sheffield's editing hides Gibbon's multiplicity behind a veil. When the veil is removed, the monochromatic historian yields to the more richly colored man.

EIGHT

LAST THINGS

The autobiography, though the most important of Gibbon's projects after the *Decline and Fall*, was not the only one. He had never troubled himself much with the question of what to do after the history was finished, and when the time came, he found himself wondering where to turn. His last fragments, jottings, and evanescent speculations about new ventures have the tentativeness of any writer's attempt to turn up the right subject at the right time. It would be an exaggeration to say that his final searchings were marked by frustration, for he never committed himself enough to the search to create a sense of having failed. At the same time, it is possible to see what he was looking for. What he wanted, after his chronicle of decline and fall, was a heroic story.

This is the hope Gibbon had harbored when young and had then nourished in his first chapter on Julian. The two main, failed projects of his apprenticeship, the history of Swiss liberty and the proposed life of Raleigh, could not have been less like the work that made his name. His attraction to these heroic stories reflects the idealizing streak that runs persistently and deeply through his character, whether in his conversion, in the portrait of Julian, or in his warm response to "the finest modern statue I have seen," Lorenzetto's Jonah.[1] If in his searches for a new subject Gibbon thinks he might now do something in the heroic line, this could almost have been predicted. In these ventures he takes refuge in an irony more wistful than astringent, intermittently giving way to the ironist's underlying desire to believe.

Of the projects he took up or contemplated, the most substantial, in terms of words on paper, was an essay on the "Antiquities of the House of Brunswick," intended for a volume of "Historical Excursions," and prompted by "the curiosity of an English subject" (*EE*, 398) regarding the origins and lineage of Britain's Hanoverian kings. In 1790, while writing on the House of Brunswick, Gibbon also worked on materials that Sheffield published under the collective name "On the Position of the Meridional Line and the Supposed Circumnavigation of Africa by the Ancients," and that Patricia B. Craddock gathers together as "The Circumnavigation of Africa" (*EE*, 375–97). And a few years later, there came a "scheme of Biographical writing," perhaps modeled on Johnson's *Lives of the Poets*, a project that Gibbon describes to Sheffield in January 1793 with a sense of liberation, having just expressed his frustration with the autobiography. This anthology would contain "the lives or rather the characters of the most eminent persons in arts and arms, in Church and State who have flourished in Britain from the reign of Henry VIII to the present age," and Gibbon claimed to view it as less demanding than the autobiography (which he had also thought of, originally, as a diversion): "This work, extensive as it may be, would be an amusement rather than a toil: the materials are accessible, in our own language, and for the most part ready to my hands: but the subject, which would afford a rich display of human nature and domestic history, would powerfully address itself to the feelings of every Englishman" (*L*, III, 312). It is a significant distance from the self-amusement Gibbon proposes at first to the powerful feelings of others that he wants to engage by the end.

Finally, later in 1793, Gibbon contemplated one more project, "the last and greatest of the still-born successors to *The Decline and Fall*":[2] an edition of medieval English historians. He had no intention of doing the work himself, but he believed he had found an editor in the Scottish antiquary John Pinkerton. If Pinkerton would handle the heavy labor, Gibbon would be a consultant and, he told Pinkerton in July, would provide "something of an ornamental frieze" for the "solid edifice" of a prospectus (*L*, III, 342). That "ornamental frieze" survives, rescued by Sheffield and described in a table of contents in the five-volume *Miscellaneous Works* (1814) as "An Address recommending Mr. John Pinkerton as a Person well qualified for conducting the Publication of the 'Scriptores Rerum Anglicarum,' our Latin Memorials of the Middle Ages."[3] This "Address &c.," as Gibbon had called it, confirms the hints that, nearing the end of his life, he hoped to find an authentic hero.[4]

Of course, England's Georgian kings were not everyone's idea of a hero, and the "Antiquities of the House of Brunswick," like the portrait of Julian, sometimes flirts with the mock-heroic. Yet Gibbon evokes the greatness of the Hanoverian line with a predominantly straight face. The House of Brunswick is a "majestic tree which has since overshadowed Germany and Britain" (*EE*, 399), and although its origins may be lost in medieval darkness, "human pride may draw some comfort from the reflection that the authors of the race of Este-Brunswick can never be found in a private or plebeian rank: their first appearance is with the dignity of princes; and they start at once, perfect and in arms, like Pallas, from the head of Jupiter" (*EE*, 400). It is wild hyperbole, but disbelief is willingly suspended.

To be sure, Gibbon cannot resist a calculated anticlimax in the tall tale of Foresto, whose history intersects both the story of the decline and fall of Rome and the story of the House of Brunswick on its Italian side: "the . . . illustrious Foresto opposed in arms the great invasion of Attila and the Huns. On the intelligence of the siege of Aquileia he marched from Este and Padua with a chosen band of subjects and allies, cut his way through the Barbaric host, and displayed the standard of the white Unicorn in every action of defence and attack till he was mortally wounded by a Scythian arrow." But the ardent, unsuspecting reader has been set up for a fall: "Eloquent in council, invincible in the field, an Hero in his life, a Christian in his death, the glory of Foresto would be compleat, if such a man had ever existed in the World." Still, Gibbon is not implacably opposed to "the lust of fiction" that creates the Forestos of this world (*EE*, 407). If on the one hand lust of fiction "is punished by the contempt of truth," on the other hand "an illustrious race must always be crowned with its proper Mythology" (*EE*, 408).[5]

Though claiming to be "fatigued with the repetition of fables"

(*EE*, 408), Gibbon now recounts with teasing euphoria the story of Ariosto's hero Ruggiero and celebrates in Ariosto, with hardly a trace of irony, the un-Gibbonian ability to transcend limits of time and space: "Such a Magician as Ariosto can annihilate time and space: and he dispenses, by the prerogative of Genius, with the laws of history, Nature and his own art" (*EE*, 409). In some marginalia on Herodotus, also from this last period of his life, Gibbon had remarked ambiguously that "we sometimes detect a Romance by the easy, though wonderful annihilation of time and space" (*EE*, 367). But here it is as if the historian who had once criticized Sallust for his geographical and chronological mistakes doubts the primacy of physical space and time, and even, therefore, the primacy of history. "After fixing on the Earth the solid foundations of the house of Este-Brunswick," he says, "I am desirous of proving that we are not less able to build in the air" (*EE*, 408). Only a moment before he had claimed to be tired of repeating fables; now he celebrates Ariosto's dissolution of time, space, and history. Did his choice of the decline and fall of Rome reflect, then, a subterranean desire to undo history, to clear away the foundations of empire, as time had done, in order to open the avenues of romance, to build castles in the air?

This wavering between the claims of history and of romance colors two separate drafts of the "Antiquities of the House of Brunswick," as Gibbon glances at William Whitehead's birthday ode to George II for 1758.[6] At least to Gibbon's ear, the ode displays "some degree of courtly and even poetic art," but it is bad history: Whitehead gets four or five things wrong in his celebration of Otbert, "the founder of the Brunswick race" (*EE*, 514). In what is probably the later of the two drafts,[7] Gibbon feels "compelled to vindicate my own accuracy by observing some Geographical and historical errors of the mortal bard": Whitehead does not know where Otbert's lands were; he mistakenly thinks the streams of the Julian Alps empty into the river Po; he has "wantonly corrupted" the motives and the date of Otbert's removal from Italy to Germany. "The poet," Gibbon says sternly, "may deviate from the truth of history; but every deviation must be compensated by the superior beauties of fancy and fiction" (*EE*, 515). In the other draft, however, Whitehead's errors drift down into a footnote, there to be absorbed as poetic license: "We must forgive the poet some historical and geographical errors" (*EE*, 416n). Gibbon is half willing, at least, to set history aside in favor of myth and heroism.

In an "Essay on the Fortunate & Canary Isles," which comprises the first part of "The Circumnavigation of Africa,"[8] is still another partial surrender to belief. To the ancients, the Canaries were known as the Fortunate Islands, and the name calls up the islands of the blessed, Elysium: "It was the duty of the Greek poets, who described the residence and rewards of departed Heroes to adorn *their* fortunate islands with the gifts of perpetual spring and spontaneous plenty." How to estimate, then, the truth of mariners' stories about the Canaries? At first Gibbon holds back. Sailors exaggerate and "the real scene of the Canaries affords, like the rest of the World, a mixture of good and evil; nay even of indigenous ills and of foreign improvements." But this Johnsonian caution yields to acceptance: "Yet, in sober truth, the small islands of the Atlantic and Pacific Oceans may be esteemed as some of the most agreable spots on the Globe. The sky is serene, the air is pure and salubrious: the meridian heat of the Sun is tempered by the sea-breeze: the groves and vallies, at least in the Canaries, are enlivened by the melody of their native birds; and a new climate may be found, at every step, from the shore to the summit, of a mountainous ascent" (*EE*, 375). The green world has been reborn; birds sing; breezes blow. Of course, Gibbon describes an Eden he has never seen, but the historian had become adept at that. Why not sport with Amaryllis in the shade of some Fortunate Island, under a serene sky, in the salubrious air? The islands of the Atlantic and Pacific—Gibbon cannot help but have had in mind narratives like Bougainville's *Voyage autour du monde* (1771), later the occasion of Diderot's famous *Supplément*, with its celebration of the instinctual and the primitive—reconstruct Eden and are a place where heroes go to rest. The Canaries and other Fortunate Islands appeal to the same longings as Ariosto, miraculously annihilating habits of space and time.

If the genealogical essay on the House of Brunswick aims to make a hero of George III, "The Circumnavigation of Africa" discovers a more authentic, modern heroism in the Portuguese who first sailed the Cape of Good Hope. The ancients, Gibbon believed, had never rounded the Cape, and he rejects with surprising vehemence the claim that, because Herodotus believed the circumnavigation of Africa was possible, therefore the Phoenicians had made the journey. The boundedness of the ancient world seems more than ever to mark a failure of nerve when set beside the heroism of Prince Henry and his sailors: "The World of the Greeks the Romans and the Arabians was circumscribed within a narrow out-line" (*EE*, 393–94). Even though the historian Arrian, in the reign of Hadrian, had supposed the Indian and Atlantic oceans to be joined, it was not Hadrian's nature to have tested the theory: he "was not ambitious of conquest; his curiosity did not grasp the knowledge of the Globe; and the endless promontory of the south would have soon exhausted the skill and patience of his mariners" (*EE*, 394). The Roman dislike of the sea, which cast its shadow over the Antonine Utopia, casts a longer shadow here. If Hadrian was not ambitious of conquest, if his curiosity was limited, if the "endless promontory" of Africa would have exhausted the skill and patience of his sailors, was it not for reasons of fearfulness? Rome under the Antonines was not a time for heroes.

To substantiate the claim that the Portuguese first rounded the Cape, Gibbon appeals not only to historical proof but to the evidence of poetic inspiration. "Listen," he had written in the margins of his Herodotus, "to the Spirit of the Cape, the dark sublime phantom created by the fancy of Camoens" (*EE*, 372). Then he had quoted lines from William Mickle's translation of the *Lusiad*, spoken by the Spirit of the Cape to the Portuguese seamen who "alone" have disturbed his reign:

> Nor Roman prow, nor daring Tyrian oar
> Ere dash'd the white wave foaming to my shore;
> Nor Greece nor Carthage ever spread the sail
> On these my seas to catch the trading gale.
> You, you alone have dared to plough my Main;
> And with the human voice disturb my lonesome reign.[9]
>
> (*EE*, 372)

Gibbon exclaims: "I would take the Ghost's word for a thousand pounds." And coming to the circumnavigation of Africa, he invokes Camoens's "sublime fiction" again, quotes the same lines from Mickle, and echoes Hamlet once more, this time in bold capitals and with an exclamation point: "I WILL TAKE THE GHOST'S WORD FOR A THOUSAND POUNDS!" (*EE*, 395) This is a remarkable burst of metaphorical risk-taking from someone who had learned prudence after having lost so many pounds gambling in Lausanne.[10]

By now, Gibbon's reasons for contemplating a biographical anthology "of the most eminent persons . . . who have flourished in Britain from the reign of Henry VIII to the present age" cannot be missed. The project that would have addressed itself powerfully to the feelings of every Englishman would have addressed itself as well to the feelings of a historian inclining as much to secular hagiography as to history. In the ranks of eminent Englishmen there would have been some true heroes.

But the most telling evidence of Gibbon's need for a hero is the "ornamental frieze" he provided for Pinkerton's never-to-be-completed prospectus. Gibbon's last hero was also his chosen successor—and as strange a successor as a hero. Pinkerton had had a checkered early career that included the literary forgery of "old" Scots ballads, singular views about the inferiority of the Celts, and a hostility to the writers of Greece and Rome. But when he met Gibbon, he had published an essay on medals (1784) and edited a collection of early Scots poetry (1786)—not, despite the suspicions of some, a forgery—and in 1797 he would publish a notable history of Scotland under the House of Stuart. Gibbon welcomed him as a son and a scholar.[11]

For years, Gibbon says, he has been hoping that "our Latin memorials of the middle age, the *Scriptores rerum Anglicarum* might be published in England, in a manner worthy of the subject and of the country." But who, in this decadent time, will take on the task? "We knew not where to seek our English Muratori in the tumult of the metropolis or in the shade of the University. The age of Herculean diligence which could devour and digest whole libraries is passed away." Like some ancient prophet in exile, Gibbon awaits deliverance: "and I sat down in hopeless despondency, till I should be able to find a person endowed with proper qualifications, and ready to employ several years of his life in assiduous labour, without any splendid prospect of emolument or fame" (*EE*, 541). But now, with a small, messianic cry of triumph, "the man is at length found."[12]

Gibbon concedes that Pinkerton may seem a curious choice. "The impulse of a vigorous mind" led him to publish too much, too soon. But, having repented youthful error and folly, Pinkerton no longer underestimates the ancients, having "long since propitiated the mild Divinity of Virgil." After all, a hero's adolescence should be rash. And though the Goths "continue to be his chosen people,"

he "retains no antipathy to a Celtic savage" (*EE*, 542). Thus puri-
fied, Pinkerton is everything a son, successor, and scholarly knight-
in-arms should be: "As soon as he was informed by Mr. Nichol the
bookseller of my wishes and my choice: he advanced to meet me
with the generous ardour of a volunteer, conscious of his strength,
desirous of exercise and careless of reward" (*EE*, 543). Gibbon has
called up the potential rival that any son and successor must also be.
Though a volunteer in the same army, Pinkerton advances to meet
him, as if on the battlefield, conscious of his strength, just as young
Gibbon had advanced to meet Breitinger. The historian seems to
remember his words to the Swiss scholar three decades before: "In
the darkness of the night, a recruit may contend with a veteran."[13]

Now Gibbon and Pinkerton strike an agreement: "we have dis-
cussed in several conversations every material point that relates to
the general plan and arrangement of the work, and I can only com-
plain of his excessive docility to the opinions of a man much less
skilled in the subject than himself." As a scholar, Pinkerton comes
from an older race of heroes: "Should it be objected that such a
work will surpass the powers of a single man, and that industry is
best promoted by the division of labour, I must answer that Mr.
Pinkerton seems one of the children of those Heroes whose race is
almost extinct: that hard assiduous study is the sole amusement of
his independent leisure; that his warm inclination will be quickened
by the sense of a duty resting solely on himself, that he is now in
the vigour of age and health" (*EE*, 543). That is to say, he comes
from the same race, now almost extinct, as the historian whose
youthful sleep had been disturbed by the chronology of ancient empires—and by dreams of heroism. In one version of the autobiography, Gibbon compared his "fortunate shipwreck" on the shores
of Lake Leman with the exile of a victor in the Olympic games,
celebrated by Pindar in an ode reminding the victor that his triumph
was the consequence of his exile.[14] Olympic champions and great
historians have something in common.

In the young Pinkerton—then in his middle thirties, as Gibbon
had been when he turned to serious work on the *Decline and Fall*—
the older historian sees a reflected image. He had not been innocent
himself of "those juvenile sallies which candour will excuse" (*EE*,
542), and his last lines in this "Address" conflate the historian of the
Roman Empire, who had once almost lost his English identity, and

his young, Scottish heir. The man is found: "*Exoriatur aliquis!* a man
of genius at once eloquent and philosophic who should accomplish
in the maturity of age, the immortal work, which he had conceived
in the ardour of youth" (*EE*, 545). Months after writing this in the
summer of 1793, Gibbon was dead.

On 30 June 1788, Gibbon wrote his Aunt Hester, on whose formidable piety he had sometimes cast the sort of quizzical glance he
generally reserved for German barbarians.[15] This time, however,
being about to leave England for Lausanne, he wanted to make
amends. The letter has a valedictory air. He assures his aunt that he
is not the rank heathen she thinks: "Your good wishes and advice
will not, I trust, be thrown away on a barren soil; and whatever you
may have been told of my opinions, I can assure you with truth,
that I consider Religion as the best guide of youth and the best support of old age: that I firmly believe there is less real happiness in
the business and pleasure of the World, than in the life, which you
have chosen, of devotion and retirement" (*L*, III, 118). D. M. Low
remarks that those who look for repentant orthodoxy in Gibbon
make too much of this. Yet too little may be made of it as well.

No doubt the sentiments are, in Low's word, artful, and perhaps
"a man is not on his oath when he writes to his aunt."[16] It is unlike
Gibbon, however, to be hypocritical or cruel, and if the letter were
merely artful, it would come close to being cruel. Though much
depends, as Low says, on what religion guides youth and supports
age, and though Gibbon, having chosen a life of devotion and retirement like his aunt's in all but its object of devotion, could say
with both art and truth that he thought such a life held more happiness than the business of the world, still it is reasonable to suppose
a measure of sincerity in his words.

A man may not be on oath when he writes an evangelical aunt,
but he may also permit himself less guarded expressions of feeling
than in other circumstances, where decorum requires him to be res-
olutely his public self. Low is quite right to dismiss the claim of one
of Gibbon's clerical acquaintances that the historian died in a religious state of mind,[17] but these lines to his aunt are nonetheless
touched by the longing to believe, whether in heroes or gods, that
marked the end, as it had marked the beginning, of his life.

Though he could never have professed a belief in immortality, Gibbon found the idea seductive. As he came to the end of his life's story, he entertained the thought of being read by "many distant readers" and the hope that "his personal existence may be extended to countries and perhaps to ages, which he will never see but to which he shall be familiarly known" (*M*, 188n). But then, knowing that his personal existence was not synonymous with his art (whatever he might on occasion feel), he rewrote the sentence, hoping instead that "one day his mind will be familiar to the grandchildren of those who are yet unborn" (*M*, 188). He had come near to exposing an unguarded wish.

When his Aunt Catherine, who had cared for him so devotedly after the death of his mother, herself died in 1786, Gibbon lamented to Sheffield: "All this is now lost, finally irrecoverably lost!" Then he added warily: "I will agree with Mylady that the immortality of the soul is, on some occasions a very comfortable doctrine" (*L*, III, 46). This concedes very little. But when Lady Sheffield died, Gibbon was willing to consider, if only in a wistful, speculative, consolatory, and rhetorical way, the possibility of an afterlife. He wrote his friend: "In four days! in your absence, in that of her children! But she is now at rest, and if there be a future state her mild virtues have surely entitled her to the reward of pure and perfect felicity" (*L*, III, 327). And in his next letter to Sheffield, written just as he left for his last trip to England, he assures him of his own good health, then closes with another venture into conditional belief, this time about the possibility of spiritual presences in the world: "If there be any invisible guardians may they watch over you and yours. Adieu" (*L*, III, 331).

"Gibbon's utterances," Low observes, "may have taken colour from the piety of the friends who surrounded him in his last years."[18] But the important thing is that, however warily, Gibbon does express hopefulness under the coloring afforded by the need to console or reassure his friends. David Hume never did anything of the sort. For Gibbon, to defer to the feelings of others was to open up channels of private desire. He could concede obliquely to Sheffield, grieving for his wife, what he could not concede to himself. Having long before taken the risky step of professing an unacceptable faith, he had learned the dangers of belief. Now, at the end of his life, he entertains, if not religious sentiments, at least a sense of what he has lost. Of course there is no afterlife. Of course there are no invisible spirits at work in the world. But could these comfortable fantasies in some obscure sense be true, just as the vision of the builders of the great cathedrals might in some sense have been true?

Henry Adams called Gibbon his idol—and was one of the historian's best readers. Adams "never tired," he reports, "of quoting the supreme phrase of his idol Gibbon, before the Gothic cathedrals: 'I darted a contemptuous look on the stately monuments of superstition.'" What Adams sees in this is not contempt but wistful humor and loss: "one would have paid largely for a photograph of the fat little historian, on the background of Notre Dame of Amiens, trying to persuade his readers—perhaps himself—that he was darting a contemptuous look on the stately monument." What Gibbon was really feeling, says Adams, was "the respect which every man of his vast study and active mind always feels before objects worthy of it."[19] Gibbon was always trying out what it would mean to believe.[20]

Belief and hope aside, however, death presented the need to come to terms. This Gibbon did, in the same way that he came to terms with pain and discomfort, by making the best of them. If, like Voltaire, he wanted to die "en philosophe" and not like a milksop, a "poule mouillée," he also wanted to avoid, like Voltaire, the "vulgar defiance of a professional *esprit fort*."[21] But unlike Voltaire, Gibbon subscribed to the proposition that the way to judge a life is by considering its end. In his marginalia to Herodotus, he challenged Voltaire for having "ridiculed the observation of Solon . . . that we should not calculate the good and evil incident to any human life, till death has finally closed the account." As infidels go, Voltaire was too astringent for Gibbon's taste. He thought Solon's proposition "clear and judicious" (*EE*, 365).[22]

In the classical version of the wisdom that a life should not be judged until death closes the account, emphasis falls on the turning of Fortune's wheel, now up, now down, perhaps down at the last. That is how Gibbon understood Solon's observation. It is also what he thought of when in the "Antiquities of the House of Brunswick" he remembered the fall of Henry the Lion: "The prosperity of Henry the Lyon had now reached it's summit; and he might justly fear the revolution of the descending wheel. A sovereign, the most opulent and fortunate of his age was reduced to the state of a culprit, a suppliant, an exile; and the last fifteen years of his life . . . exemplified the sage remark of antiquity, that no man should be pronounced happy before the hour of his death" (*EE*, 490). The affairs of state turn on the revolutions of an ascending, then a descending wheel.

By Gibbon's day, however, the saying that no one should be called happy before the hour of death had been filtered not only through the screen of Christian orthodoxy, which proclaimed that salvation depends on the final disposition of the soul, but also through the screen of Montaigne's skeptical intelligence. In it Montaigne had seen the way to a secular yet teleological psychology in which the hour of death provides the clue to a labyrinth. Death shows us as we really are:

En tout le reste il y peut avoir du masque: ou ces beaux discours de la Philosophie ne sont en nous que par contenance; ou les accidens, ne nous essayant pas jusques au vif, nous donnent loysir de maintenir tousjours nostre visage rassis. Mais à ce dernier rolle de la mort et de nous, il n'y a plus que faindre, il faut parler François, il faut montrer ce qu'il y a de bon et de net dans le fond du pot,

> Nam verae voces tum demum pectore ab imo
> Ejiciuntur, et eripitur persona, manet res.[23]

In everything else there may be sham: the fine reasonings of philosophy may be a mere pose in us; or else our trials, by not testing us to the quick, give us a chance to keep our face always composed. But in the last scene, between death and ourselves, there is no more pretending; we must talk plain French, we must show what there is that is good and clean at the bottom of the pot:

> At last true words surge up from deep within our breast,
> The mask is snatched away, reality is left.[24]

This belief system is for conservative skeptics—for Lucretius (whom Montaigne is quoting), for Montaigne, for Gibbon: the last scene is incorrigible, with no possibility of afterthoughts or apologies. Of course, the last scene might be prearranged to match some ideal notion of the self, as Julian may have done. But even then death makes further revisions impossible.

When the mask is snatched away, the reality Montaigne hopes to find in himself is that he will be able to die well, which means dying quietly:

Au Jugement de la vie d'autruy, je regarde tousjours comment s'en est porté le bout; et des principaux estudes de la mienne, c'est qu'il se porte bien, c'est à dire quietement et sourdement.[25]

In judging the life of another, I always observe how it ended; and one of my principal concerns about my own end is that it shall go well, that is to say quietly and insensibly.[26]

How to realize this end? Gibbon did it by schooling himself to take death neither too seriously nor too lightly. Not for him the terror-stricken orthodoxy of Swift or Johnson nor the devil-may-care skepticism of Hume. Death-obsessed, Swift sported with his antagonist like a gamester, turning the game into existential farce, as in the ridiculous musical parody of "A Cantata": "See, see, Celia, Celia dies, / Dies, dies, dies, dies, dies, dies, dies."[27] Johnson fought death off, making deep incisions in his body to draw off dropsical fluids when he thought his surgeon had cut too "tenderly."[28] Hume faced death like a witty, unrepentant, and philosophical highwayman; he enjoyed teasing the pious, especially the impertinent Boswell, forever poking and prying at ultimate questions, who visited him six weeks before he died, went on tiresomely about immortality, and found himself shaken by Hume's intrepid disbelief in an afterlife.[29] Beside all this urgency and swagger, Gibbon's engagement with death offers less to spectators who like to watch hand-to-hand combat but is in its reticent way a moving one.

Gibbon's skill lay in defensive maneuvers and delaying actions. Studiously he put the best face on things, not only ignoring the swelling in his groin but reporting to others over and over that he was "perfectly well." By these assurances he armed himself against any rash incursion by death. To his stepmother Dorothea, 29 March 1777, he wrote: "Even in the midst of the dissipation of this town I might have found a few moments to tell you that I have been perfectly well this winter" (*L*, II, 140). And, 24 December 1778: "I am perfectly well, and shall pass my Holydays in town" (*L*, II, 200). Again, 13 April 1781: "My health this winter has been perfect without the slightest attack of the gout" (*L*, II, 266). It became a verbal reflex to reassure his stepmother, and himself, that all was well, indeed perfectly so. Thus, 1 October 1782: "I should be apt to fix on the last month as the part of my life, in which I have enjoyed the most perfect health" (*L*, II, 309). And, 27 October 1784: "nor do I remember a year in which I have enjoyed a [more] perfect state of health: the air though sharp is pure, it may be dangerous for weak lungs; but is excellently suited to a gouty constitution, and during the whole twelfthmonth I have never once been attacked by my old Enemy" (*L*, III, 18). Though the "old Enemy" is gout, Gibbon sees another, stronger enemy waiting.

Even at the very end of his life, despite painful recurrences of gout, gathering weariness, and his eventual surgery, Gibbon goes on maintaining to anyone within hearing that, mostly, all is well. To Sheffield, 8 May 1793: "I never found myself stronger, or in better health" (*L*, III, 330). To his Swiss friend, Catherine de Sévery, 28 May 1793, from Brussels, on his way to England: "Since Frankfurt, I have been rudely jolted, but the shock has only done me good, and I have never felt better." And again, 12 July 1793, from London: "my health has never been better." And to Wilhelm de Sévery, 12 September 1793, only two months before he wrote Sheffield to confide that he had at last to consult the surgeons: "As for health, you will not be displeased to know that mine is perfect, and I would almost be tempted to believe in the influence of native air."[30]

This insistence, so relentlessly repeated, could not have fooled Gibbon's correspondents, at least not forever. On 25 July 1793, the woman who had known him longer and better than anyone else, the former Suzanne Curchod, now Mme. Necker, wrote to Wilhelm de Sévery: "Je ne suis pas dupe . . . de cette force de santé dont M. Gibbon se vante; c'est un artifice innocent des personnes de son caractère qui aiment mieux s'occuper des autres que les occuper d'eux" (I am not fooled . . . by this vigorous health of which Mr. Gibbon boasts; it is an innocent artifice of persons like him, who would rather concern themselves with others than let others worry about them; *L*, III, 350n).

Mme. Necker understands Gibbon's artifice: he diverts attention from himself and his frailties. Only a month before his death, and not long after the second of his operations, he wrote a physician who had been caring for his friend John Craufurd. Having inquired earlier after Craufurd's health and having now received a satisfactory answer, Gibbon thanks his correspondent, projecting his own strategies onto the situation of his friend. "I flatter myself," he writes, "that you will soon be able to announce his perfect recovery from an attack the symptoms of which had at first alarmed me." This hopeful outlook for Craufurd's "perfect" recovery leads, by an association with Gibbon's own case, to the patient's state of mind: "The temper of mind which can asswage or aggravate every bodily pain is not within the reach of your skill"—not, that is, within the skill of any physician; " 'therein the patient must minister to himself' and I much fear that our friend is not a very skillful practitioner. Will you be so good as to assure him, of what he has long known, the lively interest which I take in his health and happiness?"[31] Overlaying the memory of *Macbeth*—"Canst thou not minister to a mind diseas'd?" Macbeth asks, only to receive his doctor's ironic answer—is a memory of the proverbial "Physician, heal thyself."[32] Gibbon speaks as a physician of the mind to a physician of the body, knowing that in the healing of bodily pain much depends on temper of mind. Faced with another's affliction, he prescribes the treatment that he himself has followed, in his way, religiously.[33]

In his last letter to Sheffield, 7 January 1794, Gibbon comes as close as he ever does to conceding that he is not invulnerable. Then he catches himself short and passes off pain and exhaustion with a wave of the hand. He has just returned to London after a difficult journey from Sheffield Place:

This date says everything. I was almost killed between SP and East Grinstead by hard frozen long and cross ruts that would disgrace the approach of an Indian Wig-wam. The rest was something less painful, and I reached this place half dead, but not seriously feverish or ill. I found a dinner invitation from Lord Lucan, but what are dinners to me? I wish they did not know of my departure. I catch the flying post. What an effort! Adieu, till Thursday or Friday. (*L*, III, 369)

Death takes the shape of colloquial hyperbole: "I was almost killed between SP and East Grinstead"—a distance of several miles. But, though desperate, the situation is not yet very serious: half dead or not, Gibbon reports in his usual way that he is "not seriously feverish or ill." And though his journey seems in fact to have nearly killed him, he wards off fatality: "Adieu, till Thursday or Friday." He will charm death away, substituting social grace for fierce denial.

In the same spirit, he jokes in letters about occasional rumors of his death or supposes, lightheartedly, that others will think him dead—a claim disproven by his writing the letter at hand. On 1 October 1785, he wrote Sheffield, quoting an announcement of his death from an English newspaper: "It is reported, but we hope without foundation, that the celebrated Mr. Gibbon who had retired to Lausanne in Switzerland to finish his valuable history lately died in that city" (*L*, III, 30). Now, in a Bickerstaffian jeu d'esprit, Gibbon demonstrates that he is not dead at all, no matter what the newspapers have reported, or, like Mark Twain, that the report was greatly exaggerated. He begins, however, by agreeing that it might be true:

> The hope of the Newswriter is very handsome and obliging to the historian yet there are several weighty reasons which would incline me to believe that the intelligence may be true. *primo* It must one day be true, and therefore may very probably be so at present. *secundo*. We may always depend on the impartiality accuracy and veracity of an English newspaper. *Tertio*, which is indeed the strongest argument, we are credibly informed that for a long time past, the said celebrated historian has not written to any of his friends in England and as that respectable personnage had always the reputation of a most exact and regular correspondent it may be fairly concluded from his silence that he either is or ought to be dead. (*L*, III, 30–31)

However probable the reports, some evidence exists to the contrary:

> The only objection that I can foresee is the assurance that Mr. G himself read the article as he was eating his breakfast, and laughed very heartily at the mistake of his brother historian; but as he might be desirous of concealing that unpleasant event, we shall not insist on his apparent health and spirits which might be affected by that subtle politician. He affirms however, not only that he is alive, and was so on the fifth of September, but that his head, his heart his stomach are in the most perfect state, and that the Climate of Lausanne has been congenial both to his mind and body. (*L*, III, 31)

The reports having upset Gibbon's equilibrium, he sets out to reestablish it by guile. First comes an anxious mock-logic of possibilities: there is good reason to suppose him dead because he must die sometime, a logical proposition that pulls the rest of the world into its web as well. Then he moves on to a joke, customary after his long epistolary silences, that he will be thought dead or, in this case, that he ought to be, until he arrives at a reassertion of the normal: breakfast in Lausanne, sensory and immediate. This leads in turn to the usual assurances—after a nervous disclaimer that "we shall not insist on his apparent health and spirits"—that not only is he and was he alive but that his head, heart, and stomach "are in the most perfect state," notwithstanding a long siege of the gout that has "pursued him to his retreat among the mountains of Helvetia" (*L*, III, 31) and from which he has only recently recovered. Gibbon fights off disequilibrium by noticing ironically that death lies in store for everyone, then by concentrating on the reality of his surroundings, then by familiar habits of self-reassurance. In fact, he demonstrates the truth of a proposition his letter ironically denies: he is "desirous of concealing"—or at least of disarming—"that unpleasant event," his death.

This same anxiety, playful and existential at once, colors other letters, including those in which, after a long silence, he wonders whether he will have ceased to exist in the memory of others. He writes Sheffield on 18 October 1784: "Since my retreat to Lausanne our Correspondence has never received so long an interruption, and as I have been equally taciturn with the rest of the English World it may now be a problem among that sceptical nation whether the historian of the decline and fall be a living substance or an empty name" (*L*, III, 4). Anticipating that Sheffield will worry about him after the French invasion of Savoy, he writes on 5 October 1792. No, he says, the cannibals have not devoured him yet: "As our English news-papers must have informed you of the invasion of Savoy by the French and as it [is] possible that you may have some trifling apprehension of my being killed and eaten by those Cannibals, it has appeared to me that a short extraordinary dispatch might not be unacceptable on this occasion" (*L*, III, 275). And he writes Lady Sheffield, on 31 October 1782, a letter in which his anxiety reaches out to include others and shield them: "Although I am provoked (it is always right to begin first) with Your long and unaccountable silence, yet I cannot help wishing (a foolish weakness) to learn whether you and the two infants are still alive, and what have been the summer amusements of your widowed and orphan state" (*L*, II, 313). The widowed and orphan states of Lady Sheffield and her children were occasioned by nothing more than Sheffield's being away with his regiment. Death is temporary absence. Conversational hyperbole and social grace replace, even incorporate, the comforts of belief.

In the last paragraph of the only complete draft of the autobiography, Gibbon faced death most squarely. There, lacking the protective context of an exchange with friends, he could not depend on social grace. How then to come to an accommodation, while remaining at least reasonably safe? Blending anxiety and comfort with a final resort to ironic self-implication, this long last paragraph mixes forthrightness and evasion:

The present is a fleeting moment: the past is no more; and our prospect of futurity is dark and doubtful. This day may *possibly* be my last: but the laws of probability, so true in general, so fallacious in particular, still allow me about fifteen years . . . ; and I shall soon enter into the period, which, as the most agreable of his long life, was selected by the judgement and experience of the sage Fontenelle. His choice is approved by the eloquent historian of Nature, who fixes our moral happiness to the mature season, in which our passions are supposed to be calmed, our duties fullfilled, our ambition satisfied, our fame and fortune established on a solid basis. . . . I am far more inclined to embrace than to dispute this comfortable doctrine: I will not suppose any præmature decay of the mind or body; but I must reluctantly observe, that two causes, the abbreviation of time and the failure of hope, will always tinge with a browner shade the evening of life. 1. The proportion of a part to the whole is the only standard by which we can measure the length of our existence. At the age of twenty, one year is a tenth perhaps of the time which has elapsed within our consciousness and memory: at the age of fifty it is no more than a fortieth, and this relative value continues to decrease till the last sands are shaken by the hand of death. This reasoning may seem metaphysical; but on a tryal it will be found satisfactory and just. 2. The warm desires, the long expectations of youth are founded on the ignorance of themselves and of the World: they are gradually damped by time and experience, by disappointment or possession; and after the middle season the crowd must be content to remain at the foot of the mountain; while the few who have climbed the summit, aspire to descend or expect to fall. In old age, the consolation of hope is reserved for the tenderness of parents who commence a new life in their children; the faith of enthusiasts who sing Hallelujahs above the clouds . . . ; and the vanity of authors who presume the immortality of their name and writings. (*M*, 188–89)[34]

Structurally, this excursion on the theme of mortality matches Gibbon's reflections on the newspaper report of his death. First, a premonition of non-being: this may be the historian's last day. Then the recovery of a living self, this time by way of the laws of probability and the likelihood of a happy old age. Then fear slips back in; the unpleasant event cannot be altogether denied. Just as gout stirs up trouble in the paradise of Lausanne, the speeding up of time and failures of hope stir up trouble in the paradise of old age. Finally, in place of the customary, private, and saving assertion that he is perfectly well, public irony saves the day, or so Gibbon hopes: "The present is a fleeting moment: the past is no more; and our prospect of futurity is dark and doubtful." The prospect of the past, which has been his signature, fades as Gibbon touches on the paradox of history—namely, that it, and the lives that made it, are no more. The paradox throws a shadow on the autobiographical project as well as on the history of empire. It is the sort of paradox that Johnson assaulted by beating his foot against the rock of existence and that Gibbon and his age assaulted by gathering tangible remnants of the past: medals, ruins, and the rest. But here Gibbon obliterates everyday evidence, and the assurances of continuity and historical reality enforced by the *Decline and Fall*, though a history of ruin, come into question. Only a dark prospect of the future, with its certainty of death, remains.

Deprived of ruins, remnants, and breakfast in Lausanne, Gibbon turns to the analogous, if less reliable, security of probability. In a supplementary volume of Buffon's *Histoire naturelle* he had found a calculation of life expectancies in which he learned, to his comfort, that at the age of almost fifty-four, he could look forward to fifteen years more. Even more than this good news, however, he must have welcomed the implacable precision of Buffon's tables, a relentless ordering such as had been Gibbon's earliest solace for the disorder and confusion of raw history. Buffon's calculations submerge anxiety in mensuration. "La connoissance des probabilités de la durée de la vie," he says, "est une des choses les plus intéressantes dans l'Histoire Naturelle de l'homme" (the knowledge of life expectancies is one of the most interesting things in the natural history of man).[35] He then provides actuarial tables for every age from two to ninety-nine.

When Gibbon turned to the table for his own age, this is what he read: "For a person aged fifty-four, one can wager 5,204 to 170, or $30^{19}/_{17}$ to 1, that he will live one year more; 5,204 to $^{170}/_2$, or $61^3/_{17}$ to 1, that he will live six months; 5,204 to $^{170}/_4$, or $122^6/_{17}$ to 1, that he will live three months; and 5,204 to $^{170}/_{365}$, or 11,173 to 1, that he will not die within 24 hours. . . . [But one can wager] 2,969 to 2,405, or $1^7/_{30}$ to 1, that he will not live 16 years more." And so on.[36] Such precision makes the world seems stable. Furthermore, when the calculations show, as Buffon's did, that "dans notre grand âge, nous sommes toujours à trois ans de distance de la mort, tant que nous nous portons bien" (in our old age, we are always three years from death, so long as we stay healthy), they show that so long as

Pour une perſonne de cinquante-quatre ans.

On peut parier 5204 contre 170 ou 30 $\frac{10}{17}$ contre 1, qu'une perſonne de cinquante-quatre ans vivra un an de plus.

5204 contre $\frac{170}{2}$ ou 61 $\frac{3}{17}$ contre 1 qu'elle vivra 6 mois.

5204 contre $\frac{170}{4}$ ou 122 $\frac{6}{17}$ contre 1 qu'elle vivra 3 mois.

& 5204 contre $\frac{170}{365}$ ou 11173 contre 1 qu'elle ne mourra pas dans les vingt-quatre heures.

5031 contre 343 ou 14 $\frac{11}{17}$ contre 1 qu'elle vivra 2 ans de plus.

4857 contre 517 ou 9 $\frac{2}{7}$ contre 1 qu'elle vivra 3 ans de plus.

4680 contre 694 ou 6 $\frac{11}{69}$ contre 1 qu'elle vivra 4 ans de plus.

4501 contre 873 ou 5 $\frac{11}{87}$ contre 1 qu'elle vivra 5 ans de plus.

4318 contre 1056 ou 4 $\frac{9}{105}$ contre 1 qu'elle vivra 6 ans de plus.

3947 contre 1427 ou 2 $\frac{51}{71}$ contre 1 qu'elle vivra 8 ans de plus.

3568 contre 1806 ou près de 2 contre 1 qu'elle vivra 10 ans de plus.

3371 contre 2003 ou 1 $\frac{17}{21}$ contre 1 qu'elle vivra 11 ans de plus.

3175 contre 2199 ou 1 $\frac{2}{7}$ contre 1 qu'elle vivra 12 ans de plus.

2786 contre 2588 ou 1 $\frac{1}{13}$ contre 1 qu'elle vivra 14 ans de plus.

2969 contre 2405 ou 1 $\frac{7}{10}$ contre 1 qu'elle ne vivra pas 16 ans de plus.

3891 contre 1483 ou 2 $\frac{9}{14}$ contre 1 qu'elle ne vivra pas 21 ans de plus.

4711 contre 663 ou 7 $\frac{7}{66}$ contre 1 qu'elle ne vivra pas 26 ans de plus.

5137 contre 237 ou 21 $\frac{16}{23}$ contre 1 qu'elle ne vivra pas 31 ans de plus.

5289 contre 85 ou 62 $\frac{1}{8}$ contre 1 qu'elle ne vivra pas 36 ans de plus.

5350 contre 24 ou 222 $\frac{11}{12}$ contre 1 qu'elle ne vivra pas 41 ans de plus.

5372 contre 2 ou 2686 contre 1 qu'elle ne vivra pas 46 ans de plus, c'eſt-à-dire, en tout 100 ans révolus.

Buffon's life expectancy table "for a person aged fifty-four." From Georges-Louis Leclerc, Comte de Buffon, "Des Probabilités de la durée de la vie," *Supplément à l'histoire naturelle* (Paris, 1774–82), IV, 224.

we are well, a lifetime remains: "Trois années ne sont-elles pas une vie complète?" (Are not three years a lifetime?) "Ne suffisent-elles pas à tous les projets d'un homme sage?" (Are they not enough for all the projects of a wise man?)[37] As Robert Favre puts it, "Buffon distribue la petite monnaie de l'immortalité" (Buffon passes out the small change of immortality).[38] And if probability allows fifteen years, as it did to Gibbon, anxiety can almost be set aside. Now he faces the future with some of his customary cheerfulness. Fontenelle (who lived to be a hundred) and Buffon agree that old age is best. It is a comfortable doctrine, like that of the afterlife, and one Gibbon need not be skeptical about: "I am far more inclined," as he says, "to embrace than to dispute this comfortable doctrine."

At the same time, uncertainty, like gout, cannot be cured, only treated symptomatically—or dropped into a footnote. Though he may have fifteen years left, Gibbon records the plain truth that the laws of probability are fallacious in almost every particular case, hints at a quarrel with their paternalistic authority, and in a note disputes Buffon's abstracting of human realities. The laws of probability take shape as a stern parental figure "allowing" fifteen more years of life: behind the changes and chances of the world stands a judge whose sentence is only temporarily suspended. Nemesis has a ghostly human form. And in a note, fear may prevail (just as, in the *Decline and Fall*, sexuality had its freest play in the annotations): "From our disregard of the possibility of death within the four and twenty hours he [Buffon] concludes that a chance which falls below or rises above ten thousand to one, will never affect the hopes or fears of a reasonable man. The fact is true, but our courage is the effect of thoughtlessness rather than of reflection. If a public lottery was drawn for the choice of an immediate victim, and if our name were inscribed on one of the ten thousand tickets, should we be perfectly easy?" (*M*, 196).

Buffon had said of such a probability: "j'en conclus, que toute probabilité égale ou plus petite, doit être regardée comme nulle, & que toute crainte ou toute espérance qui se trouve au-dessous de dix mille, ne doit ni nous affecter, ni même nous occuper un seul instant le cœur ou la tête" (I conclude that every equal or smaller probability must be regarded as nothing, and that every fear or hope that falls below ten thousand should neither disturb us nor take possession of our heart or head for an instant).[39] But if a public lottery were held, as Gibbon imagines, with our name on one of ten thousand tickets, would we be perfectly easy? Our uneasiness would stem not only from the chance of death but, more deeply, from the fear of an extraordinary injustice should our lot come up. Gibbon has turned Buffon's statistical probabilities upside down in the insidious interrogations of a note. Anxiety steals back in.

And though more inclined to embrace than to dispute the view that old age is best, still "I must reluctantly observe, that two causes, the abbreviation of time and the failure of hope, will always tinge with a browner shade the evening of life." At first Gibbon wrote that these causes "will always colour with a dark shade the evening of life" (*M*, 189n). His revision cures the ineptitude of attributing color to darkness and also avoids taking back too much: he does not want to retreat to a prospect of the future as altogether dark and doubtful. Yet the security of probability clashes with the insecurity produced by the relative speeding up of time; and the failure of hope, with its ring of Johnsonian determinism, catches Gibbon up more intimately than he admits: "The warm desires, the long expectations of youth are founded on the ignorance of themselves and of the World: they are gradually damped by time and experience, by disappointment or possession; and after the middle season the crowd must be content to remain at the foot of the mountain; while the few who have climbed the summit, aspire to descend or expect to fall." Gibbon alludes to Augustus's words in Corneille's *Cinna*: "Et monté sur le faîte, il aspire à descendre."[40] Like Augustus, Gibbon has climbed the summit. Perhaps the fear of an imperial fall has been lodged in some remote part of his mind while he painted his breathtaking panorama of the empire. In retrospect, the *Decline and Fall* looks like a premonitory version of the historian's own history. A chasm opens.

At this point, Gibbon turns to his saving irony: consolations of hope are reserved for parents who live on in their children; for enthusiasts who sing Hallelujahs above the clouds; and for authors who in their vanity presume that their name and writings will be immortal. Though Gibbon identifies himself above all with authors, he may also see something of himself among parents and believers. In the first place, the *Decline and Fall* was the child he had conceived and delivered and, as well, a child whose story prefigured that of the father and was simultaneously the father's immortality and doom. In the second place, he intrudes on the enthusiasts' celestial scene in a self-implicating note, subtracting from the number of true believers all nominal Christians, fanatics hell-bent on avoiding hell, and, at the top of the list, "mere" philosophers:

This celestial hope is confined to a small number of the Elect, and we must deduct, 1 All the *mere* philosophers who can only speculate about the immortality of the soul. 2. All the *earthly* Christians, who repeat, without thought or feeling, the words of their Catechism. 3. All the *gloomy* fanatics who are more strongly affected by the fear of Hell, than by the hopes of Heaven. "Strait is the way, and narrow is the gate, and *few* there be, who find it!" (*M*, 196)

The true believers who remain after these exclusions resemble the primitive Christians of the *Decline and Fall*; perhaps few or none were ever in their number. Perhaps there are none but half-believers, among them mere philosophers. That "mere" gives Gibbon away. It is self-dismissive, though it glances as well at the meaning of "mere" as pure, unmixed—a meaning that was on the wane, though not altogether lost, in Gibbon's day.[41] In the ironic self-deprecation of being merely a philosopher, he concedes again some ordinary human hopes of immortality.

As for the vanity of authors who presume the immortality of their name and writings, there is no need to retrace the earlier analysis. Authors may be wholly presumptuous or merely presume what will turn out to be true. But perhaps even the immortality of a name is insubstantial. If so, can the immortality of the written word be more real? Not even history guarantees immortality because time, too, will have an end. That Gibbon never committed these flickering images of his own authorial immortality to print seems a last gesture of self-protection.

Dying like a philosopher usually meant dying in public. This was especially true in France, where, during the seventeenth and eighteenth centuries, deathbeds were public places. "When Pascal said 'on mourra seul,'" John McManners notes, "he meant that a man is alone in his last hour *in spite of* the throng."[42] Hume's dying, which took months, brought to his deathbed all manner of visitors— friends, pious tourists like Boswell, and the wife of a tallow-chandler who chastised the philosopher for his infidelity, prayed for him, then took away a large order for candles.[43] Voltaire's dying also took time, marked by public speculation about how such a man would die and, on Voltaire's part, by careful calculations about how to ensure himself decent burial without having to renounce his principles.[44] Dying like a philosopher required patience and planning.[45]

Gibbon was spared all that. His third operation took place on Monday, 13 January 1794. Sheffield was with him but left for the country the next day, believing his friend was out of danger. On Thursday, Gibbon had a visit from John Craufurd, now recovered from his own illness, at three in the afternoon. In the conversation, Gibbon said with touchingly precise imprecision, and with Buffon surely in his thoughts, that he expected to live "for ten, twelve, or perhaps twenty years." He then spent a long night of sleeplessness and pain. But when his valet Dussaut asked him, at seven in the morning, whether to send for his doctor, Gibbon said no, explaining that he was "as well as he had been the day before." After an hour and a half, he got out of bed, saying he was "plus adroit" than he had been for three months past (*MW*, I, 298). Then he returned to bed and, at nine, told Dussaut he would rise. Dussaut persuaded him to wait until the doctor came at eleven. By then Gibbon was "visibly dying" (*MW*, I, 299). He wanted Dussaut's company, and his valet stayed with him until he died early in the afternoon. It was only Dussaut he wanted. He waved another servant out of the room and, Dussaut reported, "il m'a fallu le voir expirer seul et n'ayant pas même une âme dans la maison" (I was to see him die, alone and with not a soul in the house).⁴⁶ In his own estimate, a Swiss valet did not count as a presence on the stage of death. Gibbon withdrew from the world privately, as he hoped to do.

APPENDIXES

APPENDIX A

FIVE GIBBON LETTERS

Five of Gibbon's letters, not available to Norton, are now in the Department of Special Collections, Stanford University Libraries. The first is to Gibbon's Aunt Hester on the vexatious subject of her Sussex estate. The next two are to Abigail Holroyd, written at a time when her husband was in Ireland and she was on a seaside holiday in Sussex. ("Oracle Caplin" in the first of these letters is Gibbon's indispensable butler, Richard Caplen.) The fourth, to Lady Elizabeth Foster, shows Gibbon in a mood of perhaps not entirely whimsical passion. The fifth, to the physician who had been caring for his friend John Craufurd, is characteristically solicitous of others. All are published here for the first time, although the letter to Lady Elizabeth Foster was known to Norton, from an auction catalogue, in fragmentary form (*L*, III, 267).

TO HESTER GIBBON. *Fri.* 17/2/75.

Dear Madam,

My silence, which I do not pretend entirely to justify may however be excused by several reasons, the hurry of Parliamentary business, the loss of a very dear friend Mr Clarke of Derbyshire whose will has entrusted me with a very troublesome Executorship, and above all my expectation of a satisfactory letter from Mr Holroyd. By one which I received Yesterday he informs me that nothing has been neglected with regard to your Sussex

Estate which it was time to do, a very accurate Survey has been made, and in a few days Mr H will go over with a very skilful Man to value it. But he does not think it will be expedient to give Martin any notice till immediately before Lady Day. that in case he should refuse to give the advanced Rent and have warning to quit the farm, at Michaelmas next, it may not be in his power to do the land any mischief before he leaves it. Mr H is every day more and more of opinion of the importance and even the necessity of purchasing the Tythes; since if they should fall into the hands of any neighbouring farmer or Gentleman (and many are eager to get them) it might be almost the ruin of your Estate, as no Tenant who foresaw a prospect of their being taken in kind would ever give any thing like the value of it. At present they do not pay (the Tythes) one fourth of what they would be worth in kind. We had so much difficulty and lost so much time in finding the Owner, that it seems rather difficult to conclude an Agreement as would be most desirable before your Rents are raised. But if you would immediately send Mr Holroyd, somewhat of a full power of Attorney for that purpose, it might enable him to treat with much more effect and dispatch. I will *answer* for his honour and his care of your Interest. I am sorry to hear of the storm, and the expence which it will involve you. It is Mr. H.s plan that the Tenant should pay all Taxes whatsoever, but as to the repairs of the Sea Walls, he thinks they cannot be safely entrusted to the care of a common farmer.

Poor Mrs Darrel died at Bath last November. Sir Stanier and Mrs Porten join with me in every kind wish. The former is just married to Miss Wybolt, a very amiable Woman who, I hope will make the remainder of his life happy. Mr Laws had your franks near three Weeks ago. Whenever you want any Number be so good as to let me know. I am

Dear Madam
most affectionately Yours
E Gibbon

Bentinck Street. Febr. 17.th 1775.

TO ABIGAIL HOLROYD. *Wed.* 10/5/75.

Address: Mrs. Holroyd. Brighthelmstone. Sussex.
Franked: E Gibbon. Postmarks: FREE; 10. MA; 11. MA.

I admire and rejoyce in your Heroism—Your Wastecoast is not finished, I do not understand from Oracle Caplin that either Casimeer or buttons are in *Pan's* possession. However if you chuse it something similar might be procured and sent you down—Gray shall attend you without delay Madame de Sevignè is getting her habit made, and it happens that her Taylor is no less dilatory than yours. Your letter enclosed after some difficulty is gone, but I think it bad policy to send them me. 1st It is possible that they

180

may be *mislaid*. 2.dly If I sup out there is certainly a post lost. Your Epistles shall not remain on the Mantlepiece.

EG

May the 10.th 1775.

TO ABIGAIL HOLROYD. *Mon.* 15/5/75.

Address: Mrs. Holroyd. Brighthelmstone. Sussex.
Franked: E Gibbon. Postmarks: FREE; 16 MA.

At length Grease had heard your prayer and if there be faith in Man, your Wastecoast will set off Wednesday by the Coach. You may rely still more firmly on receiving Gray to-morrow. He is but just returned from Black-heath. As to Madame de Sevignè, you had informed me at SP that you was only in the fifth Volume and that I might give the new one to be bound. It is now in Hall's hands from which books do not easily escape. To be sure they have been a few mistakes, which it is better to forget and to turn our eyes with just admiration to your intimacy with the Ocean and the Dutch-ess. The former will I fancy prove of more service than the latter. Deyver-dun is going abroad with a brother of Sir Abraham Hume and a life annuity of an hundred a year. The event was unexpected and sudden. I rejoyce on his account but grieve on my own. I may add on your's, for on a further acquaintance with him at SP, I am sure he would have pleased exceedingly. I suppose H writes in the true Way that is directly by the post. I epistolize him to night, but cannot send the Letter you enclosed because I am in Pall Mall, and the said letter is in my Bureau not on my Mantle piece in Bentinck Street. Luckily it do not require dispatch. I lay myself at your feet and re-quest farther intelligence of your august proceedings.

EG

May the 15th. 1775.

TO LADY ELIZABETH FOSTER. *Sun.* [August 1792?]

After drinking tea at the Dutchess of A's and spending the evening at a grand assembly and concert at Mrs Wynch's I find your most wellcome epistle at eleven o'Clock Sunday night, and am ordered to have my answer ready by six to morrow-morning. You must therefore accept a short but sincere expression of my gratitude. Gratitude, taste and good faith are equally en-gaged in the Yverdun journey, and it is my fixed resolution to drink tea with you next Wednesday evening about eight o'Clock. Although I am a little jealous of the various visits with which you are threatened the Princess Bellozelski, the D. of A. Mrs Nugent &c yet upon the whole we shall be more quiet than at Ouchy. A friendly, familiar, rational conversation with three women the most amiable in Europe, (I speak with the religious accuracy of an historian) is the perfection of human society. It is pity that head-achs should ever attack such a class of beings: if they were always exempt from heart-achs they would be less amiable. The English post may bring you some news but the French courier of last night was barren of events. Adieu, Vale, good night! but I do not dare tell you how much I love you.

Sunday night.

TO ?   *Sun.* 15/12/93

Dear Sir.

I return you my sincere thanks for the very satisfactory account of Mr Craufurd's case, which you have been so obliging as to send me, and I flatter myself that you will soon be able to announce his perfect recovery from an attack the symptoms of which had at first alarmed me. The temper of mind which can asswage or aggravate every bodily pain is not within the reach of your skill "Therein the patient must minister to himself" and I much fear that our friend is not a very skillful practitioner. Will you be so good as to assure him, of what he has long known, the lively interest which I take in his health and happiness? I shall not return to town, till after the Christmas Holydays.

I am

Dear Sir
Your faithful humble Servant
E Gibbon.

Sheffield place.
Dec. 15. 1793.

APPENDIX B

GIBBON'S LIBRARY CARD CATALOGUE

Gibbon maintained catalogues of his libraries in London and Lausanne. For the Lausanne catalogue, entries were made on the back of playing cards, sometimes by Gibbon himself but more often not. Their arrangement, in the main, is by author and subject. Ten cards, previously unnoticed and all in Gibbon's hand, use chronological organization to index material from collections of ancient authors. In one case Gibbon indicates an unknown date by the Latin abbreviation "incert."[1] A listing of these cards follows. Those marked Y are in the Osborn collection at Yale; those marked S, in the Department of Special Collections at Stanford. Cards marked K were first published in the second edition of Geoffrey Keynes, *The Library of Edward Gibbon: A Catalogue* (London, 1980), facing p. 25; Keynes does not take account of their unusual format in his text, which is unrevised from the first edition (London, 1940).

In the Department of Special Collections, Stanford University Libraries, is a letter from W. M. Tartt to H. R. Sandbach, dated at Cheltenham, 5 December 1872, describing Tartt's visit to Gibbon's library at Lausanne in 1830, before it was entirely dispersed. Tartt reports that "there were, in a corner of the room, one or two high baskets . . . which were filled with playing cards." The owner of the library, Dr. Schöll, told him "that the names being thus easily arranged in classes, they were to be copied to form a catalogue." A classed catalogue of Gibbon's library, dated 1785, is at the Pierpont Morgan Library, New York (*The Library of Edward Gibbon*, pp. 8–10). It is apparent that Gibbon proposed to compile a chronological catalogue as well.

AC 128
Sempronius Asellio—in
Fragmentes. Hist. Veterum   (K)

AD 55
Phurnutus sive Cornutus—
de Natura Deorum inter Opuscula
Gale. Graece et Lat.   (Y)

AD 250
Marcianus Heracleota—Periplus
Maris externi cum fragmentis
    Artemidori
et Menippi et Dissert. H. Dodwell
in Geog. Min. Tom i   (S)

AD 270
Dexippus Atheniensis————.
in Corp. Script. Byzant. Tom I in
Excerpt Hoeschel   (K)

AD 312
Nazarius—Orationes ad Imp.
Constantinum inter Panegyr.
Veteres. ix. x   (S)

AD 326
Julius Rufinianus—de
figuris sententiarum inter
Rhetoras Antiq. Capperonier   (Y)

AD 395
Rutilius Taurus Æmilianus
Palladius—de re rusticā Lxīv libri
inter Scriptores R. R. Gesneris   (K)

AD 410
Diomedes—de oratione et
partibus Orationis et vario
genere metrorum inter Gr. Lat.
auctores Putschii   (K)

AD 514
Magnus Aurelius Cassiodorius
—quae extant Grammatica
inter G. Lat Auctores Putschii   (Y)

Incert.
Julius Exuperantius—
Opusculum de bello Civili
Marii &c.—ad calcem Sallustii
Havercamp.   (S)

APPENDIX C

A DIALOGUE BETWEEN
GIBBON AND HOLROYD?

The following dialogue is among the Gibbon papers housed in the British Library, Add. Mss. 34882, ff. 49–50. Evidently in Holroyd's hand, it appears to record a dialogue between himself and Gibbon.

G—Of all the false impressions the human Mind receives, nothing astonishes me so much as the horror that some conceive at the Idea of annihilation for how can that be dreadful of which one cannot be sensible?

H—Why not? If you & no one is more so, are desirous of every hour of Life in this World, can you reckon it otherwise than dreadful to give up the hope of an Eternal existence?

G—Eternal Existence might be a blessing but still I should not think of it when Annihilated.

H—But is it not *now* a horrid idea to you What can be worse except eternal punishment. Is it not giving up the highest possible enjoyment very lightly How can you feel (as you certainly must) the wonderful abilities you possess, without supposing you have an Immortal Soul for higher purposes & attachments than you find it can enjoy here while liable to the interruptions of bodily infirmities sickness sorrow & the Evils of this World Does it not sometimes strike you that your great knowledge & yet your constant thirst for more your almost wonderful powers of the mind *must* be something more durable than your body & have more than a Brute existence Do you not believe in a God

G—O yes I do indeed

H—Then you must suppose he gave you this thinking faculty to make you continually seeking what you cannot enjoy & sensible of imperfection & weakness An existence wherein there is so much more of Evil than good that it could never be deemed a blessing & how can that be reconciled with the high attribute of Mercy in a Creator whose only aim in creating such Beings as us must naturally be for the sake of spreading happiness which he has *only* done by leaving it in our power to obtain it Everlastingly

G—I do not know that to be the case, for I enjoy my present existence

H—Let me however ask you another question What is it we feel within is [*sic*] which we call *Conscience* Is it not a soul What is the Idea also that is universally allowed to exist in all ages & all parts of the world of a future state Is it not the inspiration of an Immortal soul For my part I have the most perfect Conviction of it as I have of the being of a God From his attributes alone Reason would tell it me But I have equal Faith in Revealed Religion. I am no more staggerd by not comprehending the whole of it than at not comprehending how a plant dies & the seed revives I *see* the latter but I cannot conceive how it is operated It is therefore not surprising to me to find human knowledge limited & if this is so I find no difficulty in the rest There can be no faith where all is clear to the mind I do declare it is to me the constant object of consolation & a degree of happiness & consolation in comparison of which all others seem below the thoughts (at least) of such a mind as yours

G—smiled & said Your Thoughts I allow are pleasing whether delusive or not but you have taken me out of my line & I meant only to say I do not dread the idea of annihilation.

NOTES

NOTES

ONE

1. Patricia Morrisroe, "Portrait of a Lady," *New York*, 3 Oct. 1983, p. 58.
2. Walter Jackson Bate, *The Achievement of Samuel Johnson* (New York, 1955).
3. *Gibbon's Journey from Geneva to Rome: His Journal from 20 April to 2 October, 1764*, ed. Georges A. Bonnard (London, 1961), p. 242.
4. Ibid.

TWO

1. On the literary mood of the mid-century, see John Sitter, *Literary Loneliness in Mid-Eighteenth-Century England* (Ithaca, N.Y., 1982). Sitter mentions Gibbon only in passing, but his view of the age "as unified by its heightened uncertainties about the relation of solitary writers and solitary readers to the theater of public life" (p. 215) fits Gibbon's case precisely.
2. In all but Chapter 7, I regularly cite Georges A. Bonnard's edition of Gibbon's autobiography. Where relevant, and regularly in Chapter 7, I cite drafts of the autobiography, as reprinted by John Murray. (For Bonnard's and Murray's editions, see the Abbreviations at the front of this book.)
3. The sounds of Bond Street cannot be heard in Bentinck Street today, nor could they, probably, in Gibbon's day; New Bond Street comes to an end at Oxford Street—then, as now, a major thoroughfare lying between Bentinck and Bond streets. It is not likely Gibbon had forgotten his London geography. Apparently he aims to create the sense of sound both heard and unheard, just as the scenes of empire were for him both seen and unseen.

4. In Cicero, *De officiis* (III, 1, 1), Scipio is reported as saying, according to Cato, that he was never less indolent than when he was idle ("numquam se minus otiosum esse, quam cum otiosus") and never less solitary than when he was alone ("nec minus solum, quam cum solus"). I am grateful to Edward Courtney for this reference. Cowley, Swift, Shaftesbury, and Steele all allude to this saying, which was a commonplace.

5. In a letter to Madame de Sévery of September 1787, Gibbon refers to Wilhelm as "notre fils si vous voulez bien me permettre de lui donner ce nom" (our son, if you will allow me to give him this name; *L*, III, 73). In a letter to Wilhelm, 17 March 1792, he bids him farewell: "Adieu mon ami, mon fils, puisque vous le voulez bien. En prenant le nom de père ce n'est pas une vaine formule dont je me sers" (Adieu my friend, my son, since you do not mind my calling you son. In taking the name of father, I am not just using an empty formula; *L*, III, 250). In his will Gibbon left Wilhelm £3,000 and many of his personal belongings: "I give to Mr William de Severy of Lausanne (whom I wish to style by the endearing name of son) the sum of three thousand pounds, together with all my plate, linnen, china, carriages, horses and household furniture" (British Library, Add. Mss. 34715, f. 15v.).

6. The letter, known to Norton only in fragmentary form (*L*, III, 267), is now in the Department of Special Collections, Stanford University Libraries. Though undated, it was probably written in the summer of 1792. See Appendix A.

7. Swift to Pope, 11 August 1729: "Perhaps the increase of years and disorders may hope for some allowance to complaints, especially when I call my self a stranger in a strange land" (*The Correspondence of Jonathan Swift*, ed. Harold Williams [Oxford, 1963–65], III, 341). In the third volume of his biography, Irvin Ehrenpreis notes that Swift in Ireland was outwardly a less lonely figure than he claimed (*Swift: The Man, His Works and the Age* [Cambridge, Mass., 1962–83]).

8. Alexander Pope, "An Epistle to Dr. Arbuthnot," *Imitations of Horace*, ed. John Butt (London, 1961), p. 96. This is Volume IV of the Twickenham Edition of *The Poems of Alexander Pope*. Here and elsewhere the typographical convention of small capitals in an initial word has generally been amended; hence, "Shut" instead of "Shut." Ellipses at the close and start of lines have generally been ignored.

9. *Boswell's Life of Johnson*, ed. George Birkbeck Hill, revised by L. F. Powell (Oxford, 1934), II, 106: "His mind resembled the vast amphitheatre, the Colisæum at Rome. In the centre stood his judgement, which, like a mighty gladiator, combated those apprehensions that, like the wild beasts of the *Arena*, were all around in cells, ready to be let out upon him."

10. Gibbon's "epitaph on his dead love affair," as Robert Folkenflik calls it, has a literary resonance as well, for it perhaps owes something to a line from Corneille and something more to Gibbon's memory of Aeneas leaving Dido on his way to founding Rome ("Child and Adult: Historical Perspective in Gibbon's Memoirs," *Studies in Burke and His Time*, 15 [1973–74], 368).

11. Patricia B. Craddock interprets Gibbon's "revealing error" as a response to his parents having despaired of his life and having treated him "as in some respect replaceable" (*Young Edward Gibbon: Gentleman of Letters* [Baltimore, Md., 1982], p. 26). Other commentaries on Gibbon's error take a still darker view of its meaning. See Folkenflik, "Child and Adult," p. 367: "It conveys Gibbon's extreme sense of his own frailty, his tenuous relationship to his family, his pleasure in having been lucky enough to become who he is, and perhaps his belief that his father wanted to see him dead." See also Roger J. Porter, "Gibbon's *Autobiography*: Filling up the Silent Vacancy," *Eighteenth-Century Studies*, 8 (1974–75), 20: "Since his father continually tyrannized him, Gibbon no doubt felt the need to mobilize all his forces against him; this takes the strange form of a kind of magic— five Edwards arrayed against the father in a dramatic multiplication of the self. Making a name for himself curiously becomes making five similar names for himself. This massing or solidification of the self appears to be a gesture toward defeating the rivalry of sibling, father, and death." Since events in the psyche are overdetermined, these interpretations of Gibbon's error are not necessarily incompatible with mine. It was Gibbon's habit to make the best he could of distressing facts; perhaps in this case he generates companionship out of a sense of rejection.

12. The full title of *Automathes*, published in 1745, is: *The Capacity and Extent of the Human Understanding; Exemplified in the Extraordinary Case of Automathes; a Young Nobleman, Who Was Accidentally left in his Infancy, upon a desolate Island, and continued Nineteen Years in that solitary State, separate from all Human Society.* Kirkby's fiction was largely modeled on an earlier, anonymous *History of Autonous* (1736). For a brief discussion of *Automathes* as a Lockean fiction, see W. B. Carnochan, *Lemuel Gulliver's Mirror for Man* (Berkeley, Calif., 1968), pp. 142–43.

13. For more on Gibbon's parliamentary embarrassment and on his conversational shyness, see W. B. Carnochan, "Gibbon's Silences," in *Johnson and His Age* (*Harvard English Studies*, 12), ed. James Engell (Cambridge, Mass., 1984), pp. 367–85.

14. For Gibbon's efforts to construct an adequate picture of his father, see Chapter 7.

15. For the circumstances of Gibbon's being sent to Lausanne, see D. M. Low, *Edward Gibbon, 1737–1794* (New York, 1937), p. 46; Sir Gavin de Beer, *Gibbon and His World* (New York, 1968), pp. 18–19; and Michel Baridon, *Edward Gibbon et le mythe de Rome: Histoire et idéologie au siècle des lumières* (Paris, 1977), pp. 41f. On the moderate Calvinism of the Pays de Vaud, see Baridon, p. 47; also Ernest Giddey, "Gibbon à Lausanne," in *Gibbon et Rome, à la lumière de l'historiographie moderne*, ed. Pierre Ducrey with F. Burkhalter and R. Overmeer (Geneva, 1977), pp. 26f. When Gibbon wrote his Aunt Catherine Porten in February 1755, announcing that he had renounced Catholicism, he seemed to see something whimsical in his situation. At least that is how, given his subsequent career, one would like to read his comment that, having for a long time wavered between Catholic and Protestant, he found he had another case of conscience upon

his reconversion: "when that conflict was over I had still another difficulty; brought up with all the ideas of the Church of England, I could scarcely resolve to communion with Presbyterians as all the people of this country are" (*L*, I, 3).

16. On one terrifying occasion, Gibbon lost 40 guineas, then "demanded my revenge" (*L*, I, 4) and lost 110 guineas more, far more than he could possibly pay. For his stricken response, see Low, *Edward Gibbon*, pp. 54–57; and Craddock, *Young Edward Gibbon*, pp. 60–63.

17. The estate was not sold until 1789, almost nineteen years after Gibbon's father died. By then it had long been a major irritant. The best place to trace Gibbon's travails with Buriton is in Norton's edition of the letters (see Abbreviations). See "Index III" (*L*, III, 457); also "Appendix III" (*L*, I, 402–7).

18. On 8 April 1775, he wrote Holroyd: "I have remained silent and notwithstanding all my efforts chained down to my place by some invisible unknown invisible power" (*L*, II, 64). On 4 June 1779, he wrote Deyverdun: "Dans le Senat Je suis toujours demeuré tel que vous m'avez laissé, mutus pecus" (In the Senate, I am as you left me, a dumb sheep; *L*, II, 218). And on 15 May 1780, he wrote his stepmother, after Holroyd's successful maiden speech of 5 April: "I can only condole with you that a person, in whose fate and reputation you are perhaps more deeply interested, should still continue a dumb Dog" (*L*, II, 241).

19. On 19 January 1791, young Francis North wrote his sister Anne a letter from Lausanne with an amusing description of Gibbon's verbal posturing. Yet it is done with the ungrudging charity of youth (North was thirty) for age: "I begin to like old Gibbon very much tho he is always very affected and now and then extremely silly." The letter, apparently unpublished, is in the Department of Special Collections, Stanford University Libraries.

20. The several drafts of the autobiography are in the British Library, Add. Mss. 34874.

21. On Gibbon's medical history, see G. R. de Beer, "The Malady of Edward Gibbon," *Notes and Records of the Royal Society*, 7 (1949), 71–80; also Craddock, *Young Edward Gibbon*, p. 336, n. 87. Gibbon's malady, long supposed to be a hydrocele but in fact probably a hernia, later complicated by cirrhosis of the liver, became medical legend. See C. MacLaurin, *Post Mortem: Essays, Historical and Medical* (London, 1923), p. 180: "For many years it has been taught—I have taught it myself to generations of students—that Gibbon's hydrocele surpassed in greatness all other hydroceles, that it contained twelve pints of fluid, and that it was, in short, one of those monstrous things which exist mainly in romance; one of those chimeras which grow in the minds of the half-informed and of those who wish to be deceived."

22. This resolution, that "the influence of the crown has increased, is increasing, and ought to be diminished," was carried by a vote of 233 to 215, with Gibbon voting against it. Dunning's support was short-lived; a

few weeks later he was in a minority voting for a similar resolution that he had proposed.

23. de Beer, *Gibbon and His World*, p. 120.

24. See Craddock, *Young Edward Gibbon*, pp. 106, 161–62, 211–12, 227. It is likely that Gibbon had some experience with prostitutes in his youth. If, as is possible, he had homosexual inclinations, it is almost certain he never acted on them. The "effeminacy" of Byzantium offended him deeply. See Dennis M. Oliver, "The Character of an Historian: Edward Gibbon," *ELH*, 38 (1971), 263–64: "There is a natural enough tendency to suspect Gibbon of homosexuality. . . . [But] Gibbon's natural state is asexuality, as befits the neutral historian, who has a Tiresias-like ability to 'see both sides' of every activity."

25. British Library, Add. Mss. 34885, f. 222v. In a letter to Dorothea Gibbon, 21 November 1793, written a week after his first operation, in what Norton characterizes as a "very shaky hand" (*L*, III, 364n), Gibbon made another slip that may carry unconscious meaning. First he wrote: "You may justly reproach me with the long neglect of a growing, but I am now in the hands of the most skillful physicians and surgeons." Then he went back to insert the missing word: "a growing complaint" (Add. Mss. 34885, f. 224r).

26. Gibbon did write "summer," not "supper"; British Library, Add. Mss. 34883, f. 92v. A few lines later he makes another slip of the pen; Suzanne is "as handsome as every" instead of "as handsome as ever." Low speculates that these slips "possibly betray a nervous excitement which he would have disclaimed" (*Edward Gibbon*, pp. 192–93).

27. Gibbon twice rewrote the episode. One motive in these revisions may have been a desire to eliminate the untruth that he had recorded the moment of conception in his journal. This is his first revision: "It was on the fifteenth of October, in the gloom of evening, as I sat musing on the Capitol, while the barefooted fryars were chanting their litanies in the temple of Jupiter, that I conceived the first thought of my history" (*D*, 405–6). And the second: "It was at Rome, on the fifteenth of October, 1764, as I sat musing amidst the ruins of the Capitol, while the barefooted fryars were singing Vespers in the temple of Jupiter, that the idea of writing the decline and fall of the City first started to my mind" (*E*, 302). In these versions, Gibbon has edited out both the string of prepositional phrases that complicates the syntax of the first version and the syntactical ambiguity in his superimposition of the temple upon the church. Now the temple supplants the church altogether in his imagination. J. A. W. Bennett points out that it was Famiano Nardini, in his *Roma antica* (1666), who erroneously located the church of the Aracoeli on the site of the Temple of Jupiter (*Essays on Gibbon* [Cambridge, Eng., 1980], pp. 54–55). Of relevant interest are three engravings in my possession, apparently from a collection by the mid-eighteenth-century publisher John Bowles (though currently unrecorded in the Eighteenth-Century Short Title Catalogue). The engravings recreate, in a fantastical way, Roman architectural scenes. One of these is

"The inside of the Temple of Jupiter at Rome"; at the front of a long colonnade stands a solitary figure in eighteenth-century dress, looking out like a gatekeeper to the temple.

For comment on the several versions of Gibbon's epiphany on the Capitol, see David P. Jordan, *Gibbon and His Roman Empire* (Urbana, Ill., 1971), pp. 18f. Bonnard takes the first version for his text, discusses later versions in his notes, and asks rhetorically: "To what extent is the famous sentence fact, to what extent imagination?" (*M*, 305). See also Patricia B. Craddock, "Edward Gibbon and the 'Ruins of the Capitol,'" in *Roman Images: Selected Papers from the English Institute, 1982* (New Series, no. 8), ed. Annabel Patterson (Baltimore, Md., 1984), pp. 63–82; and P. R. Ghosh, "Gibbon's Dark Ages: Some Remarks on the Genesis of the *Decline and Fall*," *Journal of Roman Studies*, 73 (1983), 5f. Melvyn New suggests that the conception of the *Decline and Fall* may have been shaped in Gibbon's mind by a passage in Conyers Middleton's *History of the Life of Marcus Tullius Cicero* (1741); see "Gibbon, Middleton and the 'Barefooted Fryars,'" *Notes and Queries*, N.S. 25 (1978), 51–52. Finally, Patricia B. Craddock offers an explanation of why Gibbon may have settled on the date of 15 October 1764: on 15 October 1763, he was working on an entry for "Rome" in a collection of materials on ancient Italy that Sheffield eventually published in *MW* under the (not fully descriptive) title of *Nomina gentesque antiquae Italiae*. The earlier date Gibbon recorded in his journal. Craddock speculates that 15 October 1763 and 15 October 1764 may have come together in his memory (*Young Edward Gibbon*, p. 341, n. 79).

I am grateful to George Brown for information about the Vespers service that Gibbon would have heard, or overheard, on 15 October 1764.

28. More precisely, the moon was two days, fifteen and one-half hours short of being full; *The Memoirs of the Life of Edward Gibbon*, ed. Hill, pp. 331–32.

29. Max F. Schulz, "The Circuit Walk of the Eighteenth-Century Landscape Garden and the Pilgrim's Circuitous Progress," *Eighteenth-Century Studies*, 15 (1981–82), 25.

30. On "sublimated sexual drama" in Gibbon's autobiography, see Willis R. Buck, Jr., "Reading Autobiography," *Genre*, 13 (1980), 485f.

THREE

1. On Gibbon's several versions of how he came to his vocation, see Chapter 7. This one comes from the second draft of his autobiography (*B*, 193) and is used by Sheffield and subsequent editors. It is more decisive than later versions.

2. In the autobiography Gibbon transcribes several passages from the journal he kept while on militia duty but alters the original freely. In this case the original reads: "I at last fixed upon Sir Walter Raleigh for my hero, and found in his life a subject important, interesting and various" (*Gibbon's Journal to January 28th, 1763*, ed. D. M. Low [New York, 1929], p. 30). Gibbon dates this entry 4 August 1761, but the date and the facts are subject

to uncertainty: he began keeping the journal day by day on 10 September 1761, and everything before then is a reconstruction (probably derived from another written record, for it is often quite precise). In revising the original, Gibbon makes Raleigh's particular attraction for him apparent: "At length I have fixed on Sir Walter Raleigh for my Hero. His eventful story is varied by the characters of the soldier and sailor, the courtier and historian" (*M*, 120).

3. The original journal entry on which this is based reads: "I must look out for some other subject" (*Gibbon's Journal*, ed. Low, p. 103).

4. See *MW*, III, 98–155, "Introduction à l'histoire générale de la République des Suisses." For commentary, see H. S. Offler, "Edward Gibbon and the Making of His 'Swiss History,'" *Durham University Journal*, 41 (1948–49), 64–75; and Patricia B. Craddock, *Young Edward Gibbon: Gentleman of Letters* (Baltimore, Md., 1982), pp. 253–56. In the autobiography Gibbon claims to have burned the manuscript after it had been read and judged unfavorably "in a litterary society of foreigners in London" (*M*, 141). His obscure account of his participation in the reading points to the elusiveness of his strategies. Somehow he managed to be present but not known as the author: "as the author was unknown, I listened without observation, to the free strictures and unfavourable sentence of my judges" (*M*, 141–42).

5. Unlike other texts cited in this paragraph (but like the history of Swiss liberty), the *Mémoires littéraires* play no further part in this study. For a review of their history and contents, see J. E. Norton, *A Bibliography of the Works of Edward Gibbon* (New York, 1970; originally published, 1940), pp. 11–18. The first volume did not sell well, and plans for a quarterly issue were abandoned. The second volume, which had a different publisher, appeared early in 1769. By 22 September 1769 (according to Norton), twelve copies had been sold in England, and twenty-five were for sale in Germany at the wholesale price of 1s. 6d. Expenses were some £29 (ibid., p. 13). On the attribution of individual reviews, see Craddock, *Young Edward Gibbon*, pp. 257–68.

6. In particular, see Giuseppe Giarrizzo, *Edward Gibbon e la cultura Europea del settecento* (Naples, 1954); and Michel Baridon, *Edward Gibbon et le mythe de Rome: Histoire et idéologie au siècle des lumières* (Paris, 1977). David P. Jordan, *Gibbon and His Roman Empire* (Urbana, Ill., 1971) is also valuable; especially Chapters 4 and 5, "Gibbon's Jansenist Mentors" (on Tillemont and Pascal) and "Three Models of Excellence" (on Tacitus, Montesquieu, and Bayle).

7. In general, I have translated Gibbon's French into English and only given the original in the text for reasons of emphasis.

8. "Qui portent tous les caractères de l'évidence" (*MW*, III, 3).

9. Jean le Rond d'Alembert, *Mémoirs et réflexions sur Christine, Reine de Suède*, in *Mélanges de littérature, d'histoire, et de philosophie* (Amsterdam, 1759), II, 230: "Il seroit à souhaiter que tous les cent ans on fit un extrait des faits historiques réellement utiles, & qu'on brûlât le reste."

10. "Je m'oppose, sans crainte du nom flétrissant d'érudit, à la sentence,

par laquelle ce juge éclairé mais sévère, ordonne qu'à la fin d'un siècle on rassemble tous les faits, qu'on en choisisse quelques uns, et qu'on livre le reste aux flammes" (*EL*, 105).

11. "Cette Reine impérieuse, qui, non contente de regner, proscrit ses soeurs, et déclare tout raisonnement peu digne de ce nom, qui ne roule pas sur des lignes et sur des nombres" (*EL*, 85).

12. William Maitland, *The History of London, from Its Foundations by the Romans, to the Present Time* (London, 1739), p. 548.

13. "Hence some say History has two Eyes, *Chronology* and *Geography*," Aegidius Strauch, *Breviarium chronologicum* (London, 1699), p. 3. (Published first in 1664, Strauch's text was translated into English by Richard Sault, according to the title page, from the third edition.) The image was a commonplace, perhaps attributable to Isaac Vossius: "The elder *Vossius* said very well in the beginning of his Chronological Dissertations, *That Chronology and Geography, were two inseparable Sisters, and the two Eyes of History, without which she must inevitably be either Blind or very Obscure*" (Thomas Hearne, *Ductor historicus: or, A Short System of Universal History, and an Introduction to the Study of it*, 2d ed. [London, 1705], p. 128). On Gibbon and chronological learning, see Baridon, *Edward Gibbon et le mythe de Rome*, pp. 253–67; and Giarrizzo, *Edward Gibbon e la cultura Europea del settecento*, pp. 18–24.

14. Thomas Hearne's *Ductor historicus*, which Gibbon read early, may have been even more influential in his development than, at the distance of forty years, he wants to admit: he mentions it, along with the *Universal History* by George Sale, George Psalmanazar, and others (which he had read as it was reissued in octavo, 1747–54, after its original publication a decade earlier) as having "referred and introduced me to the Greek and Roman historians to as many at least as were accessible to an English reader" (*M*, 41). Hearne's compendium was the work of a learned young amateur, and Gibbon would have found in it congenial advice. Without chronological tables and geographical maps, says Hearne, "the greatest Learning will make your Head but a confus'd Library" (p. 44).

15. Edward Wells, *A New Sett of Maps* (Oxford, 1701).

16. Christoph Keller's *Notitia orbis antiqui* (Leipzig, 1701, 1706), is a learned treatise in two volumes, with an "Index geographicus" and the usual array of illustrations and maps.

17. Hearne also uses the Lockean vocabulary. Maps and tables "leave a clear and distinct Notion . . . in the Imagination, and make an Impression upon the Memory" (*Ductor historicus*, p. 43).

18. In *Some Thoughts concerning Education* (London, 1693), John Locke advises that a young student should study first geography, then arithmetic and astronomy, then geometry, and then chronology. On the one hand, without chronology and geography "history will be very ill retained, and very little useful; but be only a jumble of Matters of Fact, confusedly heaped together without Order or Instruction" (p. 217). On the other hand, Locke dismisses the learned "noise and dust" of chronological controversy: "When I speak of *Chronology* as a Science he [the student] should be perfect

in, I do not mean the little Controversies, that are in it. These are endless, and most of them of so little importance to a Gentleman, as not to deserve to be enquir'd into, were they capable of an easy Decision. And therefore all that learned Noise and Dust of the Chronologist is wholly to be avoided." From here Locke goes on to praise Strauch: "The most useful Book I have seen in that part of Learning, is a small Treatise of *Strauchius*" (p. 218).

19. For Gibbon's list of his early reading, see *M*, 43. In his notes (*M*, 251–52), Bonnard identifies Strauch, Anderson, Helvicus, and the rest (though not always reliably in matters of detail). Humphrey Prideaux's *Old and New Testament Connected* (1716–18) had gone through a dozen editions by the middle of the century.

20. Alexander Pope, "The First Epistle of the Second Book of *Horace*" ("To Augustus"), *Imitations of Horace*, ed. John Butt (London, 1961), p. 219. On the meanings of correctness in Pope, see Geoffrey Tillotson, *On the Poetry of Pope* (Oxford, 1938), pp. 1–140.

21. Gibbon adds a third article to his criticism of Sallust: "Having undertaken a particular history of the Jugurthine War; he neither informs us of the fate of the conquered province nor of the Captive King" (*EE*, 110). As well as being chronologically and geographically accurate, correctness means leaving no loose ends.

22. The catalogue of Gibbon's Bentinck Street library indicates how central chronology remained to his conception of history. It is divided into eight principal parts, of which the first is "HISTORIA." The first subhead under HISTORIA includes chronology and universal history (British Library, Add. Mss. 46141, f. 2r). Under "Chronology" appear the familiar texts: Eusebius, Newton, Scaliger, Strauch, and so on. See Geoffrey Keynes, *The Library of Edward Gibbon: A Catalogue*, 2d ed. (Dorchester, Eng., 1980), p. 20. On the partly chronological ordering of Gibbon's library card catalogue in Lausanne, see Appendix B.

23. "Il a souvent quitté le personnage d'historien pour celui de rhéteur et même de poëte" (*MW*, III, 4).

24. On Newton's chronological system and the controversies it aroused, see Frank E. Manuel, *The Eighteenth Century Confronts the Gods* (Cambridge, Mass., 1959), pp. 83–125.

25. "On peut douter . . . si cet épisode blesse la véritable chronologie. Dans le système plausible du Chevalier Newton, Enée et Didon se trouvent contemporains" (*EL*, 67–68).

26. "Quel art dans le poete de saisir le moment où Enée arrive à Carthage, pour répondre à ses critiques, de la seule maniere que la rapidité de sa marche et la grandeur de son sujet pouvoient le lui permettre! Il leur fait sentir que dans ses hypothèses la rencontre de Didon et d'Enée n'est point une licence poëtique" (*EL*, 71n).

27. "Virgile n'est point le seul qui ait revoqué en doute la chronologie vulgaire des Rois Latins" (*EL*, 71n).

28. "Quiconque ôse condamner l'épisode de Didon est plus philosophe ou moins homme de gout que moi" (*EL*, 67).

29. In 1757, Gibbon had noticed a geographic puzzle in the *Georgics*: How could Virgil, who combined a scholar's knowledge with the skill of a poet, "qui réunissoit les connoissances du savant aux talens du bel-esprit," have put Persia and the Nile next to each other? Gibbon then tried to answer the question. ("Remarques critiques sur une passage de Virgile," *MW*, III, 385f.)

30. On Gibbon as a literary critic, and his commentary on Hurd, see Hoyt Trowbridge, "Edward Gibbon, Literary Critic," *Eighteenth-Century Studies*, 4 (1970–71), 403–19.

31. From D. M. Low, "Gibbon's Correspondence with J. J. Breitinger," included as "Appendix I" in Norton's edition of the *Letters* (*L*, I, 387–90).

32. Translations of Gibbon's letters to Breitinger are by Norton.

33. Craddock, *Young Edward Gibbon*, p. 137.

34. "The præposterous mixture of an English dedication was enjoyned by Mr. Mallett" (*C*, 255; also *D*, 402). In his edition, Sheffield suppressed Gibbon's description of Mallett's advice as "foolish." I suspect Sheffield's reticence stemmed from sensitivity to Gibbon's relationship with his father; Mallett, having died thirty years earlier, was beyond insult. And perhaps Sheffield thought that Mallett's advice was not foolish in any case (for reasons that will appear).

35. Compare Martin Price's description of the opening pages of the *Decline and Fall* as marked by "a typical readiness for irony, clearly hinted but not quite precipitated" ("'The Dark and Implacable Genius of Superstition': An Aspect of Gibbon's Irony," in *Augustan Worlds: Essays in Honour of A. R. Humphreys*, ed. J. C. Hilson, M. M. B. Jones, and J. R. Watson [Leicester, Eng., 1978], p. 247).

36. Melvyn New, "Sterne, Warburton, and the Burden of Exuberant Wit," *Eighteenth-Century Studies*, 15 (1981–82), 245. For Johnson on Warburton, see pp. 245–46.

37. In *Gibbon's Antagonism to Christianity* (New York, n.d.; originally published London, 1933), Shelby T. McCloy surveys the outpouring of answers to Gibbon's treatment of Christianity. See also Norton, *A Bibliography*, pp. 78–93 and 233–47.

38. A complete account of young Gibbon's dealings with authority would include the pseudonymous letter he wrote to Hurd in the summer of 1772, more than two years after the *Critical Observations* appeared, disputing the authenticity of the Book of Daniel. The letter is more polite than the *Critical Observations*, if not quite as polite as Patricia B. Craddock claims (*Young Edward Gibbon*, p. 300). Innuendo, though not absent in Gibbon's opening address to Hurd, is muted: "I flatter myself that I am speaking to a candid critic, and to a philosophical divine; whose first passion is the love of truth. On this pleasing supposition, let me venture to ask you . . . " (*L*, I, 328). At the end of the letter Gibbon asks Hurd to address any answer to "Daniel Freeman," then adds that if his correspondent has "any scruple of engaging with a mask," he stands ready "to disclose my real name and place of abode" (*L*, I, 338–39). Hurd did not accept this invita-

tion—or is it a plea?—to ask Gibbon to disclose himself (and so to make him, perhaps, truly a "free man").

On the connection between the *Critical Observations* and the *Decline and Fall*, see P. R. Ghosh, "Gibbon's Dark Ages: Some Remarks on the Genesis of the *Decline and Fall*," *Journal of Roman Studies*, 73 (1983), 15: "the *Critical Observations* testify to Gibbon's continuing absorption in the study of ancient religion and its connection with politics, a theme foreshadowed in the *Essai* and which is, of course, a hallmark of the *Decline and Fall*." Ghosh's article is an important account of "Gibbon's hesitant shuffle towards Roman history" (ibid.).

39. On the ideal of the philosophic historian and its origin, see Frank E. Manuel, "Edward Gibbon: Historien-Philosophe," in *Edward Gibbon and the Decline and Fall of the Roman Empire*, ed. G. W. Bowersock, John Clive, and Stephen R. Graubard (Cambridge, Mass., 1977), pp. 167–81.

40. "L'histoire est pour un esprit philosophique ce qu'étoit le jeu pour le Marquis de Dangeau. Il voyoit un systême, des rapports, une suite, là–où les autres ne discernoient que les caprices de la fortune. Cette science est pour lui celle des causes et des effets" (*EL*, 94–95).

41. "Pour lier à vos yeux la chaine des évenements, et remplir votre ame des plus sages leçons" (*EL*, 103).

42. "Choisira parmi les faits contestés, ceux qui s'accordent le mieux avec ses principes, et ses vues. . . . Le désir de les émployer [*sic*] leur donnera même un degré d'évidence qu'ils n'ont pas; et la logique du coeur ne l'emportera que trop souvent sur celle de l'esprit" (*MW*, III, 46).

43. In his letter to Hurd on the authenticity of the Book of Daniel, Gibbon wrote: "I have endeavoured to form something like this chain of witnesses in favour of the Book of Daniel; but without being able to carry it higher than the first century of the Christian aera" (*L*, I, 331). To get back to beginnings is to move higher on the charts and tables of time.

44. Edward Gibbon, *An Essay on the Study of Literature* (London, 1764), p. 90.

FOUR

1. Virginia Woolf, "The Historian and 'The Gibbon,'" in *Collected Essays* (New York, 1967), pp. 115, 118; "Reflections at Sheffield Place," ibid., p. 129. Both essays, written in the spring of 1937, were published in *The Death of the Moth* (London, 1942).

A full treatment of prospect poetry and prospect situations in the eighteenth century remains to be written, as does a larger study of prospects from, say, Lucretius or Seneca to Roland Barthes. What Barthes says of the Eiffel Tower might almost be said of Gibbon's experience in the *Decline and Fall*: "the Tower can live on itself: one can dream there, eat there, observe there, understand there, marvel there, shop there; as on an ocean liner (another mythic object that sets children dreaming), one can feel oneself cut off from the world and yet the owner of a world" (*The Eiffel Tower and Other Mythologies*, tr. Richard Howard [New York, 1979], p. 17).

On the prospect situation, see Jay Appleton, *The Experience of Landscape* (London, 1975), pp. 85–95. On eighteenth-century prospects, see John Dixon Hunt, *The Figure in the Landscape: Poetry, Painting, and Gardening During the Eighteenth Century* (Baltimore, Md., 1976), especially pp. 224–45; also, on Montesquieu, Georges Van Den Abbeele, "Montesquieu *touriste*, or a View from the Top," *L'Esprit créateur*, 25 (Fall 1985), 64–74 (I am grateful to Pierre St. Amand for this reference). For a study of how Swift's vision of the world differs from that of the prospect-seekers, see Carole Fabricant, *Swift's Landscape* (Baltimore, Md., 1982), especially pp. 173–209. On *Coopers Hill*, the chief inspiration for eighteenth-century prospect poetry, and on other prospect situations, see W. B. Carnochan, *Confinement and Flight: An Essay on English Literature of the Eighteenth Century* (Berkeley, Calif., 1977), especially pp. 102f. And for a reading of *Coopers Hill* quite the contrary of mine, see James Turner, *The Politics of Landscape: Rural Scenery and Society in English Poetry 1630–1660* (Cambridge, Mass., 1979), pp. 49–64. On the evolution of prospect poetry in Germany, see Theodore Ziolkowski, *The Classical German Elegy 1795–1950* (Princeton, N.J., 1980), especially, on Schiller's "Spaziergang," pp. 3–26. On the concept of distance in the eighteenth century, see John T. Ogden, "From Spatial to Aesthetic Distance in the Eighteenth Century," *Journal of the History of Ideas*, 35 (1974), 63–78. Ogden's argument, relevant to Gibbon's situation in the *Decline and Fall*, is that distance in the eighteenth century "comes to be understood as the ground for apprehending the objective world" and, also, that "understanding distance served as a means for integrating subjective and objective realms of experience" (p. 78).

2. Frederick A. Pottle, "Synchrony and Diachrony: A Plea for the Use in Literary Studies of Saussure's Concepts and Terminology," in *Literary Theory and Structure: Essays in Honor of William K. Wimsatt*, ed. Frank Brady, John Palmer, and Martin Price (New Haven, Conn., 1973), p. 10; Roger J. Porter, "Gibbon's *Autobiography*: Filling Up the Silent Vacancy," *Eighteenth-Century Studies*, 8 (1974–75), 15; Michael Joyce, *Edward Gibbon* (London, 1953), p. 122; David P. Jordan, *Gibbon and His Roman Empire* (Urbana, Ill., 1971), p. 152; Harold L. Bond, *The Literary Art of Edward Gibbon* (Oxford, 1960), p. 112; Carl L. Becker, *The Heavenly City of the Eighteenth-Century Philosophers* (New Haven, Conn., 1932), p. 117.

3. Gibbon recorded these and a few other afterthoughts as marginalia in a copy of the *Decline and Fall* (British Library; shelf mark, C.60 m.I). Craddock reprints these marginalia and suggests that they are "probably part of Gibbon's abortive attempt at a seventh, supplemental volume for the *Decline and Fall*" (*EE*, 587), though they generally take the form of amendments to the original text.

4. On Gibbon's mixed feelings about the Antonine Utopia, see A. Lentin, "Edward Gibbon and 'The Golden Age of the Antonines,'" *History Today*, 31 (July 1981), 33–39.

5. While in Lausanne during the autumn of 1763 and preparing for his journey to Italy, Gibbon recorded a long series of notes and observations that he intended as a systematic guide to the geography, antiquities, and in

some measure the history of ancient Italy. When Sheffield rearranged these (and other) materials and published them in *MW* as *Nomina gentesque antiquae Italiae*, he obscured the centrality of Rome in Gibbon's mind even at this early stage; after some prefatory observations, Gibbon starts at Rome, then moves outward to other parts of Italy and finally to the Alps. Patricia B. Craddock points out: "This is the order of a man with a Roman imagination; Sheffield replaced it with the itinerary of an English Traveler" (*Young Edward Gibbon: Gentleman of Letters* [Baltimore, Md., 1982], p. 183).

6. *Inquiring Spirit: A New Presentation of Coleridge from His Published and Unpublished Prose Writings*, ed. Kathleen Coburn (London, 1951), pp. 181–82. Like so many of Gibbon's readers, Coleridge has his own version, a disapproving and inaccurate one, of how the historian assumes the heights: "he skips on from eminence to eminence, without ever taking you through the valleys between" (p. 181).

7. On 11 December 1772, Gibbon wrote Holroyd that "the punishment of my sins has at length overtaken me. On Thursday the third of December in the present year of our Lord one Thousand seven hundred and seventy two, between the hours of one and two in the Afternoon, as I was crossing St. James's Church Yard, I stumbled, and *again sprained my foot*, but alas after two days pain and Confinement, a horrid Monster *ycleped the Gout made me* a short Visit, and though he now has taken his leave, I am full of apprehensions that he may have liked my company well enough to call again" (*L*, I, 351–52). The worst of Gibbon's later attacks of gout came in 1790 when, from February to July, "I was not able to move from my house or chair" (*L*, III, 197).

8. On 16 October 1775, Gibbon wrote to the historian John Whitaker, who had attacked Macpherson in 1772: "With regard to your old friend Ossian, the dogmatic language of Johnson, and the acquiescence or indifference of the Scotch, particularly of Macpherson, seem to have given the bard a dangerous, if not a mortal wound. It appears to be the prevailing opinion, that truth and falsehood, the Highland ballads, and the fancy of the translator are blended together in such a manner, that unless he himself should condescend to give the clue, there is no power of criticism capable of untwisting them" (*L*, II, 91). The inextricability of truth and falsehood—that is, of ancient sources and of Macpherson's own invention in the Ossianic poems—suits Gibbon's purpose exactly. It also reflects a more accurate understanding of the Ossianic poems than Johnson's "extreme acerbities," which a modern student of Macpherson regards as a matter almost of "curiosity" (Derick S. Thomson, *The Gaelic Sources of Macpherson's "Ossian"* [Edinburgh, n.d.], p. 1).

9. Of this passage, Martine Watson Brownley comments that Gibbon is "at his best at those times when he can work not with or against facts but in spite of them" ("Gibbon's Artistic and Historical Scope in the *Decline and Fall*," *Journal of the History of Ideas*, 42 [1981], 641).

10. The sudden shift in viewpoint lodged within the parallel structure— "in a composition of some days, in a perusal of some hours"—gives force to the first person plural Gibbon has been using ("if we compute"; "our

intellectual view"). He effects a syntactical rapprochement between the historian and his readers.

11. Poggio Bracciolini, *Historiae de varietate fortunae* (Paris, 1723; reprinted, Bologna, 1969), pp. 5–6. The line from Virgil is *Aeneid*, VIII, 348. In *The Language of History in the Renaissance: Rhetoric and Historical Consciousness in Florentine Humanism* (Princeton, N.J., 1970), Nancy S. Struever implies affinities—including a shared "posture of detachment or disjunction" (p. 154)—between Gibbon and Poggio's Renaissance humanism.

12. *Aeneid*, II, 274–75; *Paradise Lost*, I, 84–85; Isaiah 14: 12.

13. Poggio Bracciolini, *Historiae de varietate fortunae*, p. 21. Cited by Gibbon, *Decline and Fall*, VII, 314n.

14. Lionel Gossman, *The Empire Unpossess'd: An Essay on Gibbon's "Decline and Fall"* (Cambridge, Mass., 1981), p. 91. Gossman's study, combining psychological and semiotic analysis, paints a monochromatic picture of Gibbon's intellectual character, yet it is a powerful one. This is how Gossman describes the relationship between Gibbon's physical disability and his view of the world: "Gibbon's sense of a flaw at the source of being appears to have been both an opportunity and a limitation: an opportunity in that it led him to assume a critical stance with respect to the world, his own disability having made him no doubt uncommonly alert to the secret flaws of others; a limitation in that the absence of a ground or origin of authority seems still to have been thought of by him as a 'flaw,' a shame to be concealed, or at best shared only with an elite who would be unlikely to abuse the confidence, and a pathological rather than a normal condition" (p. 18).

15. *Gibbon's Journal to January 28th, 1763*, ed. D. M. Low (New York, 1929), p. 70. (Gibbon was born on 27 April, old style; or 8 May, new style.) Gibbon was not indifferent to formal problems of aesthetic value and visual perception, as is evident from his commentary on the cathedral dome in Florence. While he thought it worthy of all the praise it had received—grand, simple, and sublime—he remarked that a dome, though the most beautiful form in architecture, is also the least susceptible of being seen and appreciated from different points of vantage: "la Coupole quoiqu'elle soit peut-etre la plus belle figure de l'architecture est peut-etre aussi celle qui est susceptible du plus petit nombre de points de vue avantageux" (*Gibbon's Journey from Geneva to Rome: His Journal from 20 April to 2 October, 1764*, ed. Georges A. Bonnard [London, 1961], pp. 216, 217).

16. *Lucian*, tr. A. M. Harmon (London, 1915), II, 287, 289, 293, 295.

17. Michel Baridon, *Edward Gibbon et le mythe de Rome: Histoire et idéologie au siècle des lumières* (Paris, 1977), p. 369.

18. José Ortega y Gasset, "On Point of View in the Arts," in his *The Dehumanization of Art and Other Essays on Art, Culture, and Literature* (Princeton, N.J., 1968), pp. 110, 112.

19. Ibid., pp. 129f.

20. For a commentary on the ingrained Romantic association of sublimity and bathos, see Peter Conrad, *Shandyism: The Character of Romantic Irony* (Oxford, 1978); especially pp. 134–36.

21. *The Poetical Works of the Late Thomas Warton, B.D.* (Oxford, 1802; reprinted, Farnborough, Eng., 1969), I, 68, 69.

1. With the deaths of Charles Churchill in 1764 and Laurence Sterne in 1768, the breed of English ironists virtually died out, Gibbon excepted. Satirists of the late century like "Peter Pindar" (John Wolcot) and William Gifford had little talent for irony. See W. B. Carnochan, "Satire, Sublimity, and Sentiment: Theory and Practice in Post-Augustan Satire," *Publications of the Modern Language Association*, 85 (1970), 260–67; and Thomas Lockwood, *Post-Augustan Satire: Charles Churchill and Satirical Poetry, 1750–1800* (Seattle, Wash., 1979).

2. Swift wrote Pope on 20 September 1723: "I have often endeavoured to establish a Friendship among all Men of Genius, and would fain have it done. they are seldom above three or four Cotemporaries and if they could be united would drive the world before them" (*The Correspondence of Jonathan Swift*, ed. Harold Williams [Oxford, 1963–65], II, 465).

3. Irvin Ehrenpreis's demonstration that Swift exaggerated his solitariness (see Chap. 2, n. 7) can alter but not efface the sense of his isolation. Swift was no hypocrite, and whatever may have been the external conditions of his life, he surely felt as he said he did.

4. Howard D. Weinbrot has severe views about the Augustan label (*Augustus Caesar in "Augustan" England: The Decline of a Classical Norm* [Princeton, N.J., 1978]). His argument depends on the true claim that Augustus was not loved in the English "Augustan" age. Yet it can be argued that the "Augustanism" of Swift and Pope derives, like Horace's, from ambivalent reactions to imperial power. Labels like "Augustan" have uses as well as abuses. I think Weinbrot mistakes the one for the other.

5. Quoted in Stewart Perowne, *Hadrian* (London, 1960), p. 179; I have corrected the first line from Perowne's "Animula, blandula, vagula." The source of the lyric is the life of Hadrian in the *Augustan History*. On its authenticity, see Herbert W. Benario, *A Commentary on the Vita Hadriani in the Historia Augusta* (Ann Arbor, Mich., 1980), p. 136n.

6. *The Literary Works of Matthew Prior*, ed. H. Bunker Wright and Monroe K. Spears, 2d ed. (Oxford, 1971), I, 196.

7. *Lord Byron: The Complete Poetical Works*, ed. Jerome J. McGann (Oxford, 1980), I, 70.

8. Others who translated Hadrian's farewell to his soul were Fontenelle and Pope. Pope catches the mood less successfully than either Prior or Byron, and his last line shatters the fragility of the lyric with an Augustan farewell to "Wit and Humour":

> Ah fleeting Spirit! wand'ring Fire,
>   That long has warm'd my tender Breast,
> Must thou no more this Frame inspire?
>   No more a pleasing, chearful Guest?
>
> Whither, ah whither art thou flying!
>   To what dark, undiscover'd Shore?
> Thou seem'st all trembling, shiv'ring, dying,
>   And Wit and Humour are no more!

(*Minor Poems*, ed. Norman Ault and John Butt [London, 1954], p. 93. This is Volume VI of the Twickenham Edition.)

9. In the land of the giants, Gulliver reads in "a little old Treatise" that "Nature was degenerated in these latter declining Ages of the World, and could now produce only small abortive Births in Comparison of those in ancient Times." (Jonathan Swift, *Gulliver's Travels*, ed. Herbert Davis, intro. Harold Williams, revised ed. [Oxford, 1959], p. 137. This is Volume XI of *The Prose Writings of Jonathan Swift*, ed. Herbert Davis [Oxford, 1939–68].)

10. On the conclusion of the *Tale of a Tub* and on Swift's habit of generating life out of annihilation, see W. B. Carnochan, "Swift's *Tale*: On Satire, Negation, and the Uses of Irony," *Eighteenth-Century Studies*, 5 (1971–72), 122–44; and Carnochan, "The Consolations of Satire," in *The Art of Jonathan Swift*, ed. Clive T. Probyn (London, 1978), pp. 19–42.

11. "I desire those Politicians, who dislike my Overture, and may perhaps be so bold to attempt an Answer, that they will first ask the Parents of these Mortals, Whether they would not, at this Day, think it a great Happiness to have been sold for Food at a Year old, in the Manner I prescribe; and thereby have avoided such a perpetual Scene of Misfortunes, as they have since gone through." (Jonathan Swift, *A Modest Proposal*, in *Irish Tracts, 1728–1733*, ed. Herbert Davis [Oxford, 1964], p. 117. This is Volume XII in *The Prose Writings of Jonathan Swift*.)

12. "For myself, it is my wish to depart in charity with all mankind; nor am I willing, in these last moments, to offend even the pope and clergy of Rome" (VII, 311).

13. Jonathan Swift, *A Tale of a Tub, to which is added The Battle of the Books and the Mechanical Operation of the Spirit*, ed. A. C. Guthkelch and D. Nichol Smith, 2d ed. (Oxford, 1958), pp. 230, 231.

14. Swift's feelings about Temple are matter of dispute. In the first volume of his biography, Irvin Ehrenpreis maintains that Swift admired Temple wholeheartedly, both in private and in public (*Swift: The Man, His Works, and the Age* [Cambridge, Mass., 1962–83], I, 174–75). But John Traugott claims, I think correctly, that Swift smarted under the burden of Temple's urbane authority and that some of the hurt finds its way into the spider's confrontation with the bee: "The Spider is neither inept nor pert. In his high blood runs the quickening energy of the race of radical individualists that inhabit Swift's satire from first to last. It is they who inherit the earth" ("*A Tale of a Tub*," in *Focus: Swift*, ed. C. J. Rawson [London, 1971], p. 88). For Swift and Temple, see also A. C. Elias, Jr., *Swift at Moor Park: Problems in Biography and Criticism* (Philadelphia, 1982).

15. *The Drapier's Letters and Other Works, 1724–1725*, ed. Herbert Davis (Oxford, 1966), p. 48. This is Volume X of *The Prose Writings of Jonathan Swift*.

16. Alexander Pope, "Epilogue to the Satires: Dialogue II," in *Imitations of Horace*, ed. John Butt (London, 1961), p. 325.

17. Line references are to *The Dunciad in Four Books*, in *The Dunciad*, ed. James Sutherland, 3d ed. (London, 1963), pp. 323f. This is Volume V of the Twickenham Edition.

18. *The Dunciad*, ed. Sutherland, p. 158n.

19. On 3 July 1782, Gibbon wrote his stepmother, commenting on Hayley's *Essay on Epic Poetry*: "I hope you like Mr Hayley's poem, he rises with his subject, and since Pope's death, I am satisfied that England has not seen so happy a mixture of strong sense and flowing numbers" (*L*, II, 298). In 1780, Hayley had addressed his *Essay on History* to Gibbon and, the next year, had composed a sonnet to celebrate publication of the second and third volumes of the *Decline and Fall*. Later, on the occasion of the publication of the final volumes of the *Decline and Fall*, Hayley composed verses celebrating a triumvirate of Newton in science, Shakespeare in drama, and Gibbon in history (*MW*, I, 173–74n). See p. 124.

20. Blaise Pascal, *Les Provinciales*, ed. Louis Cognet (Paris, 1965), pp. 73–74.

21. Ibid., pp. 72–73.

22. Ibid., pp. 193f.

23. Ibid., p. 193n.

24. This summary simplifies a controversy that touched a deep nerve of the age. The *Provinciales* were well-known in England, and the eleventh letter may have had direct influence. Yet the question seems not to have been tested. John Barker's study of Pascal in England does not take it up (*Strange Contrarieties: Pascal in England During the Age of Reason* [Montreal, 1975]), nor does John Redwood, *Reason, Ridicule and Religion: The Age of Enlightenment in England* (Cambridge, Mass., 1976). Raymond A. Anselment notices the eleventh letter only as a "convenient" guide to patristic sources (*'Betwixt Jest and Earnest': Marprelate, Milton, Marvell, Swift & the Decorum of Religious Ridicule* [Toronto, 1979], p. 163, n.3).

25. Pascal, *Les Provinciales*, pp. 196–97.

26. See Richard H. Popkin, *The History of Scepticism from Erasmus to Spinoza* (Berkeley, Calif., 1979), p. 213: "Pascal stressed our plight, caught between a total Pyrrhonism that we could not avoid, and a nature that made us believe nonetheless." Of Gibbon it might be said that he expressed our plight, caught between a habit of belief that he could not avoid and a modified Pyrrhonism that made him doubt nonetheless.

27. *Les Pensées de Pascal*, ed. Francis Kaplan (Paris, 1982), p. 156.

28. Patricia B. Craddock, *Young Edward Gibbon: Gentleman of Letters* (Baltimore, Md., 1982), p. 50. Craddock comments: "in this episode we see a boy capable of quixotic, disinterested, impulsive acts, of acting out a role comparable to that of the heroes of far away and long ago on whom his imagination had fed. The man that boy became had no such desire or capacity" (p. 51). I agree with this description of Gibbon the boy—but not with the description of the man.

29. Jonathan Swift, *An Argument to Prove That the Abolishing of Christianity in England May . . . Be Attended with Some Inconveniencies*, in *Bickerstaff Papers and Pamphlets on the Church*, ed. Herbert Davis (Oxford, 1966), p. 27. This is Volume II of *The Prose Writings of Jonathan Swift*.

30. Edward Gibbon, *The Decline and Fall of the Roman Empire*, ed. The Rev. H. H. Milman (New York, n.d.), I, 508.

31. Gibbon owed Bayle a great deal, as the autobiography makes clear.

Not only had Bayle been "seduced" at a young age by the Jesuits but he became "a calm and lofty spectator of the Religious tempest" (*M*, 63, 64). For Bayle's influence on Gibbon, see David P. Jordan, *Gibbon and His Roman Empire* (Urbana, Ill., 1971), pp. 159–72; also Michel Baridon, *Edward Gibbon et le mythe de Rome: Histoire et idéologie au siècle des lumières* (Paris, 1977), especially pp. 410–15; and Giuseppe Giarrizzo, *Edward Gibbon e la cultura Europea del settecento* (Naples, 1954), passim.

32. "The end of writing is to instruct; the end of poetry is to instruct by pleasing." (Samuel Johnson, *Preface to Shakespeare*, in *Johnson on Shakespeare*, ed. Arthur Sherbo, intro. Bertrand H. Bronson [New Haven, Conn., 1968], I, 67. This is Volume VII of the Yale Edition of *The Works of Samuel Johnson*.)

33. The second definition of "entertaining" in the *OED* is "agreeable; interesting; now chiefly, amusing." The citation from Berkeley, included under this definition, comes from *Hylas and Philonous*. By 1860, the meaning of "entertaining" as "amusing" had been fixed: the *OED* cites a reference from that year reporting that the word, in "olden Scottish usage," had "the sense not of amusing but interesting."

34. Louis Kampf, "Gibbon and Hume," in *English Literature and British Philosophy*, ed. S. P. Rosenbaum (Chicago, 1971), p. 111.

35. It is not clear whether Kampf intends a distinction between mock epic and "ironic mock-epic." But I think not: "*The Dunciad*, with its mocking vision of doom, rather than Voltaire's *La Henriade*, is the epic of the eighteenth century" (ibid.).

36. D. C. Muecke, *The Compass of Irony* (London, 1969); Wayne C. Booth, *A Rhetoric of Irony* (Chicago, 1974); Anne K. Mellor, *English Romantic Irony* (Cambridge, Mass., 1980); Lilian R. Furst, *Fictions of Romantic Irony* (Harvard Studies in Comparative Literature, no. 36) (Cambridge, Mass., 1984); Peter L. Thorslev, Jr., *Romantic Contraries: Freedom Versus Destiny* (New Haven, Conn., 1984); Northrop Frye, *Anatomy of Criticism: Four Essays* (Princeton, N.J., 1957). For the tally of Gibbon's appearances in these studies, I have relied, like Swift's modern reader, on their indexes, "by which the whole Book is governed and turned, like *Fishes* by the *Tail*" (Swift, *A Tale of a Tub*, p. 145).

37. Hayden White, *Metahistory: The Historical Imagination in Nineteenth-Century Europe* (Baltimore, Md., 1973), pp. 54–55, 58, 69.

38. Ibid., p. 55.

39. Thorslev, *Romantic Contraries*, p. 145.

40. See Alexandre Koyré, *From the Closed World to the Infinite Universe* (Baltimore, Md., 1957).

41. Quoted in Muecke, *The Compass of Irony*, p. 151.

SIX

1. Virginia Woolf, "The Historian and 'The Gibbon,'" in *Collected Essays* (New York, 1967), p. 115.

2. Leo Braudy, *Narrative Form in History and Fiction* (Princeton, N.J., 1970), p. 253.

3. And the footnotes, often wittily salacious, take on more than incidental value. See James D. Garrison, "Lively and Laborious: Characterization in Gibbon's Metahistory," *Modern Philology*, 76 (1978–79), 163–78. Garrison considers Gibbon's treatment of authors who provided the materials of his history, concluding that "an unstable hierarchical arrangement of characters (conceived dynamically) coexists in the notes with a comparatively stable, lateral differentiation of characters (conceived statically)" (p. 166).

4. Harold Bond agrees with Braudy: "If one revolves in his mind a few of the leading figures of the history—Julian, Athanasius, St. Ambrose, Mahomet, Justinian, Belisarius, Constantius, and Andronicus Comnenus—one will be impressed by the vitality and the extraordinary energy which they possess" (*The Literary Art of Edward Gibbon* [Oxford, 1960], p. 91).

5. Alexander Pope, *Epistles to Several Persons*, ed. F. W. Bateson, 2d ed. (London, 1961), p. 30. This is Volume III.ii of the Twickenham Edition.

6. Alexander Pope, *An Essay on Man*, ed. Maynard Mack (London, 1950), pp. 70–72. This is Volume III.i of the Twickenham Edition.

7. The poem closes:

> And you! brave COBHAM, to the latest breath
> Shall feel your ruling passion strong in death:
> Such in those moments as in all the past,
> "Oh, save my Country, Heav'n!" shall be your last.

(*Epistles to Several Persons*, p. 38.) In a note (p. 38n), F. W. Bateson points out that Pope attributes the same dying sentiment to Atterbury in an epitaph written at much the same time as this epistle. The epitaph went unpublished, probably because Pope realized the risk of attributing the same sentiment to both men. When he canceled publication, he must have recognized, if he had not before, the tendency of ruling passions to become mechanical encrustations on the living personality.

8. E. M. Forster, *Aspects of the Novel and Related Writings*, ed. Oliver Stallybrass (London, 1974), pp. 46–51. This is Volume XII of the Abinger Edition of E. M. Forster.

9. In his unfinished argument with Hurd about the authenticity of the Book of Daniel, Gibbon drafted an answer to Hurd's proposition that "the strongest belief, or conviction of the mind, perpetually gives way to the inflamed selfish passions" (*MW*, I, 458). No, says Gibbon, and his answer might be taken to imply that all ruling passions feed slowly on themselves: drunkards and prodigals "sink by slow degrees; and, whilst they indulge the ruling passion, attend only to the trifling moment of each guinea, or of each bottle, without calculating their accumulated weight, till they feel themselves irretrievably crushed under it" (*MW*, I, 464).

10. I follow P. R. Ghosh, "Gibbon's Dark Ages: Some Remarks on the Genesis of the Decline and Fall," *Journal of Roman Studies*, 73 (1983), 23, in dating the essay on Brutus.

11. "Semblable aux observateurs de la nature il auroit reconnu que les expériences valoient mieux que les systèmes, et . . . il auroit expliqué le caractère de l'homme par ses actions (. . . avec bien des précautions,) non point les actions suivant l'idée qu'on s'étoit formé d'avance du caractère.

. . . Il auroit vu que bien loin que le caractère qu'on pose à la base de la narration soit uniforme, que bien loin, dis-je, qu'il puisse nous rendre raison de la conduite d'une vie entière, rien n'est plus dissemblable à l'homme de hier que l'homme d'aujourd'hui. . . . Les messieurs qui croyent pouvoir nous développer ainsi tous les motifs des actions des hommes (qui tres souvent ne les connoissent pas eux-mêmes) ont à la fois bien bonne opinion et de la constance des hommes et de leur propre pénétration; mais qu'ils se souviennent que . . ." (*MW*, III, 372).

12. Compare Pope, *Epistles to Several Persons*, p. 19.

13. On the man in the iron mask and Voltaire's interest in him, see Marcel Pagnol, *Le Masque de fer* (Paris, 1965), pp. 48–55. Gibbon had evidently not read Voltaire's last word on the subject. Even so, he is disingenuous to claim that Voltaire "never attempts . . . to reveal the secret of that wonderful Affair" (*EE*, 204).

14. Now Gibbon relics on Libanius rather than Ammianus Marcellinus. See Glen W. Bowersock, "Gibbon and Julian," in *Gibbon et Rome à la lumière de l'historiographie moderne*, ed. Pierre Ducrey with F. Burkhalter and R. Overmeer (Geneva, 1977), pp. 197f.

15. Compare Lionel Gossman, *The Empire Unpossess'd: An Essay on Gibbon's "Decline and Fall"* (Cambridge, Mass., 1981), p. 28: "Julian is not whole. He is divided, like Rome itself, self-consciously representing himself to himself in the theater of his mind in an effort at reappropriation, which is the mark of alienation and loss. Hence his return to the ancient religion of Rome never really succeeds."

16. La Bletterie thought that Julian had prepackaged his deathbed speech, that doing so was a mark of vanity, and that his death was "labored and theatrical" (Robert J. Ziegler, "Edward Gibbon and Julian the Apostate," *Papers on Language and Literature*, 10 [1974], 146).

17. "Extraordinary" was Gibbon's customary epithet to express a sense of rare human qualities. He had begun a brief, early commentary on Julius Caesar, by quoting Montesquieu on Caesar: "cet homme extraordinaire" (*MW*, III, 359). And the epithet, though it signified greatness, also signified puzzlement, as it does in Gibbon's final judgment of Constantine: "the character of Constantine is considered, even in the present age, as an object either of satire or of panegyric. By the impartial union of those defects which are confessed by his warmest admirers and of those virtues which are acknowledged by his most implacable enemies, we might hope to delineate a just portrait of that extraordinary man, which the truth and candour of history should adopt without a blush. But it would soon appear that the vain attempt to blend such discordant colours, and to reconcile such inconsistent qualities, must produce a figure monstrous rather than human, unless it is viewed in its proper and distinct lights by a careful separation of the different periods of the reign of Constantine" (II, 214). The only way to deal with Constantine's inconsistencies is by sorting them chronologically. On Gibbon and panegyric, see James D. Garrison, "Gibbon and the 'Treacherous Language of Panegyrics,'" *Eighteenth-Century Studies*, 11 (1977–78), 40–62.

18. When Henry Davis, aged twenty-one and a recent graduate of Balliol, published his *Examination of the Fifteenth and Sixteenth Chapters of Mr. Gibbon's History of the Decline and Fall of the Roman Empire* (1778), accusing the historian of "servile plagiarism," Gibbon answered with *A Vindication of Some Passages in the Fifteenth and Sixteenth Chapters of the History of the Decline and Fall of the Roman Empire* (1779); reprinted in *EE*, 229–313. Gibbon opens his defense by quoting Davis's charge of plagiarism (*EE*, 231). The *Vindication* is an extremely successful, often witty, polemic, which I would like to have found more room for here.

19. In the *Vindication*, Gibbon identifies himself with Swift's bee, whose materials come from outside himself, unlike the spider who spins his web from his entrails: "If my readers are satisfied with the form, the colours, the new arrangement which I have given to the labours of my predecessors, they may perhaps consider me not as a contemptible Thief, but as an honest and industrious Manufacturer, who has fairly procured the raw materials, and worked them up with a laudable degree of skill and success" (*EE*, 277).

20. If the roles of Julian and Mahomet express a sense of Gibbon's own dividedness, that of Theodora expresses an identity of actor and role; see pp. 121–23.

21. J. W. Burrow remarks that Gibbon "was stepping into an eighteenth-century debate on which he lacked the equipment to pronounce" and that his account "contains elements of both views"—Mahomet as an impostor or enthusiast, Mahomet as the philosophic legislator and unitarian prophet—"not altogether, as he recognizes, harmoniously combined" (*Gibbon* [Oxford, 1985], p. 77). See also Bernard Lewis, "Gibbon on Muhammad," in *Edward Gibbon and the Decline and Fall of the Roman Empire*, ed. G. W. Bowersock, John Clive, and Stephen R. Graubard (Cambridge, Mass., 1977), pp. 61–73. The strength of contemporary interest in Mahomet can be gauged from the fact that Joseph White's Bampton Lectures, delivered at Oxford in 1784 and containing "A View of Christianity and Mahometanism in their History, their Evidence, and their Effects," went through four editions by 1792. White politely challenged Gibbon's treatment of Christianity; in turn, Gibbon rather lavishly acknowledged the worth of the lectures: "[White] sustains the part of a lively and eloquent advocate; and sometimes rises to the merit of an historian and philosopher" (VI, 16n).

22. Pope, *Epistles to Several Persons*, pp. 49–50.

23. Ibid., pp. 67, 72.

24. On Beerbohm's "The Happy Hypocrite," see John Felstiner, *The Lies of Art: Max Beerbohm's Parody and Caricature* (New York, 1972), pp. 50–51.

25. On the interplay of "role" and character in the *Decline and Fall*, see Braudy, *Narrative Form in History and Fiction*, pp. 254f. On theatricality, see Martine Watson Brownley, "The Theatrical World of *Decline and Fall*," *Papers on Language and Literature*, 15 (1979), 263–77. On Gibbon's portraits of women, see Brownley, " 'The Purest and Most Gentle Portion of the Human Species': Gibbon's Portrayals of Women in the *Decline and Fall*," *South*

Atlantic Quarterly, 77 (1978), 1–14. If Gibbon habitually sees character—his own and others'—as role-dependent, it is usually for lack of a more coherent analysis. Theodora the actress rises above consistency; it is in that sense that Gibbon has stumbled over his own metaphor.

26. Pope, *Epistles to Several Persons*, p. 46.

SEVEN

1. On the autobiography see Barrett John Mandel, "The Problem of Narration in Edward Gibbon's *Autobiography*," *Studies in Philology*, 67 (1970), 550–64; Robert Folkenflik, "Child and Adult: Historical Perspective in Gibbon's Memoirs," *Studies in Burke and His Time*, 15 (1973–74), 31–43; Irma S. Lustig, "On the Conclusion to Robert Folkenflik's Child and Adult: Historical Perspective in Gibbon's Memoirs," *Studies in Burke and His Time*, 16 (1974–75), 149–52; Roger J. Porter, "Gibbon's *Autobiography*: Filling up the Silent Vacancy," *Eighteenth-Century Studies*, 8 (1974–75), 1–26; Martin Price, "The Inquisition of Truth: Memory and Freedom in Gibbon's Memoirs," *Philological Quarterly*, 54 (1975), 391–408; Patricia Meyer Spacks, *Imagining a Self: Autobiography and Novel in Eighteenth-Century England* (Cambridge, Mass., 1976), pp. 92–126; Robert H. Bell, "Gibbon: The Philosophic Historian as Autobiographer," *Michigan Academician*, 13 (1980–81), 349–64; Willis R. Buck, Jr., "Reading Autobiography," *Genre*, 13 (1980), 477–98; Fredric V. Bogel, "Crisis and Character in Autobiography: The Later Eighteenth Century," *Studies in English Literature*, 21 (1981), 499–512; and Martine Watson Brownley, "Gibbon's *Memoirs*: The Legacy of the Historian," *Studies on Voltaire and the Eighteenth Century*, 201 (1982), 209–20. Both Mandel and Spacks analyze the autobiography, as I do, by considering its several drafts. Mandel concludes: "Gibbon never finished his life story because he was unable to commit himself emotionally to one dominant narrative form" (p. 552). What Mandel regards as a difficulty of narrative form, I regard as one of generic form and also of self-understanding. On self-doubt and self-discovery in the autobiography, see Porter, "Gibbon's *Autobiography*," pp. 4f. P. R. Ghosh disagrees that a composite version, in an imperfect situation, is essential: "For comprehensiveness and clarity, printing the six drafts of the memoirs consecutively will always be preferable to a mangled unitary account" ("Gibbon's Dark Ages: Some Remarks on the Genesis of the *Decline and Fall*," *Journal of Roman Studies*, 73 [1983], 1n). Ghosh has the interest of scholars rather than readers in mind.

2. On the history of the term, which came into being by the turn of the century, see Jerome Hamilton Buckley, *The Turning Key: Autobiography and the Subjective Impulse Since 1800* (Cambridge, Mass., 1984), pp. 18–19.

3. Gibbon nonetheless alludes to spiritual autobiography like Bunyan's in *C*: "Every man who rises above the common level has received two educations: the first from his teachers; the second, more personal and important, from himself. He will not, like the fanatics of the last age, define the moment of grace; but he cannot forget the æra of his life in which his mind has expanded to its proper form and dimensions" (*C*, 231). Reluc-

tantly he recognizes the kinship between his project and those of the "fanatics of the last age."

4. See the entry for de Thou in *Biographie universelle ancienne et moderne* (Paris and Leipzig, 1854), XLI, 441.

5. Reprinted in David Hume, *Dialogues concerning Natural Religion*, ed. Norman Kemp Smith, 2d ed. (London, 1947), pp. 231–40.

6. Louis Marin, "Montaigne's Tomb, or Autobiographical Discourse," *Oxford Literary Review*, 4 (1981), 43.

7. Louis A. Renza, "The Veto of the Imagination: A Theory of Autobiography," in *Autobiography: Essays Theoretical and Critical*, ed. James Olney (Princeton, N.J., 1980), p. 279. Originally printed in *New Literary History*, 9 (1977), 1–26.

8. *Private Letters of Edward Gibbon (1753–1794)*, ed. Rowland E. Prothero (London, 1896), II, 366; reprinted, New York, 1971.

9. In a note, Sheffield describes Gibbon's doubts that he would ever publish the autobiography as expressed "rather carelessly" and reports a conversation "not long before" Gibbon's death: "it was suggested to him, that, if he should make them a full image of his mind, he would not have nerves to publish them in his lifetime, and therefore that they should be posthumous;—He answered, rather eagerly, that he was determined to publish them *in his lifetime*" (*MW*, I, 1n). This is inconclusive evidence, given all the uncertainties of the project.

10. Gibbon had mistakenly thought himself a collateral descendant of the herald John Gibbon (1629–1718). Brydges published a series of anonymous notes on the Gibbon family in the *Gentleman's Magazine* (1788–96), the first of which (58 [August 1788], 698–700) Gibbon came upon in 1792. Having learned from John Nichols, editor of the *Gentleman's Magazine*, that Brydges was the author, Gibbon wrote him on 7 August 1793 to express his appreciation, ask questions, and, he hoped, begin a correspondence: "Your correspondence will be highly useful and agreable to me, but I shall be still more desirous of a personal interview" (*L*, III, 345). No further correspondence between the two is known.

11. When he came to the end of *E*, Gibbon called life a lottery: "When I contemplate the common lot of mortality, I must acknowledge that I have drawn a high prize in the lottery of life" (*E*, 343). See also Chapter 8, n. 10. The image is an ordinary one, but invested with a sharp and literal sense.

12. Bonnard describes the passage as "a fairly long digression" (*M*, 27n). In fact, its interest lies in Gibbon's digressive search for his exact origins.

13. The lines Gibbon quotes are *Paradise Lost*, VIII, 253–73.

14. With Descartes in mind, Gibbon wrote at first, "he suffers, therefore he exists," then crossed out "exists" and substituted "feels" (British Library, Add. Mss. 34874, f. 110v). It is doubtful which version makes less logical sense, but it is the illogic that matters.

15. The effort a chicken makes in being born had caught Gibbon's eye in 1764, as he was reading Réaumur's treatise on the hatching and raising of domestic fowl, *L'Art de faire éclorre & d'élever en toute saison des oiseaux domestiques* (Paris, 1749), which included an entire chapter on the birth of chickens, "De la naissance des poulets" (I, 311–39), with illustrations of the

chick's laborious breaking out of the shell. "Quel instinct," Gibbon exclaimed, "que celui du poulet qui travaille pendant une demie journée à l'ouvrage difficile de sa propre naissance" (*Le Journal de Gibbon à Lausanne*, ed. Georges Bonnard [Lausanne, 1945], p. 227: What a powerful instinct the chicken has, laboring half a day, with so much difficulty, to be born). Whatever the facts of Gibbon's own birth, he seems to have supposed it a difficult one. On his desire for primal knowledge, see Frank E. Manuel, "Edward Gibbon: Historien-Philosophe," in *Edward Gibbon and the Decline and Fall of the Roman Empire*, ed. G. W. Bowersock, John Clive, and Stephen R. Graubard (Cambridge, Mass., 1977), p. 168: "From the outset Gibbon conceived of the historian as a man charged with unveiling, with probing the innermost recesses, of past societies. This sense of mission might be related psychologically to a longing for primal knowledge and a metaphysical anguish about where he came from, to fantasies about his ancestry, to boyhood images of an *Ile de la félicité* and to the womb-like libraries in which he enclosed himself in London and Lausanne." Then Manuel draws back: "but I shall forgo the attempt." On the evidence of the passage at hand, Gibbon's need to return to beginnings is demonstrable.

16. In Genesis 2:19, Adam ("the man") is first called by name at the same moment when God brings him other living creatures to be named: "And out of the ground the Lord God formed every beast of the field, and every fowl of the air; and brought *them* unto Adam to see what he would call them: and whatsoever Adam called every living creature, that *was* the name thereof."

17. Buckley, *The Turning Key*, p. 29.

18. Hume, *Dialogues concerning Natural Religion*, pp. 239, 239n.

19. Ibid., p. 239.

20. Ibid., p. 240.

21. The comparison of versions of the autobiography would not have been possible but for the patience and skill of Deborah Laycock, who with inspired cut-and-paste work arranged photocopies of the drafts, as transcribed by Murray, into parallel columns on sheets of heavy paper. Much more might be done by way of comparative analysis than I have attempted. The sheets are now in the Department of Special Collections, Stanford University Libraries.

22. Virginia Woolf, "The Historian and 'The Gibbon,'" in *Collected Essays* (New York, 1967), p. 116.

23. The dream of discovering a manuscript of the *Decline and Fall* has probably crossed the mind (or haunted the imagination) of everyone who has studied Gibbon. Even J. E. Norton, the most meticulous and reticent of scholars, entertained the thought: "the present editor does sometimes wonder what happened to the MS of *The Decline and Fall*" (*L*, I, xiv).

EIGHT

1. *Gibbon's Journey from Geneva to Rome: His Journal from 20 April to 2 October, 1764*, ed. Georges A. Bonnard (London, 1961), p. 242. When he

arrived at Rome in October 1764, Gibbon gave up keeping his journal and hired a Scottish antiquary, James Byres, to introduce him to the city. In December he finished with Byres and revisited the art and sites that, he thought, "le méritent le mieux." While doing so, he kept fragmentary notes, which, unlike the journal that precedes them, are in English: "Mais à propos parlons un peu Anglois" (ibid., p. 236). The decision, at this juncture, to write in his native tongue has an assertiveness that is as important, perhaps, to the genesis of the *Decline and Fall* as was the epiphany on the Capitol.

In Florence, Gibbon had also gone into "quite uncharacteristic raptures over the *Venus de' Medici*" (Francis Haskell, "Gibbon and the History of Art," in *Edward Gibbon and the Decline and Fall of the Roman Empire*, ed. G. W. Bowersock, John Clive, and Stephen R. Graubard [Cambridge, Mass., 1977], p. 193). As Haskell says, there was nothing out of the ordinary about Gibbon's artistic tastes—like other visitors to Rome, he swooned over Guido Reni's "Aurora"—but the feeling that art could inspire in him is an unfamiliar aspect of his character.

2. J. E. Norton, *A Bibliography of the Works of Edward Gibbon* (New York, 1970; originally published 1940), p. 179.

3. *The Miscellaneous Works of Edward Gibbon, Esq.*, ed. John, Lord Sheffield (London, 1814), III, viii. Norton understands Gibbon's "ornamental frieze" to refer to a series of prefaces he would write for the completed edition (*A Bibliography*, p. 180). But Gibbon can be referring instead to the "Address," recommending Pinkerton, that he did actually write: "If you proceed in drawing up a prospectus, I will consider it with my best attention, nor shall I be averse to the crowning your solid edifice with something of an ornamental frieze" (*L*, III, 342).

4. Compare E. M. W. Tillyard, *The English Epic and Its Background* (London, 1954), pp. 510–27. In Tillyard's view, the *Decline and Fall* in several ways approaches epic. Since Gibbon never gave up his search for a hero, however, the *Decline and Fall* may best be thought of as an epic *manqué*.

5. On Gibbon's gathering appreciation for "fiction," even in the *Decline and Fall*, see Leo Braudy, "Edward Gibbon and 'The Privilege of Fiction,'" *Prose Studies*, 3 (1980), 138–51.

6. The ode, the first of many that Whitehead turned out during nearly thirty years as laureate, is reprinted in *The Work of the English Poets from Chaucer to Cowper*, ed. Alexander Chalmers (London, 1810), XVII, 252–53.

7. On the textual history of the "Antiquities of the House of Brunswick," see Craddock's notes, *EE*, 594–97.

8. Neither Sheffield nor Craddock reprints the title Gibbon gives his fragmentary "Essay on the Fortunate & Canary Isles" (British Library, Add. Mss. 34880, f. 355r). Craddock, however, indicates its partly separate identity (*EE*, 375, 593). Although Gibbon's pagination is continuous with the materials that follow, all having to do with the circumnavigation of Africa, the piece on the Canaries seems to have been conceived as a self-contained project.

9. For the original (which Gibbon cites accurately), see *The Lusiad; or,*

the Discovery of India (Oxford, 1776), pp. 211–12. In a note Mickle says that "the fiction of the apparition of the Cape of Tempests, in sublimity and awful grandeur of imagination, stands unsurpassed in human composition" (p. 206n).

10. The subject of Gibbon and gaming—for example, his likening of the philosophical historian to the Marquis de Dangeau, both of them seeing deeply into the connections of things, as if in some cosmic game of chance (Chap. 3, pp. 47–48)—might be amplified. Although his unhappy experience in Lausanne cured him of gambling, except for the trivial pleasures of whist, and although he once told his stepmother, defensively, that he neither loved nor understood play (*L*, I, 281), he was drawn to metaphors of chance. When he returned to London from Lausanne, he and his father on one occasion purchased lottery tickets and entertained themselves with fancies of winning the grand prize of £10,000. He wrote his father whimsically on 14 December 1758: "I must begin by the most disagreable news I have to tell you; all our tickets are come up blanks. All our visionary plans of Grandeur are disapointed, the dream of those who have had the ten thousand pounds will last a little but perhaps not much longer" (*L*, I, 113). Edward Gibbon, Sr., was an inveterate gambler: "against the more dangerous temptation of play he was not invulnerable; and large sums were silently precipitated into that bottomless pit" (*M*, 27).

11. For Gibbon and Pinkerton, see Norton, *A Bibliography*, pp. 179–81. In the history of Scotland, Pinkerton makes sure readers know his connection with Gibbon: "The author was happy to find that his ideas on this topic"—the interspersion, within the narrative, of retrospective chapters on cultural history—"completely corresponded with those of the late Mr. Gibbon, who was pleased warmly to express his approbation of this part of the plan" (*The History of Scotland from the Accession of the House of Stuart to that of Mary* [London, 1797], I, vii).

12. In his enthusiasm, Gibbon goes on to write, in yet another gaming metaphor, that "on the zeal and abilities of the Editor of my choice, I boldly and considerately stake whatsoever credit I may have obtained from the public opinion" (*EE*, 541n). Then he strikes out this bold wager.

13. See Chapter 3, p. 40.

14. "Whatsoever have been the fruits of my education, they must be ascribed to the fortunate shipwreck which cast me on the shores of the Leman lake. I have sometimes applied to my own fate the verses of Pindar, which remind an Olympic champion that his victory was the consequence of his exile; and that at home, like a domestic fowl, his days might have rolled away inactive or inglorious" (*C*, 239).

15. Late in May 1774, Hester Gibbon appeared unexpectedly in London, and Gibbon wrote his stepmother to tell her what had happened: "I immediately went to Surry Street where she lodged, but though it was no more than half an hour after nine, the Saint had finished her Evening Devotions and was already retired to rest. Yesterday morning (by appointment) I breakfasted with her at eight o'Clock, dined with her today at two in Newman Street, and am just returned from setting down. She is in truth

a very great curiosity; her dress and figure exceed everything we had at the Masquerade. Her language and ideas belong to the last Century. However, in point of Religion she was rational that is to say silent" (*L*, II, 17).

16. D. M. Low, *Edward Gibbon, 1737–1794* (New York, 1937), p. 269. See Paul Turner, "The 'Supposed Infidelity' of Edward Gibbon," *Historical Journal*, N.S. 25 (1982), 23–41. Turnbull concludes with an overstatement: "We would do well to interpret Gibbon's critique of christianity as belonging to a line of sympathetic religious criticisms of traditional christianity rather than seeing him as an English version of a glib philosophical modern pagan" (p. 41).

17. Low, *Edward Gibbon*, p. 270.

18. Ibid.

19. *The Education of Henry Adams*, ed. Ernest Samuels (Boston, 1974), p. 386. Adams evidently read the different drafts of the autobiography: the phrase in question comes from the third draft (*C*, 263) and was not used by Sheffield, who published a fuller version, from *B*, of Gibbon's visit to Paris in 1763; in *B*, however, Gibbon merely says that "my eye was amused" (*B*, 199). Samuels describes Adams as adapting Gibbon's words (*The Education of Henry Adams*, p. 653, n. 34), but in fact he is accurately quoting *C*. I am grateful to Kenneth Fields for directing me to Adams's comments.

20. On Gibbon's views about immortality, see Appendix C. In his fragmentary essay on Livy (1756), he had early remarked that the work of poets was likely to last longer than that of historians, because it was of more interest at all times and in all countries (*MW*, III, 374). In choosing the extensive theme of the *Decline and Fall*, Gibbon had authorial immortality in mind from the start.

21. John McManners, *Death and the Enlightenment: Changing Attitudes to Death Among Christians and Unbelievers in Eighteenth-Century France* (Oxford, 1981), p. 266.

22. For another account of the tradition that a life can be judged only at its end, see Christopher Fox, " 'Gone as Soon as Found': Pope's 'Epistle to Cobham' and the Death-Day as Moment of Truth," *Studies in English Literature*, 20 (1980), 431–48. On eighteenth-century dying, see also Morris R. Brownell, " 'Like Socrates': Pope's Art of Dying," *Studies in English Literature*, 20 (1980), 407–29. Brownell contrasts the resignation of Pope's "Socratic" death with "the éclat of the famous free-thinking deaths of Hume, Voltaire, and Gibbon" (p. 423). This is not an entirely accurate version of Voltaire's death nor, certainly, of Gibbon's.

23. Michel de Montaigne, *Essais*, ed. Jean Plattard (Paris, 1959–73), I.1, 107.

24. *The Complete Essays of Montaigne*, tr. Donald M. Frame (Stanford, Calif., 1958), p. 55.

25. Montaigne, *Essais*, p. 108.

26. *The Complete Essays of Montaigne*, tr. Frame, p. 55.

27. Jonathan Swift, *The Complete Poems*, ed. Pat Rogers (New Haven, Conn., 1983), p. 564.

28. *Boswell's Life of Johnson*, ed. George Birkbeck Hill, revised by L. F.

Powell (Oxford, 1934), IV, 399. On Johnson's dying, see O. M. Brack, Jr., "The Death of Samuel Johnson and the *Ars Moriendi* Tradition," *Cithara*, 20 (1980–81), 3–15.

29. Boswell's account of his interview with Hume is reprinted in David Hume, *Dialogues concerning Natural Religion*, ed. Norman Kemp Smith, 2d ed. (London, 1947), pp. 76–79. Boswell played along with Hume and his joking but was very uneasy: "I however felt a degree of horrour, mixed with a sort of wild, strange, hurrying recollection of My excellent Mother's pious instructions, of Dr. Johnson's noble lessons, and of my religious sentiments and affections during the course of my life. I was like a man in sudden danger eagerly seeking his defensive arms; and I could not but be assailed by momentary doubts while I had actually before me a man of such strong abilities and extensive inquiry dying in the persuasion of being annihilated" (p. 77).

30. "Depuis Francfort j'ai eté assez rudement secoué, mais la secousse ne m'a fait que du bien, et jamais je ne me suis mieux porté" (*L*, III, 335); "ma santé n'a jamais eté meilleure" (*L*, III, 339); "A propos de santé vous ne serez pas faché d'apprendre que la mienne est parfaite, et je serois presque tenté de croire à l'influence de l'air natal" (*L*, III, 350).

31. This unpublished letter, dated 15 December 1793, is in the Department of Special Collections, Stanford University Libraries. See Appendix A.

32. In alluding to *Macbeth* (as was first pointed out to me by Paul Schacht), Gibbon may have in mind not only the Shakespearean text (*Macbeth*, V.iii.40–46) but also an incident from Johnson's last sickness, eight or ten days before his death. Boswell reports that, after a bad night, Johnson greeted Dr. Brocklesby with the lines beginning "Canst thou not minister to a mind diseas'd?" Brocklesby answered, to Johnson's satisfaction, "therein the patient / Must minister to himself" (*Boswell's Life of Johnson*, ed. Hill, IV, 400–401).

33. Though John Craufurd of Auchinames is not mentioned in Gibbon's correspondence until 1783 (*L*, II, 363) and appears only once in Low's biography, the two men were acquainted by 1774, when Gibbon joined Craufurd in Parliament. In October 1777 they returned from Paris to London together. (Madame du Deffand to Horace Walpole, 22 October 1777, and 26 October 1777; in *Horace Walpole's Correspondence with Madame du Deffand and Wiart*, ed. W. S. Lewis and Warren Hunting Smith [New Haven, Conn., 1939], IV, 485, 486. This is Volume 6 of the Yale Edition of *Horace Walpole's Correspondence*.) Craufurd was also the last of Gibbon's friends to see him alive.

34. Bonnard's text reads: "In old age, the consolation of hope is reserved for the tenderness of parents who commence as new life in their children." I have corrected "as" to "a," in accord with British Library, Add. Mss. 34874, f. 96r.

35. Georges-Louis Leclerc, Comte de Buffon, "Des Probabilités de la durée de la vie," *Supplément à l'histoire naturelle* (Paris, 1774–82), IV, 149.

36. Ibid., IV, 224.

37. "Addition à l'article de la vieillesse & de la mort," ibid., IV, 412, 411.
38. Robert Favre, *La Mort dans la littérature et la pensée françaises au siècle des lumières* (Lyon, n.d.), p. 229.
39. Buffon, "Essai d'arithmétique morale," *Supplément à l'histoire naturelle*, IV, 56–57.
40. *Cinna*, II.i.370. I am grateful to René Girard for this reference.
41. Gibbon may remember Hume: "The mere philosopher is a character, which is commonly but little acceptable in the world, as being supposed to contribute nothing either to the advantage or pleasure of society; while he lives remote from communication with mankind, and is wrapped up in principles and notions equally remote from their comprehension" (*An Enquiry concerning Human Understanding*, in *Enquiries concerning Human Understanding and concerning the Principles of Morals*, ed. L. A. Selby-Bigge, 3d ed., revised by P. H. Nidditch [Oxford, 1975], p. 8).
Gibbon had referred to himself as a "mere philosopher" in the *Decline and Fall*, in a similar context: "Can the death of a good man be esteemed a punishment by those who believe in the immortality of the soul? They betray the instability of their faith. Yet, as a mere philosopher, I cannot agree with the Greeks, ὃν οἱ θεοὶ φιλοῦσιν ἀποθνήσκει νέος" (VII, 294n). The mere philosopher, that is, cannot agree that those whom the gods love die young.
42. McManners, *Death and the Enlightenment*, p. 234.
43. Ernest Campbell Mossner, *The Life of David Hume* (London, 1954), pp. 598–99.
44. McManners, *Death and the Enlightenment*, pp. 265–69.
45. Gibbon owned a 1786 edition, in Greek and Latin, of Demetrius Cydonius's treatise on the contempt of death (*Opusculum de contemnenda morte* [Leipzig, 1786]; recorded in Geoffrey Keynes, *The Library of Edward Gibbon: A Catalogue*, 2d ed. [Dorchester, Eng., 1980], p. 108). Demetrius was a fourteenth-century Byzantine statesman and theologian. Whether Gibbon acquired the volume for its historical or its homiletic value, there is no way to tell.
46. M. and Mme. William de Sévery, *La Vie de société dans le Pays de Vaud à la fin du XVIIIᵉ siècle* (Geneva, 1978; originally published 1911), II, 39. As is common with deathbed scenes, accounts of Gibbon's dying vary. Sheffield's sister Serena wrote to Maria Josepha Holroyd, her niece and Sheffield's eldest daughter, reporting that at nine in the morning "he cried out 'O! my God!' several times, in great pain and spoke no more" (*The Girlhood of Maria Josepha Holroyd*, ed. J. H. Adeane [London, 1896], pp. 264–65). Dussaut wrote two accounts of the death, the one I have cited, in a letter of 18 January 1794 to the Chanoinesse de Polier; the other, British Library Add. Mss. 34887, on which Sheffield based his account in the *Miscellaneous Works*. Serena's account is the starting point for a psychological study of Gibbon and Sheffield that is overheated but not without usefulness (Marvin Stern, "Death, Grief, and Friendship in the Eighteenth Century: Edward Gibbon and Lord Sheffield," *Advances in Thanatology*, 5, no. 3 [1984], 1–60). Serena had come to London with Sheffield, arriving after Gibbon's

death. Both were dependent on Dussaut for information, and there is no reason to weigh her version more heavily than her brother's. We discover in the deaths of others what perhaps we need to find.

APPENDIX B

1. When I first saw this particular card, I misread "incert" as "incest." I failed to dislodge the error from my mind until after I had committed it to print in a review of Geoffrey Keynes, *The Library of Edward Gibbon: A Catalogue*, 2d ed. (Dorchester, Eng., 1980). I am grateful to David Sullivan for his help in arriving at the correct reading. Connoisseurs of nonsensical error can find my review of Keynes in *Modern Language Review*, 78 (1983), 685–87.

INDEX

Index

Index

Library of Congress Cataloging-in-Publication Data

Carnochan, W. B.
  Gibbon's solitude.

  Includes index.
  1. Gibbon, Edward, 1737–1794.   2. Gibbon, Edward,
1737–1794. History of the decline and fall of the
Roman Empire.   3. Rome—History—Empire, 30 B.C.–476 A.D.
—Historiography.   4. Byzantine Empire—Historiography.
5. Historians—England—Biography.   I. Title.
DG206.G5C37 1987   937'.06   86-30200
ISBN 0-8047-1363-4 (alk. paper)